HEBREWS

A Bible Commentary in the Wesleyan Tradition

GARETH L. COCKERILL

General Publisher: Nathan Birky
General Editor: Ray E. Barnwell
Senior Editor: David Higle
Managing Editor: Russell Gunsalus
Editor: Kelly Trennepohl

All Scripture quotations, unless otherwise indicated, are taken from the HOLY BIBLE, NEW INTERNATIONAL VERSION®. NIV®. Copyright © 1973, 1978, 1984 by International Bible Society. Used by permission of Zondervan Publishing House. All rights reserved.

Scripture quotations marked (ASV) are taken from THE STANDARD AMERICAN EDITION OF THE REVISED VERSION OF THE BIBLE. Copyright © 1901 by Thomas Nelson and Sons; copyright © 1929 by International Council of Religious Education. Used by permission.

Scripture quotations marked (KJV) are taken from THE HOLY BIBLE, KING JAMES VERSION.

Scripture quotations marked (NASB) are taken from THE NEW AMERICAN STANDARD BIBLE. Copyright © 1960, 1962, 1963, 1968, 1971, 1972, 1973, 1975, 1977 by The Lockman Foundation. Used by permission.

Scripture quotations marked (NEB) are taken from THE NEW ENGLISH BIBLE. Copyright © 1961, 1970 by Oxford University Press and Cambridge University Press. Used by permission.

Scripture quotations marked (NKJV) taken from THE HOLY BIBLE, NEW KING JAMES VERSION. © 1982 Thomas Nelson, Inc.

Scripture quotations marked (NRSV) are taken from THE NEW REVISED STANDARD VERSION BIBLE. Copyright © 1989 by the Division of Christian Education of the National Council of the Churches of Christ in the United States of America. Used by permission. All rights reserved.

Scripture quotations marked (REB) are from THE REVISED ENGLISH BIBLE. Copyright © 1989 by Oxford University Press and Cambridge University Press. Used by permission.

Scripture quotations marked (RSV) are taken from THE REVISED STANDARD VERSION OF THE BIBLE. Copyright © 1946, 1952, 1971, 1973. Used by permission.

CONTENTS

EDITOR'S PREFACE

This book is part of a series of commentaries seeking to interpret the books of the Bible from a Wesleyan perspective. It is designed primarily for laypeople, especially teachers of Sunday school and leaders of Bible studies. Pastors also will find this series very helpful. In addition, this series is for people who want to read and study on their own for spiritual edification.

Each book of the Bible will be explained paragraph by paragraph. This "wide-angle lens" approach helps the reader to follow the primary flow of thought in each passage. This, in turn, will help the reader to avoid "missing the forest because of the trees," a problem many people encounter when reading commentaries.

At the same time, the authors slow down often to examine particular details and concepts that are important for understanding the bigger picture. Where there are alternative understandings of key passages, the authors acknowledge these so the reader will experience a broader knowledge of the various theological traditions and how the Wesleyan perspective relates to them.

These commentaries follow the New International Version and are intended to be read with your Bible open. With this in mind, the biblical text is not reproduced in full, but appears in bold type throughout the discussion of each passage. Greater insight will be gained by reading along in your Bible as you read the commentaries.

These volumes do not replace the valuable technical commentaries that offer in-depth grammatical and textual analysis. What they do offer is an interpretation of the Bible that we hope will lead to a greater understanding of what the Bible says, its significance for our lives today, and further transformation into the image of Christ.

David A. Higle
Senior Editor

AUTHOR'S PREFACE

The writer of Hebrews has the conviction that "God . . . has spoken to us by his Son" (Heb. 1:1). From this conviction comes his urgent concern: "Today, if you hear his voice, do not harden your hearts" (3:7-8). He writes so that his readers will hear and obey the message that God has spoken and still speaks through this Son. The writer of Hebrews has a pastor's burden for the eternal welfare of His readers and a preacher's zeal to communicate the Word of God.

The purpose of this commentary is to enable the modern reader to hear what this first-century preacher who wrote Hebrews is saying. However, when we listen to him we are drawn into something deeper. We hear the Word of God which this preacher proclaimed. God himself addresses us with the "heavenly calling" (Heb. 3:1). This address is a gracious invitation to intimate fellowship with Him, for which we will be held accountable. This commentary, then, is not intended to call attention to itself. It is a "hearing aid." Its purpose is to enable you to hear what the writer of Hebrews is saying. It is offered with the prayer that God the Holy Spirit will open your heart so that you will hear His own voice. "Do not harden your hearts" (3:8) but join with "those who through faith and patience inherit what has been promised" (6:12).

It is a joy to acknowledge my debt to the many commentators and Bible scholars who have contributed to my study of Hebrews over the past twenty-five years. Although a "great cloud" (Heb. 12:1) of Bible interpreters has enriched my own understanding of this book, few references are made to scholarly sources in the endnotes. Much of the interpretation found in this commentary has been informed by many but derived from no single commentator. I have cited scholarly sources only where I am directly dependent upon them or where it seemed additional support for a point of interpretation would be appropriate. The purpose of this commentary is to make the meaning of the text accessible to the intelligent Christian lay reader, not to direct attention to secondary sources or enter scholarly debate.

Where there are differences of interpretation, I have made frequent reference to various English translations of the Bible. These references are not intended as a criticism of the New International Version. The differences that scholars have in the interpretation of the Bible are usually reflected in the different English versions. Thus I have compared English Bibles because such comparison seemed to be a user-friendly method of explaining differences of interpretation to the intelligent but nontechnical reader. Throughout the text, frequent reference is made to the New King James Version (NKJV), the New American Standard Bible (NASB), the New Revised Standard Version (NRSV), the Revised Standard Version (RSV), and the Revised English Bible (REB). Reference is also made to the King James Version (KJV) and the New English Bible (NEB).

Of recent commentaries in English, those by William Lane,[1] Harold Attridge,[2] Paul Ellingworth,[3] and Philip Hughes[4] have been most useful. Lane gives comprehensive, balanced interpretation. Attridge offers much help in understanding the cultural background of Hebrews. Ellingworth concentrates on the Greek text. Hughes deepens readers' understanding by drawing on rich resources gleaned from the great interpreters of Hebrews down through the centuries. It is necessary to understand Greek in order to use Lane, Attridge, and Ellingworth, but the person without a Greek background will find Hughes useful.

The reader who would like to consult other commentaries in the Wesleyan tradition may want to refer to the following writers: H. Orton Wiley,[5] Andrew Murray,[6] George Turner,[7] Charles Carter,[8] and John Walters.[9] Turner is very readable. Wiley is comprehensive and scholarly. Murray writes a devotional classic of substance. Walters is very concise. My own brief notes on Hebrews can be found in *The Wesley Bible.*[10]

Wiley aptly summarizes the goal of Hebrews: "(1) The primary aim of the Epistle is to bring men into the presence of God; (2) In order to stand in the presence of God, men must be holy. The dominant note of this Epistle, therefore, is holiness. . . ."[11]

Murray describes the response that Hebrews urges upon us: "And the great object of the Epistle is to show us that if we will but follow the Lord fully, and yield ourselves wholly to what God in Christ is ready to do, we shall find in the gospel and in Christ everything that we need for a life of joy and strength and final victory."[12]

My deepest appreciation to Wesley Biblical Seminary for arranging my teaching schedule so that I would have time to complete this study of Hebrews. I am also thankful to both Sharon Camp Meeting, Sharon Center, Ohio, and Sebring Holiness Camp Meeting, Sebring, Ohio, for giving me extra time while I was a camp worker to write parts of this commentary. Thanks to the Department of Local Church Education of The Wesleyan Church for the invitation to write, and to editors Phil Bence and Kelly Trennepohl for their help and patience. I am grateful to Professor Mathias Rissi who first stimulated my interest in Hebrews and to many friends who have cultivated that interest. Most of all I am thankful to my wife and best friend, Rosa, and to our children, by birth and by marriage, to all of whom this book is lovingly dedicated.

Gareth L. Cockerill
Jackson, Mississippi
Fall 1998

ENDNOTES

[1]William L. Lane, *Hebrews 1–8*, vol. 47a and *Hebrews 9–13*, vol. 47b, Word Biblical Commentary, New Testament ed. Ralph P. Martin, gen. eds. David A. Hubbard and Glenn W. Barker (Dallas: Word Books, 1991).

[2]Harold W. Attridge, *The Epistle to the Hebrews,* Hermeneia—A Critical and Historical Commentary on the Bible, ed. Helmut Koester (Philadelphia: Fortress Press, 1989).

[3]Paul Ellingworth, *The Epistle to the Hebrews,* The New International Greek Testament Commentary, eds. I. Howard Marshall and W. Ward Gasque (Grand Rapids, Michigan: Wm. B. Eerdmans Publishing Co., 1993).

[4]Philip Edgcumbe Hughes, *A Commentary on the Epistle to the Hebrews* (Grand Rapids, Michigan: Wm. B. Eerdmans Publishing Co., 1977).

[5]H. Orton Wiley, *The Epistle to the Hebrews* (Kansas City, Missouri: Beacon Hill Press, 1959).

[6]Andrew Murray, *The Holiest of All* (New York: Fleming H. Revell, 1894; reprinted, Springdale, Pennsylvania: Whitaker House, 1996).

[7]George Allen Turner, *The New and Living Way* (Minneapolis: Bethany Fellowship, 1975).

[8]Charles W. Carter, "The Epistle to the Hebrews," *The Wesleyan Bible Commentary,* ed. Charles W. Carter (Grand Rapids, Michigan: Wm. B. Eerdmans Publishing Co., 1966), pp. 1–194.

[9]John Walters, "Hebrews," *Asbury Bible Commentary,* eds. Eugene E. Carpenter and Wayne McCown (Grand Rapids, Michigan: Zondervan Publishing House, 1992), pp. 1139–69.

[10]Gareth Lee Cockerill, "The Epistle to the Hebrews," *The Wesley Bible: A Personal Study Bible for Holy Living,* ed. Albert F. Harper, et. al. (Nashville: Thomas Nelson Publishers, 1990), pp. 1842–64.

[11]Wiley, p. 20.

[12]Murray, p. vi.

INTRODUCTION

"Well, that's what *you* believe." For thirty minutes I had been sharing the gospel with Mike. He continued, "If it works for you, that's fine, but what right do you have to say that everybody should believe like you do?" Our conversation was coming to an end.

How many times do we hear people like Mike? "What you believe is your business, but don't expect me to believe it. After all, there isn't any truth in matters of religious faith. It is just what you believe and what I believe, or don't believe. Believing in Christ is a matter of taste, not truth. Whether I believe or don't believe is no more important than whether or not I like broccoli. Don't bother me about what you believe, and I won't bother you about what I believe."

To an age that believes we cannot really know God's truth, the book of Hebrews gives a resounding challenge: "In the past God spoke to our forefathers through the prophets at many times and in various ways, but in these last days he has spoken to us by his Son" (Heb. 1:1-2). We can know the truth about God because God has revealed himself in His Son, Jesus Christ. As the Son, Christ brings us God's final and complete revelation of himself.

Through this revelation, the living God calls us to trust in His goodness and integrity, and to live in faithful obedience to Him (see Hebrews 2:1-3). God calls us to holiness! Thus the message of Hebrews destroys another modern idol—we can no longer "do our own thing." We are called to live according to God's command rather than choose our own lifestyle, to believe God's truth rather than follow our own taste. The book of Hebrews has a vital message to people in today's pluralistic age who believe in the relativity of truth and morality.

But God's revelation in His Son is more than a call to faithful obedience. Through the Son, God has provided the grace necessary for us to be obedient from the heart (see commentary on 4:14-16; 9:14; 10:16-18). If God has revealed himself in His Son, what is the content of that revelation? The content of the revelation is found in the High Priesthood of the Son. As our High Priest, the Son has made an adequate sacrifice that cleanses our hearts from sin and brings us into fellowship with God (see Hebrews 10:19-22). He enables us to overcome temptation so that we can reach the promised homeland of God's presence and live in joyful fellowship with Him forever (see commentary on 2:18; 4:14-16). This wonderful provision makes it all the more imperative that we continue in faithful obedience!

Many other aspects of the teaching of Hebrews help us significantly. From Hebrews we learn that there is one people of God throughout history: We Christians are heirs of God's faithful people in the Old Testament. That is why the Old Testament saints described in Hebrews 11:1-40 are examples for us to follow. God's destiny for His faithful people has always been eternal joy in the promised land of His presence (see commentary on 4:1-13; 11:13-16).

Hebrews is very helpful in understanding how the Old Testament applies to Christians. The other books of the New Testament tell us little about how to understand the priesthood and sacrifices of the Old Testament in light of Christ's coming. From Hebrews we learn the true significance of the Most Holy Place and the Promised Land as pictures of our eternal dwelling place with God. Hebrews also helps us to understand how the faithful of the Old Testament are examples for us to follow. The writer to the Hebrews is confident that God addresses us "Today," through the words of the Old Testament; we are to "hear his voice" (Heb. 3:7).

CHARACTERISTICS OF THE LETTER TO THE HEBREWS

The title of Hebrews in the King James Version calls the book an "epistle," or letter, and Hebrews is associated in the New Testament with the other letters. The letter-like conclusion in 13:20-25 makes it clear that Hebrews was sent to a particular group of people as a letter would be sent. Hebrews, however, is not like most of the other letters of the New Testament. If we are used to reading Paul's letters, we are surprised by the fact that Hebrews lacks the traditional letter opening. First-century letters in the Roman world began by identifying the writer and the readers, followed by greetings to, and a word of thanks for, those readers (see for example, Philippians 1:1-3). The powerful introduction in Hebrews 1:1-4 sounds more like the beginning of a sermon.

In Hebrews 13:22, the writer refers to his work as a "word of exhortation," which is probably a way of calling his book a sermon.[1] In Acts 13:15-42, the term "word of exhortation" (13:15 NASB) is applied to Paul's exposition of the Scripture in a synagogue service. Stephen's speech in Acts 7:2-53 is another possible example of a synagogue sermon. The way in which the Old Testament is quoted and expounded,[2] the repeated warnings and encouragements spread throughout the book, and the extensive use of examples are all features reminiscent of synagogue preaching in the Greek-speaking world. The author of Hebrews may have drawn on his own earlier preaching, as many preachers do. After preparing this sermon for his friends, he appended a letter-type conclusion (see Hebrews 13:22-25) and sent it to them. By continual reference to speaking and hearing, instead of to writing, he gave them a sense of his presence with them (see 2:5; 5:11; 6:9; 8:1; 9:5; 11:32). When we read his words, we hear him speaking to us. Thus you will often hear the writer referred to as the "preacher" and the addressees as the "hearers."

Let us now turn to several other questions: Who was the preacher that wrote this book? To whom was it addressed? When was it written? How does the author use the Old Testament?

AUTHORSHIP OF THE LETTER TO THE HEBREWS

At first glance it might seem easy to determine who wrote Hebrews. In the King James Version, the book's title reads, "The Epistle of Paul the Apostle to the Hebrews." However, the reference to Paul is omitted in the oldest Greek manuscripts of Hebrews, and a number of the church fathers did not think Paul was the author.

When we begin to compare Hebrews with Paul's letters, such as Romans or 1 Corinthians, we see many differences. Hebrews does not discuss many of the issues that were important to Paul. Paul was concerned with the question of how non-Jews became Christians, with the issues of circumcision and justification by faith (Romans 1:1–5:11); he emphasized the Resurrection (1 Corinthians 15:1-58) and living in the Spirit (Romans 8:1-17; Galatians 3:2-5, 14). The writer of Hebrews has no apparent concern with how non-Jews become Christians. He[3] speaks extensively about the High Priesthood of Christ (Hebrews 2:17; 4:14–5:10; 7:1–10:18). He focuses on Christ's ascension to the Father's right hand (1:3, 13; 4:14; 8:1; 10:11-15) and describes the Christian life as entering into the presence of God (see commentary on 4:14-16; 12:22-29). He is more interested in the kind of faith that enables Christians to persevere in the face of difficulties (11:1-40) than in Paul's more frequent theme: the kind of faith through which one becomes a Christian (Romans 1:16; 5:1-5; Ephesians 2:8-9).

The writer of Hebrews spoke cultured Greek and was trained in the highly valued art of persuasive speech. The style of Hebrews is more polished that the style of Paul's letters. The author of Hebrews makes a striking impression on the ears of his hearers by using words with the same sound. In Hebrews 1:1, five of the seven main words in the verse begin with a *p* sound. The following three English phrases each translate a single Greek *p*-sounding word: "In the past, at many times, in various ways." The Greek words for "forefathers" and "prophets" also begin with this sound. The author of Hebrews also arranged his words for effect. The arrangement of the famous declaration in Hebrews 13:8 is a case in point: "Jesus Christ is the same yesterday and today and forever." The Greek word order is literally, "Jesus Christ yesterday and today the same and for ever." The effect in Greek is to make the words "the same" stand out emphatically. It also associates the "yesterday" of the earlier leaders of the people to whom Hebrews was addressed very closely with their own "today." Sometimes Paul used these literary devices as well, but he was neither as accomplished nor as thorough in his use of them.

The vocabulary of Hebrews is very different from Paul's vocabulary. One hundred sixty-nine of the 1,038 words used in Hebrews are found nowhere else in the New Testament.[4]

In light of these differences, it is likely that one of Paul's colleagues who knew Timothy (see Hebrews 13:23) wrote Hebrews. Early church tradition suggests the names of Luke, Barnabas, or Clement of Rome (a late, first-century church leader not mentioned in the New Testament). Martin Luther thought that Apollos was the author. Acts 18:24 describes Apollos as a person with the eloquence and education that would have enabled him to write a book with the literary quality of Hebrews.

The multiplicity of suggestions shows how scanty the evidence is for determining the author of Hebrews. After surveying many possibilities, Origen, a church father from the third century and one of the greatest biblical scholars of antiquity, said of Hebrews, "But who wrote the epistle, in truth God knows."[5]

We may not know the name of the person who wrote Hebrews, but we do know that he was a great Christian who had received the gospel from those who had heard Jesus firsthand (see Hebrews 2:3), perhaps the apostles themselves, and to whom the Holy Spirit had given deep insight into the person and work of Christ. He was steeped in the Greek Old Testament and had a deep and urgent pastoral concern for his friends whom he addressed. We are in his debt for a trustworthy and highly creative contribution to the New Testament.

RECIPIENTS OF THE LETTER TO THE HEBREWS

"To the Hebrews," from the King James Version's title, was not a part of the original book, but was probably an early attempt to describe the people to whom it was sent. What does the content of the book tell us about who they were? There can be no doubt that the readers were Christians. They had not heard the Lord Jesus themselves, but had been converted through the preaching of those who had heard Him (see Hebrews 2:3) and convinced through the miraculous signs that accompanied this preaching (2:4). They had "shared in the Holy Spirit" (6:4) and experienced "the goodness of the word of God and the powers of the coming age" (6:5). They had a reputation for showing God's love by ministering to other Christians (6:10). Indeed, at some time in the past, shortly after their conversion, they had faced public shame, imprisonment, and the seizure of their property for Christ's sake (10:32-34), but none of them had yet suffered martyrdom (12:4).

Now, however, the writer is worried that they may drift away from their commitment to Christ (2:1). Apparently they had become lax and were in danger of sinking into a state of spiritual immaturity, of stunted growth (5:11-14). At the same time, their Christian distinctiveness had brought them shame from the outside world (13:12-13). They were suffering (12:4-11) and may have been facing another round of persecution that would require them to give their lives (11:35-38). This combination of spiritual lethargy, external pressure, and impending trials exposed them to the danger of apostasy—of turning away from the "great salvation" (2:3) provided by Christ. Such willful disobedience would cut them off from salvation and cause them to miss the heavenly homeland as the wilderness generation had done (3:16–4:11). They were vulnerable to great spiritual peril through this combination of spiritual lethargy and impending trial. The preacher is urgent—they should be careful that none of their members become lost (3:12, 13; 4:1, 11; 6:11; 12:15).

The way in which the writer addresses his readers would indicate that they represented a particular congregation living in an urban center of the Roman Empire. He is aware of their history and problems (2:1-4; 5:11-14; 6:9-12; 10:32-34; 13:1-25). The practical concerns addressed in Hebrews 13:1-6 are the kind that would have been most pressing to urban Christians. It was in the large cities that church members would need to provide hospitality for traveling Christians and help those who were in prison or persecuted for their faith. Indeed, we would expect the recipients of Hebrews to be city dwellers. The urban nature of early Christianity is demonstrated by the fact that Paul wrote all thirteen of his letters, with the possible exceptions of Galatians and Titus, to churches or church leaders in urban centers.

Yet the preacher does not address them as if they are the entire church in the city where they live. Most other major New Testament letters were addressed to churches in particular cities (Romans 1:7; 1 Corinthians 1:2; 2 Corinthians 1:1; Ephesians 1:1; Philippians 1:1; Colossians 1:2; 1 Thessalonians 1:1; 2 Thessalonians 1:1) or to people in a variety of locations (James 1:1; 1 Peter 1:1). The church in a city of the first century would often be made up of a number of house churches (Romans 16:5; 1 Corinthians 16:19; Colossians 4:15; Philemon 2) or local fellowships that met in someone's house and consisted of people connected with that household. The way in which the preacher encourages his hearers to submit to their leaders (Hebrews 13:17) and to greet *all* the saints and *all* the leaders (13:24) suggests that they were such a house church.[6] Part of his concern is that they not cease to identify with the larger group of Christians in their city.

Rome is a likely suggestion for the city in which these people lived. Clement of Rome quoted Hebrews along with some of the epistles of Paul near the end of the first century. Thus Rome is the first place where Hebrews was quoted by a church leader in an authoritative way. The statement in Hebrews 13:24b, "Those from Italy send you their greetings," would imply that this letter was written either to or from Italy. If the author was writing from Italy, he would probably have been more specific in naming those from whom he sends greeting. On balance, then, it is likely that Hebrews was sent to Christians in an Italian city. Other evidence suggests that the first-century church in Rome was made up of a number of loosely associated house churches (see Romans 16:3-15).[7] It is quite possible that this letter was addressed to such a house church in the capital city.

The suggestion of a Roman destination is also supported by the fact that "To the Hebrews" appears to be addressed to Christians of Jewish heritage. The early Roman church had strong Jewish roots. The recipients of Hebrews were steeped in the Old Testament. The writer talks about Old Testament people and events in a way that assumes his readers know the context to which he refers. For instance, if they had not known how Jacob cheated Esau (see Genesis 25:27-34), they would not have known what was being said in Hebrews 12:16-17. The way in which the author argues for the superiority and finality of Christ by comparing Him with the Old Testament covenant and priesthood seems to imply that his readers put special emphasis on these institutions. Furthermore, Hebrews 13:9-16 may imply that the readers were tempted to continue their participation in certain Jewish meals that were associated with the sacrificial ritual.[8]

Yet if their heritage was Jewish, it was the heritage of the Greek-speaking Jews who had synagogues scattered throughout the cities of the Roman Empire. The literary character of the Greek of Hebrews indicates that they were very much at home with the Greek language. It was the Greek version of the Old Testament with which they were familiar.[9] (See commentary on 2:9 for an example of a place where the writer's argument depends on the wording of the Greek text.) Greek-speaking Jews also made much of the fact that God had revealed himself through Moses in an unmediated way. The writer of Hebrews uses this understanding of Moses to his advantage when he compares Christ with Moses in such places as Hebrews 3:1-6.[10]

We cannot be sure what precipitated the crisis of faith that confronted the readers of this letter. If they had Jewish roots, they may have been tempted to blend back into the general Jewish environment. Hebrews 13:9-16 suggests that they were tempted to participate in certain ceremonial meals that were celebrated by Jews throughout the Roman world and were associated with the sacrificial rites in the Jerusalem Temple. By participating in these activities, they would have been shielded from the ire of their fellow Jews who looked askance at Christianity. They also would have been protected from persecution by non-Jews, since the Roman government recognized Judaism as an accepted religion.

The preacher gives an antidote to his readers' lethargy and to much contemporary apathy toward Christianity: God gave His final revelation of himself in His Son, Jesus Christ. Christ was the true culmination of all of God's earlier revelations. Therefore it is necessary to persevere in a holy life of faithful obedience to God's revelation in His Son. Only in this way can a person be one of God's people, who inherit the promises. The writer also emphasizes the availability of God's resources to live this holy life. Through His High Priesthood, the Son has made the promised full atonement for sin which cleanses the heart. This High Priest is at God's right hand ready to help all His people overcome every temptation and bring them to the promised heavenly homeland. This message is as vibrant today as it was to its first readers.

In Hebrews 13:1-19 the preacher gives his hearers a number of practical things they can do to help them persevere in Christ. They must continue to show love for each other in concrete ways (13:1), practice hospitality toward needy believers (13:2), minister to those suffering for their faith (13:3), avoid sexual immorality and greed (13:4-6), and imitate and obey their leaders (13:7, 17). They must be willing to separate from whatever false teachings and religious practices were tempting them (13:8-9) and bear the shame and derision that would come from taking a stand for Christ (13:10-16). All of these instructions have application to Christians in the modern world.

The preacher has a deep sense of the immediacy of God's Word. He addresses his hearers first of all as Christians. Some understanding of the background of the first recipients of Hebrews is helpful, but much of what the preacher says speaks directly to our own condition as God's people today.

PURPOSE OF THE LETTER TO THE HEBREWS

In light of what has been said about authorship above, Hebrews need not have been written during the lifetime of Paul. It was, however, written during the lifetime of some of his colleagues (see Hebrews 13:23).

An early Christian letter called "1 Clement" shows clear dependence on Hebrews in a number of places, the most extensive of which is 1 Clement 36:2-5. Scholars group this letter with the documents known as the Apostolic Fathers, the earliest Christian writings after the New Testament. Most scholars believe that Clement, a leader in the church at Rome, wrote 1 Clement between A.D. 95 and 97 to correct problems in the church at Corinth. The recent "misfortunes and reversals" referred to in 1 Clement 1:1 are normally thought to refer to persecution under the emperor Domitian (A.D. 81–96). If this is so, then we know that Hebrews was in existence by the last decade of the first century and had had time to become well known in Rome. The way in which Clement refers to Hebrews is similar to the way he refers to Paul's letters, suggesting that he considered Hebrews to have come from the same time period and to have the same authority Paul's letters had. In any case, 1 Clement was known and used by Polycarp, bishop of Smyrna, around A.D. 120. There is no reason to believe that Hebrews was written later than the last decade of the first century.

It is reasonable to suggest an early date for Hebrews by relating it to several historical events of the first century: the expulsion of the Jews from Rome by the emperor Claudius in A.D. 49, the persecution of Christians by Nero in A.D. 64 through 66, and the destruction of the Jerusalem Temple in A.D. 70.

The way Hebrews speaks may sound as if the Old Testament sacrifices were still going on: "For this reason it [the law] can never, by the same sacrifices repeated endlessly year after year, make perfect those who draw near to worship. If it could, would they not have stopped being offered?" (Heb. 10:1-2). However, this way of speaking does not mean that these sacrifices were still being performed in the Jerusalem Temple. Hebrew's discussion about priesthood and sacrifice relates to the Levitical priesthood and Tabernacle in the Old Testament, not to the Temple. The Old Testament describes these sacrifices as being continually offered. Hebrews bases what it says on these descriptions in the Old Testament. Hebrews offers biblical interpretation, not commentary on the contemporary political and religious situation in Jerusalem. Unlike the people who wrote the Dead Sea Scrolls, the writer of Hebrews was not concerned about the corruption of the particular priests then in power in Jerusalem. From the writer's point of view, the whole Levitical priesthood had been shown to be inadequate in view of the High Priesthood of Christ the Son. Thus it is best not to push the issue of the present-tense description of the sacrifices. This is the present tense of biblical exegesis. However, it does seem likely that the writer of Hebrews would have mentioned the destruction of the Temple, if that destruction had occurred, as a supplementary support to his argument that the Old Testament sacrifices had ceased, even if he wrote long after it had taken place.

If the recipients of Hebrews were members of a house church of Jewish heritage in Rome, as was proposed above, Hebrews may have been sent to them just before the persecution of Christians under Nero, which began in A.D. 64. Several passages hint that the writer was preparing them to face stiff persecution, perhaps martyrdom (see 11:35-38; 12:4). The earlier persecution mentioned in 10:32-35 would then have been under the emperor Claudius in A.D. 49. The Roman historian Suetonius tells us that Claudius ordered all Jews to leave Rome because of disturbances instigated by one named Chrestus. Most scholars think that Suetonius mistook the common slave-name "Chrestus" for the name "Christus," the Latin word for Christ. The disturbance probably arose as contention between Jews who believed in Christ and those who did not. It is possible that Claudius evicted only those Jews who were causing disturbance. The public shame and confiscation of property described in 10:32-35 would have been typical of such an expulsion. Thus it is reasonable to think that the book of Hebrews was written to a house church of people from a Jewish background who were facing pressure to identify with the larger Jewish community by participating in various ritual observances. If they participated, they would escape the shame and ostracism of their fellow countrymen. Since the Roman Empire recognized Judaism as an official religion but did not recognize Christianity, they would also escape the persecution befalling and soon to befall Christians in the city of Rome. The preacher has encouraged them by showing that Christ is the fulfillment of the Old Testament. To turn from Him is not to turn back to being the people of God but to fall "away from the living God" (3:12).

THE OLD TESTAMENT IN HEBREWS

Every book in the New Testament builds on God's revelation in the Old Testament. Hebrews, however, is almost totally biblical exposition. By studying the author's use of the Old Testament, we can survey the content of his sermon, get a basic understanding of the logic of his thought, and grasp his perspective on the fulfillment of the Old Testament in Christ.

We have already seen above that the people to whom Hebrews was sent were steeped in the Old Testament. The preacher builds on their knowledge. He focuses their attention on the experience of God's people in the wilderness after they had been delivered from Egypt and were on their way to the Promised Land. The preacher uses three great pictures that come out of this wilderness experience. If we are going to understand Hebrews, we need to review these Old Testaments images and "see" these three pictures through the eyes of the author of Hebrews and his hearers.

The first picture shows God's people gathered around Mount Sinai. We find this picture in Exodus 19:1 through 20:21. Sinai was the most important moment in Israel's relationship with God. It was at Sinai that all of the people of Israel heard God speak to them in a voice of thunder. It was there that they became His covenant people. All the rest of Israel's history is determined by how they kept the covenant made at Sinai. The second picture portrays God's people in the wilderness traveling to the Promised Land, as depicted in Numbers 10:11 through 14:45. The third picture shows the ministry of the high priest, with special emphasis on his entry into the Most Holy Place on the Day of Atonement (see Leviticus 16:1-34). We could call picture 1 "the Sinai Picture," picture 2 "the Pilgrimage Picture," and picture 3 "the High Priest Picture."

The author of Hebrews shows each of these pictures in light of Christ's coming—His death, His resurrection, His ascension to heaven, and His sitting at the Father's right hand. The Sinai Picture emphasizes Jesus' role as the "Son" through whom God has spoken. In the Pilgrimage Picture, He is the "Pioneer"[11] who brings His people into the true promised land. In the High Priest Picture, He is the "High Priest" who cleanses from sin and provides access into the heavenly most holy place.

Each of these pictures dominates a different part of the book. In 1:1 through 2:4, the Sinai Picture is in focus. The writer compares the word of God spoken through the Son when He was on earth with the word of God spoken through angels on Sinai.[12] Sinai comes into focus again in 12:14-29 at the end of the main part of the book.[13] In that passage, the word that God now speaks through the Son from heaven is compared to the word spoken on Sinai. In both of these passages, the writer emphasizes the urgency of obeying the word spoken through the Son. If the previous word, now superceded, was serious, what about this new word?

The difference of perspective between the two passages showing the Sinai Picture—1:1 through 2:4, and 12:14-29—is also significant. By use of the Pilgrimage and High Priesthood Pictures in 2:5 through 12:13, the author has made clear the exceeding greatness of the salvation that Christ has provided and the grace He has made available to Christians. By the time the hearers get to chapter 12, they have a much better idea of the "great salvation" mentioned in 2:3. Since greater spiritual privilege brings greater responsibility, the exhortation in 12:14-29 is much stronger than that in 2:1-4.

The Pilgrimage Picture appears in 2:5 through 4:13 and in 10:32 through 12:13. In these passages, Jesus is primarily the Pioneer (2:10; 12:2) who enters the promised land, the heavenly homeland. By His achievement, He opens the way for and enables His people to enter. Hebrews 2:5-18 introduces the picture of the Pioneer leading His people to the homeland, and points forward to the picture of High Priesthood. In 3:1-6, Jesus is compared with Moses, who led God's people on their pilgrimage through the wilderness. In 3:7 through 4:13, the author of Hebrews urges his readers not to follow the example of the disobedient wilderness generation who, despite Moses' faithful leadership, failed in their pilgrimage. They thus lost the privilege of entering the Promised Land. If the readers of Hebrews likewise disobey, they will not enter the true heavenly homeland.

The Pilgrimage Picture continues in 10:32 through 12:13, but the preacher no longer speaks of God's disobedient people in the wilderness. He begins to describe God's faithful people on the way to the promised land, now clearly understood as the heavenly homeland. In 11:1-40 we have the examples of faithful pilgrims who, in contrast to the wilderness generation, persevered in obedience despite hardship and persecution. The main examples of faith cluster around the lives of Abraham (11:8-22) and Moses (11:23-31) as they look forward to the Promised Land. However, believers are to fix their gaze on Jesus their Pioneer (12:1-3), who through His sacrifice has entered the heavenly homeland and enables His followers to enter. The suffering that comes from obediently following the Pioneer shows that Christians are God's children whom He is perfecting in holiness (12:4-13; compare 2:10-18).

Picture 3, the High Priest Picture, dominates the central section of the book, 4:14 through 10:31. In this section, the person and work of Christ are compared to the person and work of the high priest after the order of Aaron. In short, Christ's sacrifice effectively deals with sin because He is the eternal Son of God who became human and lived a completely obedient human life up to and including His death (see 5:1-10; 10:8-10). This obedience culminating in His death was the effective sacrifice. By contrast, the Aaronic high priest was not only mortal, but sinful, and thereby incapable of offering such a once-for-all sacrifice (see 5:1-10). Just as our Pioneer has entered into the heavenly homeland, so our High Priest has entered into the heavenly most holy place. By His High Priestly work, He enables us to enter God's presence in this present life and to enter it more fully at the consummation. As High Priest, Jesus fulfills the Pioneer's mission of bringing us into the presence of God.

The self-sacrifice of this great High Priest is compared to and contrasted with three different Mosaic sacrifices. The most obvious comparison is with the Day of Atonement sacrifice in 9:1-14. As that sacrifice made annual ritual atonement for the sins of the people, so Christ's sacrifice provides true atonement for sin once-for-all. Because Christ's sacrifice has definitively dealt with sin, it initiates a new order of relationship between God and humanity. Therefore, 9:15-22 describes it as a covenant sacrifice bringing the prophesied new covenant into being.

It is easy to overlook the third comparison. Christ's sacrifice is also seen as His inauguration or consecration to High Priesthood (see 10:1-18). Even though it does not show in our English translations, such passages in the Greek Old Testament as Exodus 29:9, Leviticus 16:32, and most clearly Leviticus 21:10 use the same word for the consecration of priests that

Hebrews uses for Christ's being "perfected" (Heb. 5:9) as our savior or High Priest.[14] By an animal sacrifice, the Old Testament priest was consecrated to his office. It is, however, by Christ's sacrifice of complete obedience that He has become our effective High Priest, able to give us victory over present temptation (see 2:17-18; 4:14-16; 8:1-2). His priesthood is based on His sacrifice and guarantees the new order (see 7:22).

When we understand how these three pictures interrelate, we will understand the overall logic of Hebrews. The Sinai Picture reminds us that the same God who addressed His people at Mount Sinai now addresses us through His Son and calls us to obedient faithfulness. The Pilgrimage Picture encourages us to obey this word of God by giving us examples of those who did and did not respond in obedience. Finally, the High Priest Picture shows us the resources available that enable us to be cleansed of sin and live in faithful obedience.

The Pilgrimage and High Priest Pictures show the goal to be obtained by obedience to God's word. The high priest offers the Day of Atonement sacrifice in order to enter the Most Holy Place, the place where God dwells. God's people traveled through the wilderness in order to enter the Promised Land, the place where they were to dwell with God. In Hebrews, both the Most Holy Place and the Promised Land represent dwelling in God's presence through the work of Christ—both now and for eternity.

It is important to observe the order in which the author deals with these pictures:

> Sinai Picture (1:1–2:4)
> > Pilgrimage Picture (2:5–4:13)
> > > High Priest Picture (4:14–10:31)
> > Pilgrimage Picture (10:32–12:13)
> Sinai Picture (12:14-29)

The historical and logical order is Sinai before Pilgrimage. God spoke to His people at Sinai, and then they made their pilgrimage to the Promised Land in response to His word. The same logic is followed in the first part of Hebrews: God spoke to us through His Son when His Son was on earth (1:1–2:4), and we are to respond by faithful obedience until we enter the heavenly homeland (2:5–4:13).

But the order is reversed in the last part of Hebrews: pilgrimage (10:32–12:13) precedes the mount of God's speaking (12:14-29). What has been said about Jesus in the central High Priest section (4:14–10:31) explains this reversal. He is the High Priest who has offered the only effective sacrifice and now sits at the Father's right hand in heaven. Our gaze is not to be on Him as He was on earth in the past, but on Him as He now is at the Father's right hand (12:1-3). As Christians we do not journey from the mount where God spoke to us, but to the mount, made accessible by our exalted High Priest, from which God now speaks (12:14-29).

This sermon does not minimize Christ's humiliation, suffering, and death. It is only through these historical events that He has become what He is at the Father's right hand. But the preacher emphasizes what Christ is and His ability to enable us today: "The point of what we are saying is this: We do have such a high priest, who sat down at the right hand of the throne of the Majesty in heaven, and who serves in the sanctuary, the true tabernacle set up by the Lord, not by man" (8:1-2).

The preacher concludes the main thrust of his argument with a solemn warning (12:25-29) which intensifies his opening exhortation (2:1-4). In chapter 13 he applies the exhortation given in this conclusion by instructing his hearers in some practical concerns of Christian living (13:1-17). In light of Christ's sacrifice which has cleansed them from sin, they are to draw near to God continually and offer the sacrifices of praise and loving deeds. Then the preacher asks for prayer (13:18-19), prays for their spiritual stability (13:20-21), and gives them a final greeting (13:22-25).

The flow of images is cinemagraphic. The drama begins with God's word at Sinai (1:1–2:4), followed quickly by the wilderness generation's tragic rejection of that word (2:5–4:13) and failure to enter the Promised Land. In a similar manner, we have heard God's word in the Son and are urged not to repeat that tragic disobedience and thus fail to enter the promised heavenly homeland. The development of the High Priest Picture in 4:14 through 10:31 is a documentary giving us the information behind the drama. Here are our resources to persevere in obedience. Through Christ we can be cleansed of sin and enter into God's presence (9:14; 10:10, 14, 19-22). These resources in Christ make us all the more responsible to obey, but they are also a great encouragement! Without forgetting the possibility of tragedy, the drama resumes in 10:32 through 12:13 with an emphasis on encouragement. Remember the long catalog of faithful pilgrims (11:1-40). Most of all, keep your eyes on Jesus and remember all that He has done (12:1-3). When the drama concludes, Sinai has become the heavenly Mount Zion. God's faithful people have the glorious and awesome privilege of approaching the God who speaks to us from the heavenly Zion through the Mediator of the new covenant (12:18-29).

The following chart is a visual representation of these great movements in the book of Hebrews:

HEBREWS 1:1–12:29 VISUALIZED

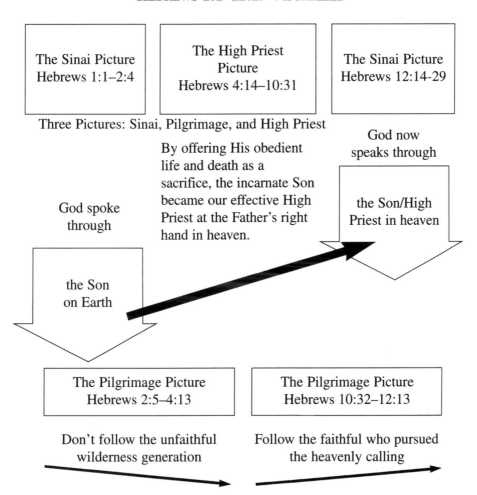

The Sinai Picture
Hebrews 1:1–2:4

The High Priest Picture
Hebrews 4:14–10:31

The Sinai Picture
Hebrews 12:14-29

Three Pictures: Sinai, Pilgrimage, and High Priest

God now speaks through

By offering His obedient life and death as a sacrifice, the incarnate Son became our effective High Priest at the Father's right hand in heaven.

the Son/High Priest in heaven

God spoke through

the Son on Earth

The Pilgrimage Picture
Hebrews 2:5–4:13

The Pilgrimage Picture
Hebrews 10:32–12:13

Don't follow the unfaithful wilderness generation

Follow the faithful who pursued the heavenly calling

Enough introduction. Now you, the reader, may approach this living God through the text of the book of Hebrews. My prayer is "that you may not be sluggish, but imitators of those who through faith and patience inherit the promises" (Heb. 6:12 RSV).

ENDNOTES

[1]For a thorough discussion of the reasons why Hebrews should be considered a sermon, see William L. Lane, *Hebrews 1–8,* vol. 47a, Word Biblical Commentary, New Testament ed. Ralph P. Martin, gen. eds. David A. Hubbard and Glenn W. Barker (Dallas: Word Books, 1991), pp. lxx–lxxv. For a simpler presentation, see William L. Lane, *Hebrews: A Call to Commitment* (Peabody, Massachusetts: Hendrickson Publishers, 1985), pp. 20–24.

[2]In such sermons the preacher would often interpret Old Testament passages phrase by phrase, as Hebrews does in 3:1 through 4:11 or in 7:1-25, or join a selection of Old Testament quotations to make a point, as Hebrews does in 1:4-14. Synagogue preachers also were fond of citing and listing Old Testament examples, such as we find in 3:7 through 4:11, 11:1-40, and 12:14-17.

[3]Although Priscilla has been suggested as the author of Hebrews, the masculine participle in the Greek text of Hebrews 11:32 shows that the author was male. William L. Lane, "Hebrews," *Dictionary of the Later New Testament and Its Development,* eds. Ralph P. Martin and Peter H. Davids (Downers Grove, Illinois: InterVarsity Press, 1997), p. 443.

[4]Lane, "Hebrews," p. 444.

[5]Quoted in Eusebius, *Ecclesiastical History* 6.25.

[6]Lane, *Hebrews 1–8,* p. liii.

[7]Lane, "Hebrews," p. 447.

[8]See commentary on Hebrews 13:9-16.

[9]At least the first five books of the Hebrew Old Testament were translated into Greek in the third century B.C. This translation took place in Alexandria, Egypt. Alexandria was the leading city of Greek learning. At the center of its vibrant intellectual life was the greatest library of the ancient world. Alexandria also had a large Jewish population, many of whom were prominent in city affairs. It is reported in a document called the *Letter of Aristeas* that Ptolemy II Philadelphus, who ruled Egypt from 285 to 246 B.C., ordered the Hebrew Old Testament to be translated into Greek and put in this library, and that this translation was done by seventy or seventy-two scholars. Thus this translation of the Greek Old Testament is often referred to as the Septuagint, the Greek word for "seventy." Sometimes it is referred to by the abbreviation LXX, the Roman numeral for seventy. Scholars today believe that the Pentateuch (the first five books of the Old Testament: Genesis, Exodus, Leviticus, Numbers, and Deuteronomy; also known as the Five Books of Moses, the Decalogue, or the Law) was translated in the third century B.C., although some of the other books may not have been translated until later. This translation of the Old Testament was the Bible of the Jews in the Greek-speaking world and was of inestimable value in the spread of the gospel.

[10]For the role of Moses in Hellenistic or Greek-speaking Judaism, see *The Epistle to the Hebrews* by Harold W. Attridge, Hermeneia—A Critical and Historical Commentary on the Bible, ed. Helmut Koester (Philadelphia: Fortress Press, 1989), pp. 104–5.

[11]The word which the New International Version translates "author" in 2:10

and 12:2 is more accurately translated by the Revised Standard Version and New Revised Standard Version as "pioneer." Pioneer includes the nuances of founder and champion or hero. It fits well with the imagery of movement toward the Promised Land. As Pioneer, Jesus overcomes all obstacles and enters the true promised land. By so doing He opens the way for others to enter.

[12]See Lane, *Hebrews 1–8,* pp. 37–38; Attridge, pp. 64–65. This seems to be the point of the comparison between the Son and the angels, even though Sinai is not mentioned per se in 1:1 through 2:4.

[13]In Hebrews 13:1-25, the writer applies the truth of what he has been saying to the very specific needs of his readers. The main part of Hebrews runs from 1:1 through 12:29 (see commentary on Hebrews 13:1-25).

[14]See Hebrews 2:10; 5:9; 7:19, 28; 9:9; 10:1, 14; and *The Epistle to the Hebrews* by Paul Ellingworth, The New International Greek Testament Commentary, eds. I. Howard Marshall and W. Ward Gasque (Grand Rapids, Michigan: Wm. B. Eerdmans Publishing Co., 1993), pp. 162–63.

HEBREWS OUTLINE

I. **THE SINAI PICTURE: HEAR THE WORD OF GOD SPOKEN THROUGH THE SON 1:1–2:4**
   A. God Has Spoken Through His Son 1:1-4
   B. The Incomparable Majesty of the Son 1:5-14
   C. The Compelling Urgency of Obedience 2:1-4

II. **THE PILGRIMAGE PICTURE: DON'T FAIL TO ENTER GOD'S REST THROUGH UNBELIEF 2:5–4:13**
   A. Our Pioneer Suffered to Lead God's Children Into Rest 2:5-18
      1. 2:5-9   Jesus, the One in Charge of the World to Come
      2. 2:10-13   The Pioneer and His Brothers
      3. 2:14-18   The Pioneer and the High Priest
   B. Our Pioneer Is Faithful Over God's Household As a Son 3:1-6
   C. Don't Follow the Example of God's Faithless Household in the Wilderness 3:7–4:11
      1. 3:7-19   Don't Harden Your Hearts As They Did
      2. 4:1-11   Enter the Rest That They Forfeited
   D. We Are Accountable Because God Has Spoken to Us Through His Son 4:12-13

III. **THE HIGH PRIEST PICTURE: DRAW NEAR TO GOD WITH A CLEANSED CONSCIENCE 4:14–10:31**
   A. Our High Priest Has Entered Heaven for Us 4:14-16
   B. The New High Priest and the Old 5:1-10
   C. Prepare Your Hearts to Receive the Truth 5:11–6:20
      1. 5:11–6:8   Don't Continue to Be Baby Christians
      2. 6:9-20   Trust in God's Promises
   D. The New High Priest Has an Eternal Priesthood 7:1-28
      1. 7:1-10   Melchizedek
      2. 7:11-19   The Priest Like Melchizedek
      3. 7:20-25   This Priest Provides Full Salvation
      4. 7:26-28   This Priest Is Just the Priest We Need
   E. The New High Priest's Sacrifice: A Different Dimension 8:1-13
      1. 8:1-2   A Heavenly Sanctuary
      2. 8:3-6   The Unique Sacrifice
      3. 8:7-13   An Appropriate Covenant

Part One

THE SINAI PICTURE: HEAR THE WORD OF GOD SPOKEN THROUGH THE SON

Hebrews 1:1–2:4

This first section of Hebrews lays the foundation for all that follows: The God who spoke in the Old Testament has now spoken through One who is His Son (see Hebrews 1:1-4). We see how great this Son is by comparing Him with the angels (see 1:5-14). It was through the angels that God revealed himself on Sinai. Hebrews 2:1-4 brings the truth home to us: Those who disobeyed God's angel-mediated word at Sinai perished (see 3:7–4:11). How much worse it will be for us if we disobey God's gracious word through His Son!

The rest of Hebrews teaches the importance of continued obedience to this revelation and the means of obedience available through our High Priest, Jesus Christ.

1

GOD HAS SPOKEN THROUGH HIS SON

Hebrews 1:1-4

These four compact verses are the keynote statement for the book of Hebrews. Their theme is clear: The God who revealed himself to His people in the Old Testament has now given His final revelation in One who is His Son. Verses 1 and 2 focus on what God the Father has done through the Son; verses 3 and 4 on the nature and accomplishments of the Son himself.

Hebrews 1:1-2a show how what God has said to us in the Son is both the continuation and the climax of what God said to His people in the Old Testament. It is helpful to contrast Hebrews 1:1 with Hebrews 1:2a in chart form.

Hebrews 1:1	Hebrews 1:2a
a. In the past . . . at many times and in various ways	a. but in these last days
b. God spoke	b. he has spoken
c. to our forefathers	c. to us
d. through the prophets	d. by his Son

Lines b and c in the chart show the *continuity* between what God said in the Old Testament and what He has now revealed in His Son.

First, the speaker is the same: The writer of Hebrews emphasizes the word **God** (1:1)—the **God** who spoke in the Old Testament has now spoken through His Son. It is the same God!

Second, there is continuity in those addressed: He spoke then to **our forefathers** (1:1) but now **to us** (1:2). **Forefathers** is a general way of referring to all of God's people in the Old Testament. The same Greek word, translated "fathers" or **forefathers,** is used in Hebrews 3:9 (quoting Psalm 95:9) and Hebrews 8:9 (quoting Jeremiah 31:32) to refer to the Sinai generation. In a sense all of God's Old Testament people were identified with those who stood before Mount Sinai (see Deuteronomy 5:3). However, the preacher is also thinking of the catalog of the faithful in Hebrews 11:1-40, many of whom lived before the Sinai revelation. They, too, are included in the **forefathers** to whom God has spoken (Heb. 1:1).

Forefathers is also a relational word. They are **our** spiritual forefathers. The writer of Hebrews was concerned with spiritual, not physical descent. **Our** refers to the writer and first readers of Hebrews, but it also refers to all of us who are faithful Christians. God's faithful Old Testament people are **our** spiritual **forefathers** because both they and we have received the word of God. Thus the response of the Old Testament faithful to God's word becomes an example for us to avoid (3:7–4:13) or imitate (11:1-40).

Items a and d in the chart emphasize the greater quality, the finality, of God's word now spoken through His Son and addressed to us. God gave the Old Testament word **in the past** (1:1). Several translations have "long ago" (NASB; NRSV) or "of old" (RSV). The Old Testament word belongs to a past era before the "today" (3:7) of God's speaking. It was partial and preliminary. It was given **at many times and in various ways** (1:1). That revelation was partial and fragmentary, never complete in itself. It was like a puzzle that no one could put together because the most important pieces were missing.

On the other hand, the final revelation of God has been given **in these last days** (1:2). The Greek words behind the term **last days** occurred frequently in the Greek Old Testament (with which our author was familiar) as a description of the time when prophesy would be fulfilled.[1] **These** days, the time since Christ has come, are the **last days** when the words of God's prophets are fulfilled. All earlier revelation has looked forward to what God has now revealed!

God spoke in those past times **through the prophets** (1:1). **Prophets** is a general term like **forefathers.** It refers primarily to the Old Testament prophets and to words they spoke, but it is here used to include all those through whom God revealed himself before Christ came.[2] Moses is usually distinguished from the prophets (see Acts 28:23), but passages like Acts 3:22-23 imply that he was a prophet. The prophets looked forward to a fulfillment!

Now, however, God has spoken through One who is **Son** (Heb. 1:2). The finality and fullness of God's revelation are guaranteed because of the quality and nature of the Person through whom He has revealed himself. It is because of who the **Son** is that this revelation is complete. This revelation brings all of the pieces of the Old Testament puzzle together. The last part of 1:2 underlines the greatness of the Son by showing what else God has done through Him.

First, God has **appointed** Him **heir of all things** (1:2). It was natural for the Father to appoint His Son as heir. **All things** is a broad term that includes everything visible and invisible. The Son is not only the heir to the visible world that we see, but He is the heir of the "world to come" (2:5). This world to come is the "Sabbath rest" that God has prepared for His people from the creation (4:3-8), the permanent city which God built (11:10), the heavenly homeland (11:16), the only thing that will remain after the judgment (12:27-29). Just as Israel was to inherit the Promised Land, so the Son has become heir to the heavenly homeland. He is the leader, the Pioneer (see the introduction and the commentary on 2:10 below) who brings God's people into that land and gives them their portion of the inheritance. Through Him they "inherit salvation" (1:14).

Heir points forward to the Son's role in the consummation of all things. **Through whom he made the universe** (1:2) reminds us of John 1:3 and points backward to His role in creation. God worked through Him to accomplish both the beginning and the end. The word translated **the universe** is a plural form which some translate as "the worlds" (NKJV; NRSV) and another as "all orders of existence" (NEB). In certain contexts the word can be translated "ages" (9:26). Here it is probably meant to include the visible universe that we see, as well as the coming age of salvation.[3]

Who is better able to reveal God than the One through whom God created the present and future worlds? This is the One who inherits and opens the way for us to share in the inheritance of that future world of salvation where we will dwell in intimate fellowship with God.

This affirmation of the Son's role in creation establishes His pre-existence and points toward His eternal deity. Hebrews 1:3 affirms the full deity of His nature while maintaining the separateness of His Person from that of the Father: **The Son is the radiance of God's glory and the exact representation of his being. . . .** These two descriptions of the nature of the Son are tied closely together. **Glory** refers to the essential nature of God in all of His majesty and greatness. God's glory is like a great beacon light. The Son is the **radiance,** the rays of light, that shine out from that beacon. Just as the radiance of a light is one with the light and yet distinct from it, so the Son is One with the Father in essence, yet is distinct from Him. Just as the light rays reveal what the light truly is because they are part of that reality, so the Son reveals what God truly is because He is One with the Father. The New Revised Standard Version translates the second description as "the exact imprint of God's very being." Just as the die used to strike a coin makes an exact imprint on that coin, just as a rubber stamp makes an exact reproduction of the words on it, so the Son is the exact **representation** of God's essential **being.** The Son is the perfect picture of God because He partakes of the reality of God. The author of Hebrews could not have stated this truth in stronger terms.

No wonder the Son is God's final revelation of himself! Sometimes we talk with people on the phone that we have never met. We hear their voices. They tell us things about themselves. We form a mental picture of what they are like. Then we meet them face to face. What they told us on the phone may have been true, but we understand them so much better after we have met them! We can hear God speak through the prophets. They offer His authentic voice. But when the Son of God became a human being, people saw God face to face. This Incarnation made it possible for us to know Him in the deepest way. All of those "phone conversations" through the prophets now fit together and make sense.

But there is more. The Son is also the One who sustains **all things by his powerful word** (1:3). The Son is involved not only with the Father in the creation and consummation, but also in the sustaining and governing of the world. He bears the world along toward God's intended purpose.[4] He directs the world merely by His **powerful word.** He exercises the same sovereign authority that God did when He spoke the world into being (see 11:3; also Genesis 1). The Son's word is identical with the Father's all-powerful creative word.

So far these verses have described what the Son is. But *how* is He the perfect revelation of God? How has He carried out God's plan for the world by becoming the heir of all things and opening the way for God's people to enter their inheritance? Hebrews 1:4 introduces the preacher's answer to these questions: **After he had provided purification for sins, he sat down at the right hand of the Majesty in heaven.**

The whole discussion of the Son's High Priesthood from Hebrews 4:14 through 10:31 explains this sentence. It is through the Son's High Priestly work that He provides **purification for sins.** The Old Testament writers often used "purification" to describe ritual or ceremonial purity (see, for example, Leviticus 12:1-8). However, the writer to the Hebrews sees the ritual purity of the old covenant as a preview of the inner heart purity that Christ brings. The Son's **purification for sins** includes both forgiveness for past sins and a heart cleansing that empowers Christians to live a life of holiness (see 9:14; 10:10, 15-18). The Son has provided this purification. The author of Hebrews is anxious that his hearers appropriate this purity.

By means of the same sacrifice with which He provided purification for sin, the Son **sat down at the right hand of the Majesty in heaven** (1:3). Here the writer clearly refers to Psalm 110:1. He quotes that verse in Hebrews 1:13 and alludes to it as he begins and finishes his discussion of Christ's sacrifice (see 8:1; 10:12) and in support of Christ's work as Pioneer (see 12:2). **Majesty in heaven** is an indirect way of speaking about God himself. This phrase emphasizes His utter greatness. **The right hand** indicates the primary place of honor and privilege. The Son completely shares in the authority of the Father. The incarnate Son who sacrificed himself to provide our purification now sits in the place of all authority. Therefore He can enable us to live faithful, holy lives and to reach our goal of joining Him in God's presence.

Thus the Son reveals the Father's hatred of sin and abundant grace to overcome sin by becoming a human being and providing for our purification. By purifying us, He brings us into direct experience of the Father himself!

Hebrews 1:4 serves as a bridge. It connects what has been said about the Son in verses 1 through 3 with the comparison of the Son and the angels in verses 5 through 14. As the eternal Son, He has always been **superior to the angels.** But in another way, He became superior to them when He provided purification for our sins, entered heaven, and sat down at the Father's right hand. It was He, and not they, who made purification and attained this exalted position. At the exaltation, He **inherited** openly what was already His, the **name** "Son." His superiority was proclaimed for all heaven to see.

This comparison with the angels gives added emphasis to the preceding description of the eternal divine nature of the Son (see 1:2-4). It also supports the preacher's contention that God's word in the Son infinitely surpasses God's word at Mount Sinai, for the angels were understood to be the mediators of the Sinai revelation (see 2:2). His eternal Sonship is indicative of how superior He is to the created angels.

ENDNOTES

[1] See Genesis 49:1; Numbers 24:14; Deuteronomy 4:30; 31:29; Daniel 2:28; 10:14; Micah 4:1.

[2] Luke 24:25 and John 6:45 are possible parallels for the use of **the prophets** to mean all Scripture.

[3] In Hebrews 6:5, another form of the root from which this word comes is used to refer to **the coming age** of salvation.

[4] The New Revised Standard Version margin reads "bearing along" instead of **sustaining.** "Bearing along" is a possible, and perhaps more literal, translation of the original Greek.

2

THE INCOMPARABLE MAJESTY OF THE SON

Hebrews 1:5-14

The writer of Hebrews develops a comparison between the Son and the angels by using a series of Old Testament quotations. He shows how these quotations relate to one another and how they demonstrate the superiority of the Son.

In Hebrews 1:5-6, the preacher quotes Psalm 2:7 and 2 Samuel 7:14 (compare 1 Chronicles 17:13) to demonstrate that God has proclaimed the Son to be the Son, and Deuteronomy 32:43[1] to confirm the submission of the angels to Him. In Hebrews 1:7-12, the preacher cites Psalm 104:4; 45:6-7; and 102:25-27. Psalm 104:4 shows that the angels are created servants. Psalm 45:6-7 and 102:25-27 describe this Son, whom God the Father has addressed, as eternal, uncreated, and sovereign. Hebrews 1:13-14 focuses on the the Son's exaltation. Psalm 110:1 (see Hebrews 1:13) is a triumphant statement of His victorious exaltation to the Father's right hand.

Note how Hebrews 1:5, 13 mark the beginning and end of this section by introducing Old Testament quotations with the words **to which of the angels did God ever say. . . .** Verse 14 concludes this section with a final description of the subservient nature and function of the angels. This description stands in contrast with what has already been said about the Son in 1:2-3.

Psalm 2:7, 2 Samuel 7:14, Psalm 45:6-7, and Psalm 110:1 are united in their Old Testament contexts by a common thread. They all refer to the kings who would descend from King David. Even within the Old

Testament, people began to look for one great king of David's line who would fulfill all of God's promises. All the kings were anointed with oil as a symbol that God had chosen them and given them His Spirit. But this king would be "God's Anointed" par excellence, called in Hebrew the "Messiah," in Greek the "Christ." The preacher who writes this sermon knows that the Old Testament's predictions of this Messiah could never be fulfilled by one who was merely human. These psalms find their fulfillment in One who is truly the Son of God.

For to which of the angels did God ever say . . . (Heb. 1:5) is clearly a question that expects the answer, "None of them." In Psalm 2:7, God speaks to the Son. In 2 Samuel 7:14, God speaks about the Son. In both He declares His divine Sonship.

Within the Old Testament context, both Psalm 2:7 and 2 Samuel 7:14 refer to a king in Jerusalem who was a descendant of King David. Psalm 2:7 is the word of God spoken to a king through a prophet. God declares that He has taken this king to be His **Son** (Heb. 1:5). The king is brought into closest relationship with God. The psalm may have been read to each succeeding king of David's line at his coronation. However, the psalm ultimately looks forward to the great king of David's line who would be the Son of God in a much greater way. This Son is One with the Father because He shares in the divine nature and is the complete revelation of God's very being (see 1:3). He is the One who would truly receive the nations as an "inheritance" and the very ends of the earth as His "possession" (Ps. 2:8), for God has appointed Him "heir of all things" (Heb. 1:2).

The "today" of the psalm is the day of coronation. It is the day of the Son's exaltation to the Father's right hand. Certainly He has always been the Son. As we have seen, Hebrews 1:2 affirms His role in creation, and 1:3 His closest identity with the Father. The eternal nature of the Son is given further support by Old Testament quotations cited in 1:7-12. However, by exalting the Son to His right hand, God has acknowledged and proclaimed to the world that He is the Son's **Father** and that the Son is indeed God's **Son** (Heb. 1:5). Later in Hebrews we will see that we live in the "today" (3:7) of the Son's exaltation. It is the "today" of opportunity. We have the opportunity to draw on the grace of our ascended Lord so that we can live in faithful obedience to Him.

The proclamation in Psalm 2:7 that the king was God's **Son** was based on God's promise to David in 2 Samuel 7:14, quoted in Hebrews 1:5b. In 2 Samuel 7:14, the prophet Nathan spoke the word of God to David. God promised David that one of his descendants would continue to sit on his throne. God would always be **Father** to this descendant, and David's descendant would always be God's **Son.** This promise also looked forward to a greater fulfillment in the descendant of David who was the eternal Son of God. Only this eternal Son would be able to "provide a place" for God's people and "plant them so that they" could "have a home of their own and no longer be disturbed" (2 Samuel 7:10). This He does by bringing them into the "rest" (Heb. 4:9), the heavenly "country" (11:13-16) that God has provided for them.

Hebrews 1:6, by contrast, gives us what God did say in relation to the angels, as found in Deuteronomy 32:43. The way in which this quotation is introduced is of great importance. The Son is referred to as the **firstborn** (Heb. 1:6). This term fits well with what has already been said about Him as the eternal Son. It emphasizes His identity with the Father in contrast to all others. He has the full privileges and prerogatives of the Father. The firstborn is head over his father's house and is his heir. So this Son is the "heir of all things" (1:2).

When does God **bring** this **firstborn into the world** (1:6)? The word used for **world** is the same word that is used for the "world to come" in 2:5. The preacher thus may be making reference to the world of salvation, God's rest (4:9), the heavenly country (11:13-16) that God has prepared for His faithful. Jesus entered that world at His exaltation. Indeed, the entrance of the **firstborn** and heir is what enables God's faithful children to share in that inheritance.

So, at the very time when the Son entered the heavenly world, the very presence of the Father, at the time when He opened the way for His followers to enter that blessed world, God commanded, **Let all God's angels worship him** (1:6b). Deuteronomy 32:43 refers to the time when God will come in judgment to punish the wicked and cleanse the "land" for His people. The Son's entrance into heaven and sitting at the Father's right hand is the decisive moment in God's saving work which fulfills this prophecy. He has cleansed His people from sin and opened the heavenly homeland for them.

At the exaltation, God proclaims to all the identity of His eternal Son. At that same time, He commands the angels to worship this Son. How great is the contrast between the Worshiped One and the worshipers!

In Hebrews 1:5-6, two quotations in reference to the Son precede one quotation in reference to the angels. In 1:7-12, one quotation in reference to the angels precedes two in reference to the Son: **In speaking of the angels he says . . .** (1:7); **But about the Son he says . . .** (1:8). The angels are temporal, changeable, created beings who are God's servants (1:7). The Son is eternal (1:8-12).

In 1:7, the preacher cites Psalm 104:4 in relation to the angels.[2] Unlike Psalm 2:7 and 2 Samuel 7:14 quoted above, Psalm 104:4 is not a word spoken directly by God within its Old Testament context. It is the word of the psalmist. However, the preacher is convinced that all Scripture is the word of God, which speaks to God's people. Thus he introduces this quotation with **he** [God] **says** (1:6-8, 10). The present tense is also important. God continues to speak through this psalm today! Psalm 104 is a description of the majesty of God as Creator and Sovereign. Hebrews 1:7 shows His complete sovereignty over the angels. They are part of creation. **He,** and He alone, **makes** them take the form of **winds**[3] or of **flames of fire.** He can cause His angels to take any form in order to serve Him. God created the angels. He is sovereign over them. They are indeed His **servants.** It might be better to translate the Greek word used here for servants as "ministers" (see the REB). This Greek word is often used for those who "minister" to God by worshiping Him in His sanctuary. The angels worship in His presence. But they are also His ministers in the sense that a king has ministers who carry out His commands. They exist to do His will (see commentary on 1:14 below).

Psalm 45:6-7 gives the words of God addressed to **the Son.** "But to the Son" (1:8 NKJV) may be a better translation than the **But about the Son** of the New International Version. Like Psalm 2:7 and 2 Samuel 7:14 cited above, Psalm 45:6-7 is directed to the king of David's line. Psalm 2 was probably written for his coronation, Psalm 45 for the royal marriage. The psalmist may be addressing the king as "God" (Ps. 45:6). The king was like God to the psalmist. It was the king's task to represent God. However, the preacher who wrote Hebrews knows that Christ the Son is the One ultimately addressed as God in this verse. He is eternal. Therefore His and only His **throne will last for ever and ever** (Heb. 1:8). His rule and the Father's rule are identical. The words of Psalm 45 and Psalm 2:7 describe a King who is greater than any human being. No merely human son of David could ever fill these shoes.

The preacher has cited Psalm 45:6-7 in order to affirm the deity of the Son and the sovereignty of His eternal kingdom, in contrast to the created status of the angels and their servant role. But note what kind of Kingdom the Son's kingdom will be. The ruling principle of this Kingdom is **righteousness** (Heb. 1:8). This Kingdom is founded on justice as no other has ever been. Those who live in this Kingdom practice righteousness. Our minds are drawn forward to Hebrews 12:14b: "Without holiness no one will see the Lord."

The preacher has proclaimed the deity and the eternity of the Son, but he does not forget the incarnation and the exaltation: When the eternal Son became a human being, He **loved righteousness;** He was exalted when **God set** Him **above** His **companions** (1:9).

The preacher is probably describing the Son's earthly obedience by the phrase, **You have loved righteousness and hated wickedness** (1:9). This form of statement is very strong. Jesus clung to and pursued everything that was right; He abhorred and completely avoided all that was wicked. He came to perfectly do the will of God (see 10:9; 4:15).

Because of this obedience unto death, God has exalted Him to the right hand, **has set [Him] above [His] companions by anointing [Him] with the oil of joy** (1:9). Hebrews 1:9 does not specify who these **companions** are. The psalmist's quoted words, however, depict a great and joyful celebration. The Son has accomplished His mission of salvation and, with great celebration, has sat down at the Father's right hand! Indeed, God will reward all "those who earnestly seek him" (Heb. 11:6) by bringing them into this great celebration through the work of the Son (see 12:22-24).

In 1:9, the Revised English Bible reads, ". . . Therefore, O God, your God has set you above your fellows. . . ." This translation may be more accurate than the New International Version's **. . . Therefore God, your God, has set you above your companions. . . .** The psalmist's words address the Son as God, just as they did in Hebrews 1:8. Through Psalm 45:6-7, the preacher has demonstrated that the Son is God. The Son is separate from the Father, but One with the Father in His deity.

Since the preacher has established the deity of the Son, he can now apply Psalm 102:25-27 to Him. These verses are a clear description of God as the eternal, unchanging Creator and Judge of the universe! The preacher uses this psalm to describe the work of the Son in both the creation (1:10, quoting Psalm 102:25) and consummation (1:11-12, quoting Psalm 102:26-27) of all things. He is the One "whom he [God the Father] appointed heir of all things, and through whom he made the universe" (1:2).

Hebrews 1:10, quoting Psalm 102:25, affirms the Son's work in creation. **In the beginning** takes readers back to the Genesis account of creation—"in the beginning God created" (Gen. 1:1). The Son is identified with the **Lord** of the Old Testament (Heb. 1:10). In the original language, **you** is emphatic[4]: **YOU** [the Son] **laid the foundations of the earth** (my emphasis). By their intricate beauty the **heavens** display the skill of their Maker's **hands.** The preacher encompasses the whole of the visible universe in the terms **heavens** and **earth** (see Genesis 1:1). The Son is its Creator.

The word **foundations** implies a degree of permanence. But this created world is not permanent. At the judgment God will shake this same "heaven" and "earth," and it will be removed (see Hebrews 12:26-27). Hebrews 1:11-12, quoting Psalm 102:26-27, proclaims the Son's role in the final end of the current visible universe. It will be helpful to diagram the structure of Hebrews 1:11-12 as follows:

(A) **They will perish,**
(B) **but you remain;**
(C) **they will all wear out like a garment.**
(D) **You will roll them up like a robe;**
(C_1) **like a garment they will be changed.**
(B_1) **But you remain the same,**
(A_1) **and your years will never end.**

With these words, the preacher contrasts the permanence of the Son of God with the transitory nature of the universe. This movement of thought is caught by the first and last phrases of these verses, lines A and A_1 above: **They** [the heavens and earth] **will perish, but . . . your** [the Son's] **years will never end.**

Lines B and B_1 strongly affirm the eternity of the Son: **you remain . . . you remain the same.** Later on the preacher shows that the eternity of the Son, His unchanging permanence, is part of the reason why we can have confidence in Him for salvation and for victory over temptation: "But because Jesus lives forever, he has a permanent priesthood" (7:24); "Jesus Christ is the same yesterday and today and forever" (13:8).

Lines C and C_1 are also parallel: **They will all wear out like a garment . . . like a garment they will be changed.** The universe is not eternal. It will not last forever. The imagery is clear. Clothes don't last. They wear out. We throw them away and get new clothes. Someday this visible universe will become threadbare. It will be **changed,** removed. The Son is permanent, but the universe is not. Later the preacher shows that the essence of unbelief is living as if this world were permanent (see commentary on 11:1-40; especially 11:1-6, 27) and the Son of God were not.

We have seen that line A parallels line A_1; line B parallels line B_1; and line C parallels line C_1. At the center of these verses is the first statement in verse 12, line D: **You** [the Son] **will roll them** [the heavens and earth] **up like a robe.** This is the main thrust of these verses. The Son is not only the One who created the universe. He is the One who will bring it to an end. It will be no harder for Him to bring it to an end that it would be for a human being to roll up a shirt and put it in a drawer. He is indeed the Beginning and the End. This understanding of the Son is vital, the necessary foundation for this whole sermon called Hebrews. If we are going to have someone we can trust, He must be eternal and permanent in the midst of this changing and temporal world. Only thus can we be steady when the world pressures us to turn aside from following God. God's eternal Son is such a Person!

This series of Old Testament quotations reaches its climax in Hebrews 1:13 with the quotation of Psalm 110:1: **Sit at my right hand until I make your enemies a footstool for your feet.** Jesus himself implied that this verse referred to Him (see Mark 12:35-37). New Testament writers often cited or alluded to this verse in reference to Jesus (see Acts 2:34, 35; Romans 8:34; 1 Corinthians 15:25; Ephesians 1:20; Colossians 3:1). Psalm 110:1 is God's invitation for the Son to sit at His right hand. The preacher has already alluded to this psalm in Hebrews 1:3 above. All the threads of thought in Hebrews 1 are brought to their high point in this verse. The eternal Son became a human being and died to make purification for our sin. He is now exalted. He sits at the Father's right hand. This is the place of ultimate authority. He fully shares the authority of the Father. He ministers from this place until the Second Coming (see 9:28), when the Father will **make [His] enemies a footstool for [His] feet.** His **enemies** are those who refuse to trust Him with a faith that leads to obedience. His own part in the judgment is assured by the fact that they will be subjected to Him, for He is the "heir of all things" (1:2).

Some have argued that Psalm 110 is the text for this sermon called Hebrews.[5] The preacher himself declares that the main point is this: "We do have . . . a high priest, who sat down at the right hand of the throne of the Majesty in heaven" (Heb. 8:1). The Son has sat down at the Father's right hand as our High Priest (see 10:12-13) and thus enables us to enter the most holy place of God's presence. He has sat down as our Pioneer (see 12:2) and thus enables us to enter the promised homeland where God dwells. Psalm 110:1 underlies the main themes of Hebrews.

God has spoken these words to the Son. They are now in effect. The Son is now at the Father's right hand with all the authority in the universe to help us come into the Father's presence. Thus Psalm 110:1 is also the key to understanding our own situation. We live between the exaltation and the final judgment. Christ has finished His saving work. He has provided for us to be cleansed from sin. He now sits at the Father's right hand with the power to bring us into God's presence. Thus we differ from the Old Testament faithful who lived before Christ and did not have this great privilege (see 11:39-40). But our situation is similar to theirs in that we live before the judgment, before His enemies are made a footstool for His feet. Thus, like the Old Testament faithful, we must walk by faith and not by sight. The significance of living between the exaltation and the Second Coming will be made clearer by the interpretation of Psalm 8:4-6 in Hebrews 2:5-9.

In Hebrews 1:14, the position of the angels is once more contrasted with this exalted position of the Son. He and He alone is the One who provides our salvation. What is said here about the angels also contrasts with what has been said about the Son in 1:2-3. Those earlier verses reminded the readers that the Son is eternal, associated with the Father in both the creation and end of all things, the exact expression of God, the One who has provided for cleansing from sin and now sits in authority at the Father's right hand. **All** is emphatic. Every one of the **angels** is included. They are **all** nothing more and nothing less than **ministering spirits. Spirits** emphasizes their noncorporeal nature. **Ministering**[6] suggests that they minister to God by worshiping in His presence. They also remind us of the ministers of a king who are **sent** by him **to serve** by carrying out his will.

They do not lead. They do not provide for human salvation. They **serve. Serve** is a very broad term, which includes the many ways in which the angels, at God's direction, helped His people in the New Testament. They may have brought messages from God (Acts 8:26; 27:23-24) or delivered one of God's people from harm (Acts 12:6-10). They may have given physical strength (Luke 22:43). But they did not and do not provide for cleansing from sin. They do not give grace to overcome temptation. They do not make the way for us to enter into God's presence. Only the Son does these things. Just as the Son has sat down at the right hand and now provides the grace necessary for us from heaven, so they have now been sent to help us in other ways.

God's people are described here as **those who will inherit salvation,** those who are on their way to inherit salvation (Heb. 1:14). His people are following the path that leads to that inheritance. What a wonderful prospect! We, and not the angels, will inherit this **salvation.** The Son is the "heir" of all (1:2). As "the pioneer of . . . salvation" (2:10 NRSV) and the "source of eternal salvation" (5:9), He brings us into this inheritance of **salvation. Salvation** includes the cleansing from sin and access to God that we now enjoy through Christ. The focus of this verse, however, is on the future aspect of this salvation, the final entrance into God's presence in the heavenly homeland, the final inheritance of those who are faithful (see 6:12; 9:15). Throughout this sermon, the preacher is determined to spur his hearers on so that they enter this inheritance. He makes this plain by the way in which he exhorts them in 2:1-4.

ENDNOTES

[1] If you look at Deuteronomy 32:43 in most English translations, you will not find the phrase, **Let all God's angels worship him,** because it is not included in the standard Hebrew text of the Old Testament. The author of Hebrews is quoting from a Greek translation of the Old Testament, which did include this statement. A Hebrew manuscript has now been discovered among the Dead Sea Scrolls which includes this line. Many scholars now believe that it was part of the original Hebrew text of Deuteronomy 32:43. The New Revised Standard Version includes this line in Deuteronomy 32:43 and translates it "worship him, all you gods." The Greek translation which Hebrews quotes has accurately interpreted "gods" in this passage as a reference to angels.

[2] If we look at Psalm 104:4 in our Old Testament, it reads as follows: "He makes winds his messengers [angels; see the margin], flames of fire his servants." Hebrews 1:7b, on the other hand, says, **He makes his angels winds, his servants flames of fire.** Hebrews is following the Greek translation of Psalm 104:4. Our English versions translate directly from the Hebrew Old Testament. However, the way in which Hebrews understands this verse is a possible way of translating the Hebrew. The Latin Vulgate also translates Psalm 104:4 in this way. See Harold W. Attridge, *The Epistle to the Hebrews,* Hermeneia—A Critical and Historical Commentary on the Bible, ed. Helmut Koester (Philadelphia: Fortress Press, 1989), p. 18, note 83.

[3] The King James Version reads "spirits" instead of **winds.** The same Greek word can be translated either way depending on the context in which it is used. It makes more sense to translate it as **winds** here since it is parallel to **flames of fire.** The same ambiguity underlies the corresponding Hebrew word in Psalm 104:4.

[4] The Greek verb contains its own subject: "you laid" is one word. However, there is a separate word that can be used for "you" to give emphasis. The preacher has used this separate word for "you" and put it first in the sentence for even stronger emphasis.

[5] George Wesley Buchanan, *To the Hebrews,* The Anchor Bible, eds. William Foxwell Albright and David Noel Freedman (New York: Doubleday, 1972), pp. xxi–xxii.

[6] **Ministering** translates a word that comes from the same root as the word translated **servants** in 1:7. I have suggested above that "ministers" would be a better translation in that verse.

3

THE COMPELLING URGENCY OF OBEDIENCE

Hebrews 2:1-4

The author of Hebrews can go no further without applying the truth to the lives of his hearers. In 2:1, he exhorts them on the basis of what he has said in 1:1-14. Hebrews 2:2-4 supports his exhortation and shows how it relates to 1:1-14. He argues in the form of an "if-then" statement. Hebrews 2:2 is the "if"; verses 3 and 4 the "then." *If* people were punished when they disobeyed the message spoken by God through the angels on Mount Sinai—and we know they were—*then* we will certainly be punished if we disobey God's word spoken through the Son.

Hebrews 2:1 offers a strong exhortation—**We must pay more careful attention. We** refers to the readers but also to all of us who have received God's blessings in Christ. The preacher emphasizes **we** in contrast to those who heard God's word at Sinai. It is a moral and spiritual imperative that we pay attention to what God has said! Our response is a matter of ultimate loss or blessing. We should certainly be **more careful** than those who heard God's word at Sinai through the angels and then disobeyed. The preacher will tell us more about them in 3:7 through 4:11. Indeed, it would be better to translate these words more strongly— "We must pay the most careful attention."[1] We should be immeasurably **more careful.** We must direct our attention **to what we have heard** God speak through His Son (2:1). All the while the writer has been thinking about what he said in 1:1—God has spoken His final word through and in His Son. This preacher wants his hearers to understand this word more deeply than ever before. He wants this word to direct their lives. Much of the rest of his sermon is a deeper explanation of this word. We will learn that it is a gracious word that invites us to be cleansed of sin and enter God's presence. This invitation comes to us only through the work of the Son who is also our High Priest.

If the preacher's hearers let their attention grow slack, they may **drift away** (2:1). At this point, the preacher does not imagine that they will deliberately turn their backs on what God has said through His Son. He doesn't think they are going to get up one day and say, "We aren't going to follow God's Son anymore." However, if they don't keep their whole attention on obeying God's Son, they may gradually go astray. Ancient mariners kept their attention on the sun and stars in order to stay on course. If they failed to pay accurate attention to these direction indicators, they would **drift away** from their intended path. They could end up somewhere very different than they had planned. If the preacher's hearers drift away from Christ, they are as truly away from Him as they would have been if they had simply denied Him and walked off.

For if could be translated "since" (2:2). Both the preacher and those who heard him were certain that the message spoken by angels was valid. This if-then statement offers one clear reason why the preacher went to so much trouble to compare the Son with the angels in 1:5-14. He wanted to compare two divine messages: the one spoken through angels and the one spoken through His Son (see 1:1-4).

God spoke His **message . . . by angels** on Mount Sinai (2:2; see Acts 7:53; Galatians 3:19). The Bible often refers to God's revelation at Mount Sinai as God's "law." The Greek words in Hebrews 2:2 translated **binding, violation, disobedience,** and **just punishment** were common legal terms. Nevertheless, God was not just concerned that His people keep certain laws and regulations. His covenant involved the deeper issue of their following Him in faith and obedience.

Every violation and disobedience is a comprehensive phrase (Heb. 2:2). Every time God's people turned away from Him, they received the appropriate punishment. The preacher is thinking of those people who stood before Mount Sinai but later refused to go into the Promised Land. They were the same people whom God had delivered from slavery in Egypt under the leadership of Moses. He will use them as an example in 3:7 through 4:11. They are often called the "wilderness generation" because they died in the wilderness. The appropriate chapters in Exodus, Leviticus, and Numbers describe their violations. Exodus 32 gives a prime example. That chapter describes how they turned to idolatry while they were still at Mount Sinai. Over and over again, this wilderness generation refused to trust God. They deliberately neglected to do what He said. That disobedience reached a climax at Kadesh Barnea (see Numbers 13–14), where they refused to enter the Promised Land. That refusal was uppermost in the preacher's mind. The **just punishment** that they received was failure to enter God's promised inheritance.

What God did when those who had heard His word at Sinai rejected Him shows us that He is serious about sin. He doesn't play around. His word is **binding** (Heb. 2:2); He always does what He says He will do. But this truth is also an encouragement. God's promised blessings are equally sure. Hebrews 6:18-19 tells us that, because God's promise is certain, we have an "anchor for the soul" that is "secure." The word translated "secure" in 6:19 is the same word translated as **binding** in 2:2. God calls His people to respond to Him with the same constant faithfulness that He shows toward us.[2]

God's people at Sinai did not escape punishment for disobedience. We certainly will not **escape if we ignore such a great salvation** (2:3). They failed to enter the Promised Land. We will fail to enter God's "rest" (4:11), the heavenly "country" (11:13-16) that He has prepared for us.

A number of translations read "if we neglect" (NKJV; NASB; NRSV) instead of **if we ignore** (2:3). The preacher fears that they might fail to take advantage of the **great salvation** that God has provided through Christ. Careless drifting (see 2:1) may lead to a "neglect" that is not totally unintentional. They are in danger of ignoring what Christ has done for them because they do not want to face the consequences of discipleship. Following Him could mean shame, difficulty, and suffering (see commentary on 10:32-34; 11:32-38; 12:4-11; 13:13).

The rest of Hebrews will show how this **salvation** is **so great** (2:3). God enacted this salvation through the Son's High Priestly work which provides blessings never before available: cleansing from sin and entrance into God's presence (see commentary on 9:14; 8:7-13; 10:15-18). The preacher shows the greatness of this salvation so that his hearers will not neglect it.

The very way in which God communicated this salvation to those who first read Hebrews indicates its certainty and effectiveness. The last half of 2:3 and all of 2:4 describe how this salvation came to them.

It **was first announced by the Lord** (2:3). Much is lost by the New International Version's translation of this statement. We could translate the original as "The beginning of its being proclaimed was through the Lord." The words and deeds of the **Lord** Jesus were the beginning, the source, and the origin of the message of salvation. He is both its content and its first proclamation. By giving himself to cleanse us from sin and bring us into God's presence, He has both provided and proclaimed this **great salvation.** God the Father provided and proclaimed this salvation through Him in order to bring "many sons to glory" (2:10). Thus our great salvation is firmly rooted in the saving work of God through Christ.

Those whom the preacher addressed had not heard or seen Jesus themselves. Neither have we. They received the message from credible witnesses—**those who** actually **heard him** (2:3). These credible witnesses **confirmed** the truth of the message to the hearers (2:3). The hearers were satisfied with these witnesses and convinced that they spoke the truth. Through books like Hebrews, we have direct access to those who heard these first witnesses.

But their faith did not depend merely on human witnesses, no matter how trustworthy. **God** himself **also testified** to the truth of this salvation. He did this through **signs, wonders and various miracles** (2:4). It is not necessary to distinguish between these three terms. They are reminiscent of the great miracles which God performed as He brought His people out of Egypt and through the wilderness to Sinai (see Exodus 7:3; Deuteronomy 4:34; 6:22; 7:19). Together these words describe various miraculous and extraordinary events that accompanied the proclamation of salvation to the hearers of this sermon.

This statement offers solid evidence for the miraculous in early Christianity. The preacher is not trying to convince his hearers that miracles happened. He argues from their knowledge of miracles. "You know the message is true because it was accompanied by miraculous signs" (see Galatians 3:5).

Signs, wonders and various miracles accompanied the first proclamation of salvation. God also gave **gifts of the Holy Spirit** to various people in the early church (Heb. 2:4). The preacher does not give any further description of these gifts. Whatever they were, they were given for the upbuilding of God's people. They were abilities given by God that went beyond the human abilities of those to whom He gave them.

The truth of the gospel rests on the historical reality of what God has done in Christ and on the credibility of the witnesses who brought the message to us. Its trustworthiness is also validated by what God does in our lives. His gospel produces what it professes to produce, cleansing us from sin and bringing us into intimate fellowship with God.

The preacher is no sensationalist. He shows no interest in the miraculous or the gifts of the Spirit for their novelty or for their own sake.

They were and are a confirmation of the message of salvation. Both the miracles and gifts were **distributed according to his** [God's] **will** (2:4). They were not given for the exaltation, manipulation, or fascination of human beings, but for the people's edification and God's glorification.

Notice how all three Persons of the Trinity are involved in the confirmation of the message of salvation. God the Father began this salvation by what He did through **the Lord** Jesus Christ (2:3). He confirmed it by **gifts of the Holy Spirit** (2:4). This message of salvation is certain. How important that we not neglect it!

For the moment, the preacher has finished applying the truth to his hearers. He is anxious to help them understand more about this **great salvation** (2:3). He plans to offer a deeper intellectual and spiritual understanding of how the Son has "provided purification for sins" (1:3) by becoming a human being and suffering death. The preacher begins to explain this truth by quoting and interpreting Psalm 8:4-6 in Hebrews 2:5-9.

ENDNOTES

[1]Compare the "much closer attention" of the New American Standard Bible.

[2]The Greek word translated **binding** in 2:1 and "secure" in 6:19 is used of our response to God in 3:14, where the New American Standard Bible translates it as "firm"—"if we hold fast the beginning of our assurance firm until the end."

Part Two

THE PILGRIMAGE PICTURE: DON'T FAIL TO ENTER GOD'S REST THROUGH UNBELIEF

Hebrews 2:5–4:13

We saw in part 1 how God's word spoken to us through His Son is much greater than God's word spoken through angels at Mount Sinai. Because Christ is the Son, He has brought the final and complete revelation of God to us. In Hebrews 2:1-4, the preacher warned that this greater revelation implied greater responsibility.

In part 2 (Hebrews 2:5–4:13), the writer continues to develop this idea of greater responsibility. He does so by comparing the response of Christians to the Son with the response of God's people who heard God speak at Sinai.

What were the Old Testament people of God to do after they heard God's word at Sinai? In obedience to that word, they were to make a faithful pilgrimage into the land God had promised them. They were to trust God to care for them on their journey and bring them into that land where they would live in fellowship with Him.

How should Christians respond to God's revelation in His Son? In obedience to this complete revelation of God, we are to make a faithful pilgrimage into the heavenly and eternal promised land, the very dwelling place of God. As our Pioneer and High Priest, the Son of God enables us to make this pilgrimage. In part 2, the preacher introduces the High Priesthood of the Son, but focuses on the Son as the Pioneer who brings God's people into the heavenly promised land.

Hebrews 2:5-18 introduces the Son as our "Pioneer" (see RSV; NRSV). In 3:1-6, the preacher shows that the Son is much greater than Moses, the pioneer who led God's people on their pilgrimage from Sinai toward the Promised Land. In 3:7 through 4:11, the preacher describes the failure of those who heard God's word at Sinai to complete their pilgrimage. He offers this as a warning to his hearers. We must not harden our hearts against God as did those who heard Him speak at Sinai (3:7-19). We must enter the rest of God that they forfeited (4:1-11). Part Two concludes with a solemn reminder of our accountability before the God who has spoken His heart-penetrating word to us (4:12-13).

4

OUR PIONEER SUFFERED TO LEAD GOD'S CHILDREN INTO REST

Hebrews 2:5-18

In Hebrews 1:1-4, the writer described the eternal Son of God, who is God's final and complete revelation of himself. In 1:5-14, he contrasted the Son with the angels. He portrayed the Son as the Creator (1:2) and Sustainer of the universe (1:3), the Heir of all things (1:2), and the One now exalted to God's right hand (1:3). The angels, on the other hand, are created and temporal (1:7), they serve those who are the heirs of God's blessings (1:14), and they worship the One exalted to God's right hand (1:6). Thus in every way the Son is superior to them.

But the preacher has not yet explained the phrase "After he had provided purification for sins" (1:3). It is the Son's providing purification for the sins of humanity that the preacher begins to explain in 2:5-18. This provision for purification is closely associated with and a prerequisite for His ascending to the Father and sitting "down at the right hand of the Majesty in heaven" (1:3). In providing purification, the Son again stands in contrast to the angels. God sent them to "serve" (1:14) those who would receive His eternal salvation. But the Son actually became a human being so that by providing purification He might make that eternal salvation available.

Hebrews 2:5-18 can be divided into three closely related paragraphs: 2:5-9; 2:10-13; and 2:14-18. The first paragraph (2:5-9) shows that the one who rules the coming world of salvation is none other than the incarnate Son Jesus who died for everyone. The following two paragraphs begin to explain why, in light of God's character and the human situation, the Son had to die in order to open for us this world of salvation. Paragraph 2 (2:10-13) shows that this Person who rules the world of salvation is the Pioneer who identifies with God's people to lead them into the promised salvation. However, according to paragraph 3 (2:14-18), identification with mortal, sinful humanity means that the Pioneer had to die. Since sin is the effective barrier that keeps God's people from their eternal homeland, it was only by becoming High Priest that the Pioneer could fulfill His mission. The work of the High Priest was to sacrifice for sin.

1. JESUS, THE ONE IN CHARGE OF THE WORLD TO COME 2:5-9

The world to come (2:5) is another description of the "salvation" (1:14) that Christians will inherit, the "great salvation" (2:3) which we must not neglect. It is the new order of salvation established by Christ, which we begin to enjoy now but which will come in its fullness at His return.[1] This salvation is the same thing as the "glory" into which, according to 2:10, God is bringing His people. The author of Hebrews will describe it as the "rest" that the Old Testament wilderness rebels lost (3:7-19) and the heavenly "homeland" that has always been the goal of God's people (11:13-16).

God is the implied subject of 2:5. He has not subjected this coming world of salvation to the angels. They may help Christians along the way, but they did not provide the means of entrance to that present but yet coming order of salvation, nor do they rule over it. Who then is in charge of this salvation? The answer is implicit in Psalm 110:1, a verse alluded to in Hebrews 1:3 and quoted in 1:13: the Son, to whom God has said, "Sit at my right hand." Psalm 8:4-6 is quoted in Hebrews 2:6-8a and interpreted in 2:8b-9 in order to elucidate this answer and ultimately to show that the One who thus sat down is Jesus who died for all (see Hebrews 2:9).

Psalm 8 is a hymn addressed by a human being to God. However, the preacher is interested in the content of this psalm, not its human author. Note how indefinite he is in his identification of the author—**there is a place where someone** (Heb. 2:6), but the word **testified** indicates that the content of the psalm is very important. The preacher uses that same word a second time when he introduces a quotation from Jeremiah 31:33-34 at the conclusion of his discussion of Christ's High Priesthood in Hebrews 10:15. It is a stronger form of the word translated "declared" and used to affirm the witness of Scripture in 7:8 and 7:17. The Revised English Bible catches the awesome nuance of this introduction: "There is somewhere this *solemn assurance"* (my emphasis).

However, when we first read the psalm quoted in Hebrews 2:6-8, it does not appear that the Son is the one who rules the world to come. Rather, the psalm seems to say that **man** or **the son of man** is in charge (Heb. 2:6). In a sense this is so. The preacher has already said that it is redeemed human beings who will inherit salvation (see 1:14). He knows that **man** and **son of man** are synonymous terms which refer to humanity in general.[2]

The preacher is aware that Psalm 8 was written to give thanks for the position God has given humanity in His creation. In the light of God's glory displayed in the wonders of the heavens (see Psalm 8:3), the psalmist marvels at the fact that God is mindful of and cares for humanity (Psalm 8:4, quoted in Hebrews 2:6). God has shown that care by giving human beings an exalted position just a little lower than the angels[3] (Psalm 8:5, quoted in Hebrews 2:7) and has crowned them with glory and honor (Psalm 8:5, quoted in Hebrews 2:7) by putting the whole creation under their feet (Psalm 8:6, quoted in Hebrews 2:8). However, in the light of Christ's coming, the preacher sees a new depth in this psalm, both in the way it relates to humanity in general and in its relationship to Jesus the perfect human being.[4]

The preacher gives no interpretation of Psalm 8:4, quoted in Hebrews 2:6: **What is man that you are mindful of him, the son of man that you care for him?** The psalmist was amazed at God's care for human beings who seemed so insignificant in light of the vastness and glory of the created heavens. Perhaps the preacher is amazed because of the great salvation of **the world to come** (Heb. 2:5) which God has provided for humanity through His Son.

In Hebrews 2:8b-9, the preacher interprets the three lines quoted from Psalm 8:5-6 in Hebrews 2:7-8a: (1) **You made him a little lower than the angels;** (2) **you crowned him with glory and honor** (3) **and**

put everything under his feet. He begins in verse 8b with the last of these three lines, **and put everything under his feet.** In verse 9 he interprets lines 1 and 2: **You made him a little lower than the angels; you crowned him with glory and honor.** His purpose is to show how this psalm in praise of God's blessings on humanity applies specifically to Jesus.

And put everything under his feet (Psalm 8:6b, quoted in Hebrews 2:8a)—in verse 8b the preacher defines the **everything** that God has subjected by saying that it excludes nothing. The Greek term here translated **everything** is very inclusive. Other translations read "all things" (KJV; NKJV; NASB; NRSV; compare the RSV). The psalmist, however, defined the "all things" of Psalm 8:6 in Psalm 8:7-8 as "All sheep and oxen, and also the beasts of the field, the birds of the heavens, and the fish of the sea, whatever passes through the paths of the seas" (NASB). By not quoting these verses, the author of Hebrews is able to expand **everything.** **Everything** includes the world of salvation made available in Christ which culminates in the heavenly homeland God has made for His people.[5]

There is one key question in regard to Hebrews 2:8: To whom do the three **him**'s of 2:8b refer? Who is the **him** to whom God has subjected everything but under whom we do not yet see all things subjected? Is the preacher still speaking about humanity, or is he already speaking about Jesus, as he does in 2:9? The Revised English Bible makes it clear that the writer is referring to humanity by substituting "man" for the third **him.** The New Revised Standard Version does the same by using the plural pronoun "them" throughout.[6]

The preacher's ambiguity is probably intentional. In the first place, he is speaking about humanity. Although Psalm 8 describes the exalted place given to humanity in God's creation, humanity has fallen into sin. A look at the newspaper will verify the preacher's observation that at present we do not see everything subject to him (humanity). Certainly humanity has fallen short of the great salvation which God has provided and of dwelling in God's presence in the heavenly homeland.

But the psalm also applies to Jesus, as Hebrews 2:9 makes clear. He is the man par excellence, the representative of humanity.[7] He is the One who, as a man, will enable humanity to fulfill the destiny to which the psalm points. We will not see everything subject to him (see 2:8b) until He comes again and we fully enter into the final salvation we are to inherit.

However, 2:9 indicates that the two statements of Psalm 8:5, quoted in Hebrews 2:7, do apply to Jesus now. The following diagram shows how the three statements from Psalm 8:5-6 apply to Jesus:

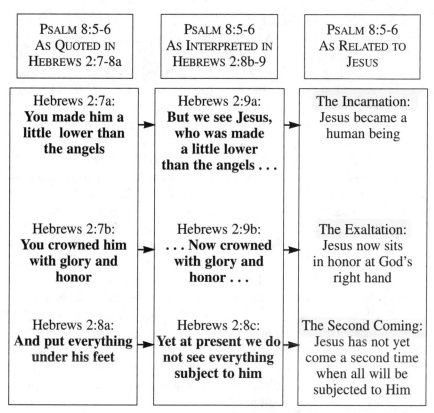

PSALM 8:5-6 AS QUOTED IN HEBREWS 2:7-8a	PSALM 8:5-6 AS INTERPRETED IN HEBREWS 2:8b-9	PSALM 8:5-6 AS RELATED TO JESUS
Hebrews 2:7a: **You made him a little lower than the angels**	Hebrews 2:9a: **But we see Jesus, who was made a little lower than the angels . . .**	The Incarnation: Jesus became a human being
Hebrews 2:7b: **You crowned him with glory and honor**	Hebrews 2:9b: **. . . Now crowned with glory and honor . . .**	The Exaltation: Jesus now sits in honor at God's right hand
Hebrews 2:8a: **And put everything under his feet**	Hebrews 2:8c: **Yet at present we do not see everything subject to him**	The Second Coming: Jesus has not yet come a second time when all will be subjected to Him

The psalmist said, **You made him a little lower than the angels** (Heb. 2:7a). The preacher explains these words: **We see Jesus, who was made a little lower than the angels** (2:9a) when He became a human being. The perfect tense of the Greek verb translated **was made a little lower** suggests that, although Jesus is now at the Father's right hand, the effects of His having become a human being continue.

The psalmist said, **You crowned him with glory and honor** (Heb. 2:7b). The preacher explains that Jesus is now **crowned . . . with glory and honor** since He has been exalted to heaven and is sitting in authority at the Father's right hand. Again, the perfect tense of the verb translated **crowned** implies that Jesus continues in this position of **glory and honor.** Thus **you crowned him with glory and honor** in Psalm 8:5 refers to the same event as the first part of Psalm 110:1, quoted in Hebrews 1:13: "Sit at my [God's] right hand."

The psalmist said, **[You] put everything under his feet** (Ps. 8:6, quoted in Heb. 2:8a). The preacher explains, **. . . We do not [yet] see everything subject to him** (Heb. 2:8), for this subjection will only occur at Jesus' second coming when He brings His own into the fullness of eternal salvation. Thus, this **everything [being] subject to him** refers to the same event as the last part of Psalm 110:1 (Heb. 1:13), "until I make your enemies a footstool for your feet." When all is subject to Jesus, it will be subject to His people as well, for they will then "inherit salvation" (1:14). In Him and in them humanity will reach its destiny.

The English versions rearrange the phrases of Hebrews 2:9 in order to offer good English style. It is helpful, however, to look at these phrases in their original Greek word order. Here is a more literal, but less smooth, English translation: "The one who has been made a little lower than the angels, we see Jesus, because of the suffering of death, with glory and honor crowned." This translation is awkward in English because it separates the clause "the one who has been made a little lower than the angels" from the word **Jesus** with which it belongs. But it shows that the phrase "we see Jesus, because of the suffering of death" comes between the two references to Psalm 8:5: **who has been made a little lower than the angels** and **crowned with glory and honor.** Jesus' death is the link between these two phrases. It is the essential link between His incarnation and His subsequent glorification. He became a human being **a little lower than the angels** so that He could suffer death (Heb. 2:14-16). Because of that death, He is now **crowned with glory and honor** at the Father's right hand. His death is the culmination of His incarnation and the cause of His exaltation to God's right hand.

The use of the name **Jesus** is significant. **Jesus** is the name the Son of God received when He became a human being **a little lower than the angels.** It was as **Jesus** that He died. The preacher uses the name **Jesus** when he speaks of His humanity and suffering.[8]

The last phrase of 2:9 brings verses 5 through 9 to their climax: **so that by the grace of God he might taste death for everyone. So that** refers back to the whole argument of the preceding verses. Why did the Son of God become a human being, suffer death, and then ascend and be seated at the Father's right hand? He did all this **so that** He might fully **taste** or experience **death** for the benefit of every human being! Even His exaltation is necessary for the benefits of His death to be available for all. The preacher's teaching on the High Priesthood of Christ in 4:14 through 5:10 and 7:1 through 10:18 will show how this is so. However, we already know that the One in charge of the coming world of salvation (see 2:5) became the human being Jesus and died in order to open that world of salvation for us!

Jesus' death was totally **by the grace of God.** The death of Jesus for us was motivated totally by God's own goodness and His desire for our good. He sought to bless us by bringing us to himself. We are reminded of John 3:16: "For God so loved the world. . . ." Hebrews 2:10-18 will show more clearly how the death of Jesus expresses the character of God and provides for our salvation.

2. THE PIONEER AND HIS BROTHERS 2:10-13

The New International Version has rearranged the original word order of Hebrews 2:10 for ease of reading. The phrase **it was fitting that God** translates the first words in the Greek text (compare the NKJV and NASB). The preacher is concerned to show that the death of Jesus was appropriate for the God whose character is revealed to us in the Bible.

This verse tells who God is and what He accomplished through the death of Jesus. This is the God **for whom and through whom everything exists** (2:10). This description sets the eternal God in sharpest contrast with the suffering of death and emphasizes His sovereign power to accomplish His purpose.

What did He sovereignly intend to accomplish? **Bringing many sons to glory** (2:10). Entrance into **glory** is the destiny of the redeemed humanity pictured in Psalm 8. It is the blessing that Jesus' death brings to the faithful. As Jesus' death enabled him to be "crowned with glory and honor" (2:9), so it is the means by which God brings **many sons to glory.** We will share the glory of Jesus at the Father's right hand! We will be **sons,** with a small *s,* through Jesus who is the Son, with a capital *S.*

The rest of Hebrews describes how Jesus enables us to enter this blessed place of the presence of God and how we who enter it must live. The preacher paints two great pictures of this place of glory in God's presence: It is the heavenly homeland into which Jesus the Pioneer leads God's pilgrims (see 3:1–4:13; 11:1–12:13; 12:22-24); it is the heavenly most holy place opened to true worshipers through the High Priest, Jesus, the Son of God (see 4:14–10:31).

It is not just any death that is appropriate to the God whose character and purpose the preacher describes. It is the **author** of His sons' eternal **salvation** who suffered death. He suffered in order that He might be made **perfect** as their Savior (2:10). By His death He was made perfectly able to save them.

As previously noted, the word that the New International Version here translates as **author,** the Revised Standard Version and New Revised Standard Version translate "pioneer." "Pioneer" catches much of the flavor of the Greek word.[9] A pioneer is often a person who enters and enables

63

others to enter a new country. Thus it is a particularly appropriate description of the Son who, through His entrance (see 10:19-22), enables us to enter the true heavenly promised land of God's presence (see commentary on 3:1–4:13; 11:1–12:13). Like other pioneers, He opened the way to this promised land only through hardship and suffering. We will experience the **salvation** He provides in its fullness when we complete our entry into that heavenly homeland at Christ's return. However, we begin to enjoy that **salvation** now as we enter into intimate fellowship with the Father.

The Son of God, of course, was, is, and always will be perfect. However, by becoming a human being and dying He became **perfect** as our Pioneer or Savior.[10] That is, He accomplished everything necessary so that He would be able to save us to the fullest and bring us into the promised homeland. The word used here for Jesus being made **perfect** as our Savior is the same word used for the consecration of priests in the Greek translation of the Old Testament used by the preacher (see Leviticus 21:10). Jesus' being made **perfect** as our Savior was His consecration to High Priesthood. It is as High Priest that He is able to save us.

The preacher affirms that it is completely in line with—indeed an expression of—the character of the eternal God to use the Pioneer's suffering of death to bring God's people into closest fellowship with Him. But why? Here is a nutshell summary of the preacher's answer to this question as given in 2:11-18: It was fitting because of God's relationship with His Son and with His people (see 2:11-13) and because of the mortal, sinful condition of those people (see 2:14-18).

Hebrews 2:11 gives the basic premise which is expanded in 2:12-13: Because the Son of God and the people of God are both related to God, they have a relationship with each other. **The one who makes men holy** is the Son of God (see 9:14; 10:10, 14), the One who as the Pioneer of their salvation will bring them into God's glory (see 2:10). **Those who are made holy** is obviously a designation for God's people (2:11). He makes them **holy** by cleansing them from sin so that they can have fellowship with a holy God. Thus, although the Son of God and the people of God **are of the same family,** their relationships to that family are not the same (2:11).

Instead of **are of the same family,** the New Revised Standard Version reads "all have one Father" and the New American Standard Bible, "are all from one Father." The New American Standard Bible, however, places "Father" in italics to show that there is no word for "Father" in the Greek text. The New King James Version renders the Greek, literally, "are all of one." The "One" referred to is, no doubt, God.[11] The relationship, however, is expressed in an indefinite way because, as indicated above, the relationship of the Son to the Father differs greatly from the relationship God's people have with Him.

It may be necessary to adjust our thinking a bit in order to grasp what is being said here. We are used to thinking of Jesus as the founder of the church and thus of the people of God. But the writer of Hebrews reminds us that God had a people long before Christ came, even if they could not yet enter God's presence through the work of Christ (see 11:39-40). Hebrews 11:1-40 chronicles a number of those who were part of the pre-Christ people of God. Hebrews 2:11 may be dealing first of all with pre-Christ relationships, with relationships before the Incarnation. Before the Incarnation, God had a people who needed to be made **holy.** He also had a Son who would make them **holy.**

What then was the relationship between the pre-incarnate Son and the people of God? Here is the astounding thing: Because the pre-incarnate Son and the people of God both were related to God, the Son **is not ashamed to call them brothers** (2:11). The Son defines their relationship to God by elevating them to the status of being His **brothers** and thereby God's sons! The double negative included in the phrase **not ashamed** offers a strong affirmation. The Son is not ashamed before others to own God's people as His **brothers.** His elevating them to the status of being His brothers and God's children is closely related to His making them holy. Only through His making them holy can they enjoy the fruits of their brotherhood with Him and enter into the privileges of Divine sonship. Thus, this brotherhood is rooted in the pre-incarnate relationships between God and His Son and between God and His people. However, it becomes a reality through the saving work of the Son who as the Pioneer brings God's people to glory.

It is unfortunate that the New International Version and the New Revised Standard Version supply the name **Jesus** in 2:11 to prevent readers from mistaking God as the subject of the sentence. The New King James Version and the New American Standard Bible represent the Greek text by using "He." The writer of Hebrews uses the name "Jesus" when he wants to emphasize Christ's earthly life and suffering (see commentary on 2:9 above). As we will see in the discussion of 2:12 below, Christ declares that God's people are His "brothers" when He is exalted to God's right hand.

The Pioneer acknowledges God's people as His brothers in the words of Psalm 22:22, quoted in Hebrews 2:12: **I will declare your name to my brothers; in the presence of the congregation I will sing your praises.** It is important both to look at this psalm in its Old Testament context and to see how Jesus and the Gospel writers used it.

Psalm 22 is a "prayer for help by one undergoing deep suffering."[12] It begins with a cry of abandonment: The psalmist has a deep sense that God has deserted him (Ps. 22:1-2). He compares his present distress with God's past goodness (Ps. 22:3-11), describes in great detail his present misery and suffering (Ps. 22:12-18), and then climaxes his prayer with an urgent plea for deliverance (Ps. 22:19-21). Psalm 22:22, quoted in Hebrews 2:12, begins a new section of the prayer where the psalmist declares his praise for God's deliverance.

Jesus understood this psalm as a description of His own suffering. Its opening words were His cry of dereliction from the cross: "My God, my God, why have you forsaken me?" (see Matthew 27:46; Mark 15:34).[13] The Gospel writers saw other verses in this psalm as descriptive of Jesus' passion: Psalm 22:7-8 describes the mockery thrown at Him by His tormentors (Matthew 27:39-43); and Psalm 22:18 predicts that His garments will be divided by lot (Matthew 27:35; John 19:23-24). Thus it is very likely that the understanding of this psalm as a description of the suffering of Jesus was part of the Christian tradition which the preacher received. He appropriately develops this tradition in line with Jesus and the Gospel writers when he interprets Psalm 22:22 as the exalted Son's declaration of God's deliverance. If the cry of abandonment fit the cross, then the cry of victory must be descriptive of the exalted Son sitting at the Father's right.[14]

The psalmist's **brothers** are **the congregation,** the people of God gathered for worship (Heb. 2:12). The psalmist declares God's **name** to them and praises God by telling them all that God has done for him. The Pioneer who has now entered God's presence declares to God's people all that God has done through Him for their salvation. By so doing, Christ confirms that they are His **brothers.**

Two additional Old Testament citations are attributed to the Pioneer of our salvation in Hebrews 2:13. It was not hard to see how Christ could have spoken Psalm 22:22. It is not as easy to see how these next two quotations could be attributed to Him. Nevertheless, they support and elucidate the quotation from Psalm 22:22. They, too, affirm the speaker's identity with the people of God and his confidence in divine vindication despite rejection by those who oppose God. Isaiah originally spoke both of these statements, and they are found in Isaiah 8:17-18.

There is a difference of wording between the Hebrew Old Testament which our English translations follow and the Greek translation used by the writer of Hebrews. Here is a translation of the Greek of Isaiah 8:17-18. The part which the author of Hebrews quotes in Hebrews 2:13 is emphasized: "And one shall say, I will wait for God who has turned away

His face from the house of Jacob, and **I will put my trust in him. Here am I and the children which God has given me:** and they shall be for signs and wonders in the house of Israel from the Lord of hosts, who dwells in mount Zion."[15]

As can be seen by observing the translation above, the writer has divided one Scripture passage into two quotations by inserting the phrase **and again he says** between **I will put my trust in him** (see Isaiah 8:17b)[16] and **Here am I, and the children God has given me** (see Isaiah 8:18a). It appears that the preacher has divided this passage because he wants to make a separate point with each part. Psalm 22:22 is both a declaration of confidence in God's deliverance and an affirmation of identity with God's people. The preacher uses Isaiah 8:17b to reinforce the former of these emphases and Isaiah 8:18a to support the latter.

A look at the broader context in Isaiah shows that, although Isaiah has faithfully proclaimed God's message, he has been rejected by "the house of Jacob" (Isa. 8:17). Despite this rejection, Isaiah was certain that God would judge the disobedient and bring salvation to the faithful just as Isaiah had prophesied. God would vindicate him. Thus Isaiah says, "I will put my trust in him." In the same way, Christ the Pioneer, who suffered rejection in order to become our Savior, expresses confidence in His vindication by God, a vindication that occurred when He sat down at the Father's right hand. His faithful trust in and obedience to the Father were crucial to accomplishing the salvation of His brothers (see Hebrews 5:6-10; 10:5-10). His trust and obedience are the basis of their assurance that He has opened the way for them into God's presence (see commentary on 10:19-25).

"Here am I and the children which God has given me" (Isa. 8:18a) immediately follows Isaiah's declaration of trust in God (see Isaiah 8:17b). Isaiah's own children were a living embodiment of his message. Isaiah had prophesied God's judgment on God's wicked people. He had also prophesied that a righteous remnant would remain. Isaiah named one son "a remnant will return" (Isa. 7:3). The name of another meant "hasten booty, speed spoil" (Isa. 8:3) and was a reminder to all of God's coming judgment. Isaiah's own children were the beginning of God's faithful remnant. Thus Isaiah identified himself with the righteous remnant of God's people. Similarly, our Pioneer uses these same words to affirm His identity with God's people, those God has given Him as His **children** (Heb. 2:13). The preacher divided this quotation because he wanted to be sure that his readers got both points. Our Pioneer was confident in the fact that God would vindicate Him and raise Him to the Father's right hand. Our Pioneer also identified with the faithful people of God.[17]

It seems a bit odd to speak of God giving **children** to the Pioneer who is also God's Son. After all the Pioneer/Son has just referred to them as **brothers** (2:11-12). However, the word here translated **children** is often used to express a close loving relationship without any hint of physical descent.[18] Jesus used this word in the original Greek to describe His disciples (see John 21:5). Thus the term complements and enriches the term **brother.** By His own declaration the Son made them His **brothers** (2:11-12). By God's gift they are His dear **children.** The gracious divine initiative is the basis of the privileged position given to God's people.

3. THE PIONEER AND THE HIGH PRIEST 2:14-18

Since God's Son is One with God, and since God's people belong to God, the Son, who is also their Pioneer, has elevated them to be His "brothers" and received them from the Father as His dear "children" (Heb. 2:13). What did this gracious action require of Him? Hebrews 2:14-18 shows what was involved in the Pioneer/Son's making God's people His brothers and accepting them as God's children. They had been beset by the fear of death (2:15) and by sin (2:17). Thus, as their Pioneer, He had to become fully human so that He could, through His own death, deliver them from the fear of death (2:14-15). This He could only do by delivering them from their sin as their High Priest. Thus this section ends by introducing the High Priest theme which dominates the central section of Hebrews (4:14–10:18).

Hebrews 2:16-17 is parallel to and helps explain 2:14-15. The chart below lays out these two pairs of verses in parallel clauses.

Hebrews 2:14-15	Hebrews 2:16-17
Since the children have flesh and blood,	**For surely it is not angels he helps, but Abraham's descendants.**
he too shared in their humanity	**For this reason he had to be made like his brothers in every way,**
so that by his death he might destroy him who holds the power of death—that is, the devil—	**in order that he might become a merciful and faithful high priest in service to God,**
and free those who all their lives were held in slavery by their fear of death.	**and that he might make atonement for the sins of the people.**

The first clause of each pair of verses makes a statement about the people of God: **Since the children have flesh and blood** (2:14) and **For surely it is not angels he helps, but Abraham's descendants** (2:16). Each of these statements provides the reason for the clause that follows.

The second clause of each pair is a description of the Incarnation: **He too shared in their humanity** (2:14) and **for this reason he had to be made like his brothers in every way** (2:17). The second of these two clauses clarifies the first.

The third and fourth clause of each pair describe the saving purpose of the Incarnation as portrayed in the second clauses. The third clause of each pair gives the purpose of the Incarnation in a general way: **So that by his death he might destroy him who holds the power of death— that is, the devil** (2:14) and **in order that he might become a merciful and faithful high priest in service to God** (2:17). Notice that the first of these two clauses relates Christ's work to the Devil; the second, to God.

The fourth pair of clauses shows how the saving purpose of the Incarnation applies to God's people: **And free those who all their lives were held in slavery by their fear of death** (2:15) and **that he might make atonement for the sins of the people** (2:17). This last pair highlights a basic issue in relating 2:16-17 to 2:14-15, the relationship of sin to death.

Let us turn now to 2:14-15. What does the Pioneer's acceptance of God's people as His "brothers" and **children** entail? **Since the children have flesh and blood,** it required that **he too** must share **in their humanity. Flesh and blood** is a phrase that emphasizes the finiteness and weakness of humanity. It conveys the exact opposite of the description of God in 2:10: "for whom and through whom everything exists." The New American Standard Bible offers a more descriptive translation: "the children share in flesh and blood." They partake of it. The tense of the Greek verb meaning "to share" implies that it is the continual condition of their existence. It is their nature. Most important of all, those who share in **flesh and blood** are mortal and destined to die! It is this transient, mortal **humanity** in which the Son **shared** (2:14). The aorist tense of this verb **shared** is also important. It helps us see that this humanity was not a part of His nature but, *at a specific time and place,* He entered into it and made it His own.

The Son shared in our dying humanity so that we might "share in the" undying "heavenly calling" (3:1; compare 3:14). He took on our mortal humanity with the intention of dying because it was only **by his death** that **he might destroy him who holds the power of death—that is, the devil** (2:14). The Greek word in 2:10 which the New International Version translates "author" and which we have been translating "pioneer" also includes the idea of "champion." Our Pioneer is our Champion who overcomes the one who has the power of death over us, but only at great cost, the cost of His own death. At this point, there is no explanation of how the Devil had the power of death or how our Champion's death destroyed him.

Hebrews 2:15, however, helps us to understand the *effect* of our Pioneer/Champion's destroying the Devil. The Devil can no longer hold us **in slavery by** the **fear of death.** To be **flesh and blood** means to be subject to death. Before our Pioneer assumed mortal flesh and blood, our humanity also implied slavery to **fear of death** for **all** our **lives.** Fear of death characterized our existence. It is important to notice that our Pioneer does not save us from physical **death.** Even Christians are still "destined to die" (9:27). But He did save us from slavery through the **fear of death.** Because of what He did, His people need never fear death!

If we would know *how* our Pioneer delivered us from the fear of death, it is important to know how the Devil enslaved us by the fear of death. The answer is given to us in 2:16-17—sin. The sinfulness of humanity makes death fearsome. Not only are human beings "destined to die," but after death "to face judgment" (9:27). By following the Devil's enticement to sin, human beings receive God's condemnation and punishment at the Judgment which they must face after death. Hebrews 9:27 does not say whether this Judgment occurs immediately after death or at Christ's return, but the latter seems to be implied (see commentary on 9:27). Through the work of Christ, however, the Christian will receive not condemnation, but the fullness of "salvation" at Judgment (9:28). Thus Christ replaces humanity's common, foreboding fear of punishment and separation from God after death with the assurance of joy in God's presence (see commentary on 12:22-24).

Hebrews 2:16-17 describes how our Pioneer/Champion deals with sin. However, in order to deal with sin He must be our High Priest. Before Christ came, any of God's people who wanted to be cleansed from sin would naturally go to a priest and offer sacrifice. A priest was a person, by definition, whose business it was to deal with the sin which prevented one from approaching God (see commentary on 5:1). Therefore, only as a High Priest who deals with sin can Christ fulfill His role as Pioneer, the role of entering himself—and thereby enabling our entry—into the presence of God. Just as Christ's dealing with sin is the key to His dealing with the fear of death, so Christ's High Priesthood is the key to His success as Pioneer.

Hebrews 1:5-14 shows how high Christ is above the angels. Hebrews 2:5-15 has shown Christ's concern for the human people of God and His identification with them. He is concerned about saving them and not angels: **Surely it is not angels he helps** (2:16). They are not subject to sin and the fear of death, so they don't need His help. The purpose of this negative statement is to reinforce the following positive one: He does help **Abraham's descendants** (2:16). This term describes the people of God both before and after Christ's coming. They are the heirs of the promise given to Abraham (see 6:13-20) who are on their way to the heavenly promised land that Abraham sought (see 11:13-16). Christ came as their Pioneer to enable them to enter that heavenly homeland. The word that the New International Version (and most modern versions) translates as **he helps** can have several other shades of meaning. The Revised Standard Version translates that word "is concerned with," and the New Revised Standard Version, "come to help." The word can literally mean "take hold of." Many of the church fathers understood this word as a reference to the Incarnation.[19] The Son "takes on, takes hold of, takes charge of" God's people in order to bring them into the fullness of salvation that He has provided. This term is particularly appropriate for the Son as the Pioneer who "takes hold of" God's people by the hand and leads them into the heavenly promised land.[20]

Because our Pioneer was taking hold of God's people to bring them into the fullness of what God has for them in God's own presence, **he had to be made like his brothers in every way** (2:17). The word **brothers** reminds us of Christ's declaration in 2:12 which made God's people His **brothers.** If they are His brothers He must become **like them in every way.** This statement intensifies and clarifies what has already been said about the Incarnation. His humanity is absolutely complete. He is completely like us, except that He never yielded to temptation (see 4:15; 7:26).

The purpose of His complete identification with humanity was **that he might become a merciful and faithful high priest in service to God** (2:17). Those who first heard Hebrews would now understand more clearly why the Son had to become completely human. To them it was axiomatic that a priest must be part of the group he represents (compare 5:1).[21] How else could he accomplish his work of representing that group to God? The New International Version translators may have chosen the phrase **in service to God** because it flows smoothly in the English language. But the representative character of a high priest's work is brought out more clearly by the more literal New American Standard Bible translation, "in things pertaining to God."

The Greek word order puts emphasis on the word **merciful.** A more literal English rendering of this word order would read like this: "in order that a merciful he might become and faithful high priest." **Merciful** implies that the Son will be a High Priest who can help *His people*. **Faithful** indicates that he will be fully obedient *to God*. The letter to the Hebrews will show that it is the Son's complete faithfulness to God that enables Him to be merciful toward God's people (see 10:5-18). Thus, if He had yielded to temptation He could not have saved us (see 4:15). Hebrews 4:14 through 10:18 is the preacher's discussion of the Son's merciful High Priesthood based on His faithful obedience. After completing the paragraph at hand, the preacher speaks about our High Priest's faithfulness in 3:1-6, followed by encouragement for us to be faithful in 3:7 through 4:13. He continues to urge us to faithfulness in 10:32 through 12:13.

As noted earlier, this whole section—Hebrews 2:5-18—begins the explanation of the Son's making "purification for sins" first mentioned in the prologue (1:3). Thus, this entire discussion has been moving toward the last phrase of 2:17: **and that he might make atonement for the sins of the people.** There is no word in the Greek text for the **and** at the beginning of this clause in the New International Version. The addition of this word and the way in which the New International Version has translated the words following **and** make it sound as if there were two purposes for the Son's becoming like His brothers in every way: first, **that he might become a merciful and faithful high priest;** and second, **that he might make atonement for the sins of the people.** It is better to understand this second clause as dependent on the first, as in the New American Standard Bible: "that He might become a merciful and faithful high priest in things pertaining to God, [in order] to make propitiation for the sins of the people." His purpose in becoming completely human was to become **a merciful and faithful high priest.** His purpose in becoming **a merciful and faithful high priest** was to **make atonement for the sins of the people.** The preacher subsequently demonstrates that this High Priest, and this High Priest alone, has truly made **atonement for the sins of the people.**

The people is a shorthand way of referring to the Old Testament phrase **the people of God.** These are the same people who were called **Abraham's descendants** in verse 16. But what does it mean to **make atonement for . . . sins?** Two other expressions have been used in translating this verse, "make propitiation for . . . sins" (NKJV; NASB) and "make expiation for . . . sins" (RSV; REB).

The modern English reader may have some idea what **atonement** means, but probably no idea at all about "propitiation" or "expiation." **Atonement** is the most general of these terms. It refers to righting what has been wrong in order to bring estranged people together. Atonement can be used for both propitiation and expiation. "Propitiation" is God directed. This word refers to making a sacrifice or offering to God which satisfies His justice and thus removes His condemnation of the worshiper. "Expiation" is human oriented. It describes the purging of sin from the human heart.

The word here translated variously **atonement,** "propitiation," or "expiation" is first of all God directed.[22] This nuance is present throughout Hebrews. The people who stand under God's judgment are those who have disobeyed and not done the will of God (3:7–4:11; 12:14-17). With them God is angry (see commentary on 3:17). Disobedience brings the wrath of God's judgment (2:1-4; 12:25-29). Christ's sacrifice is pleasing to God ultimately because He has perfectly done the will of God (10:5-10).

Yet the preacher is very concerned with the cleansing of the heart from sin. He portrays the ceremonial outward purity of the old covenant as a picture of true inner heart purity (9:13-14). Thus, Christ's sacrifice cleanses the heart of sin (9:11-14; 10:10, 14) and establishes the new covenant (9:15-22) under which God's laws are written in our hearts (10:15-18)—that is, we are given hearts willing and able to obey God.

The main thrust of Hebrews is the holiness of heart and life that Christ's High Priesthood provides and that is expected of all the people of God. It is probably best to use the word **atonement** as the New International Version does because it includes both the satisfying of the justice of God and the cleansing of the human heart from sin. We must not, however, lose sight of the fact that the preacher puts a heavy emphasis on heart cleansing.

It is important to notice that the Pioneer does not deliver His people from the Devil's power by fighting a battle with him or by paying him a ransom. The above exposition of 2:16-17 makes it clear that He delivers them by adequately satisfying the just displeasure of God against sin and effectively cleansing the heart of sin. When sin is removed, the enslaving power of the Devil disappears because the believer's fear of judgment after death has vanished.[23]

The preacher has much more to say about the High Priesthood of Christ and the atonement for sin that it effects. He has introduced this subject here, which then dominates 4:14 through 10:18, the central section of this sermon. However, faithful preacher that he is, he cannot leave this subject without making some application to his hearers. He wants to encourage them to be faithful despite the pressure they face to turn away from Christ. Hebrews 2:18 gives his immediate application of

73

the truth of Christ's High Priesthood and atoning sacrifice. Christ can **help** them now to reject any temptation to turn from Him.

Verse 18 raises two important interpretive questions. First, the translations differ in the way they arrange the first clauses of the verse. The New International Version offers **Because he himself suffered when he was tempted.** The New American Standard Bible reads, ". . . He Himself was tempted in that which He has suffered. . . ." Which idea is meant to be primary—suffering or temptation? **Because he himself suffered** or "since He himself was tempted"? Second, is it better to use the word **tempted** (NIV; NASB; NKJV) or "tested" (NRSV; REB)?

Greek grammar allows either arrangement of these two clauses. At first it appears that the arrangement of the New American Standard Bible would be best: "For since He himself was tempted . . . He is able to come to the aid of those who are tempted" (compare the NRSV; REB). There seems to be a logical parallel between Christ's being **tempted** and His ability to help those who are tempted. However, it is not merely the fact that Christ was tempted that enables Him to help those who are tempted. Everyone is tempted. What is unique about Christ is that He did not yield to temptation. He was completely obedient unto and including His death (see 4:15; 10:5-10; compare 5:8). This obedience led to His suffering, especially His suffering of death. The writer of Hebrews can actually say that "he learned obedience from what he suffered" (5:8). That is, He fully experienced what it meant to be obedient through enduring what He suffered, especially His death. Thus **because he himself suffered** is a shorthand way of referring to Jesus' complete obedience up to and including His willing suffering of a sacrificial death. It is this obedience, this overcoming of temptation, that enables Him to help those who are tempted. Thus the New International Version's ordering of these clauses is best. Here is an interpretive expansion of the NIV: "Because he himself was completely obedient when he was tempted even to the suffering of death, he is able to help those who are being tempted." And that means you!

The second question is this: Is the **tempted** of the New International Version, New American Standard Bible, and New King James Version, or the "tested" of the New Revised Standard Version and Revised English Bible the best translation? Either word has the possibility of misleading the reader. If we use **tempted,** we may think that the verse is a general reference to any kind of temptation to sin. Such temptations are included, but do not exhaust the preacher's meaning. If we use "tested," we may think that the preacher is referring to any kind of difficulties or troubles that we may face in life, whatever they may be. Christ certainly helps us in all of these difficulties, but they are not really the preacher's point in this verse. He is referring to the kinds of tests or trials that try our loyalty to Christ, that tempt us to give up our faith and turn away from Him. These were the kinds of challenges which God's people faced in the wilderness after they left Sinai. When they lacked food or water and when they were challenged with entering the Promised Land despite the dangers, their loyalty to God—their faith—was put to the test. Would they trust God to supply food and water; would they trust Him to give them the Promised Land? The preacher discusses their story in 3:7 through 4:11. They failed to trust God. They turned away from Him and thus lost the privilege of entering the Promised Land.

It appears that those who first received Hebrews were confronted with such tests of faith. They faced shame from the larger community and possible physical persecution because of their Christian commitment. Thus they were tempted to give up their faith and turn back to their old way of life (see commentary on 10:32-36; 11:32-38; 12:4-11; 13:13).

Any time we face pressure to compromise our stand for Christ, we are facing the kind of testing or temptation that the preacher is addressing. Christ was victorious in the face of all such pressure. He can help us to be victorious also.

To conclude, in 2:5-18 the preacher begins to show us how the Son of God became a human being in order to deliver us from sin and bring us into the presence of God. He is our Pioneer who enters God's presence and thereby makes a way for us to enter. Because sin prevents our entrance, our Pioneer fulfills His role by becoming our High Priest.

The preacher now leaves the High Priest theme until Hebrews 4:14. In 3:1-6, he continues with the theme of the Son as our Leader or Pioneer who takes us to the heavenly homeland. He compares Him with Moses, who led God's people through the wilderness from Sinai toward the Promised Land.

ENDNOTES

[1] F. F. Bruce, *The Epistle to the Hebrews,* The New International Commentary on the New Testament, ed. F. F. Bruce (Grand Rapids, Michigan: Wm. B. Eerdmans Publishing Co., 1990), pp. 71–72; Philip Edgcumbe Hughes, *A Commentary on the Epistle to the Hebrews* (Grand Rapids, Michigan: Wm. B. Eerdmans Publishing Co., 1977), p. 82.

[2] Some commentators believe that the writer of Hebrews understood **son of man** in 2:6 as a title for Christ rather than as a synonym for **man.** See Donald A. Hagner, *Hebrews,* New International Biblical Commentary, ed. W. Ward Gasque (Peabody, Massachusetts: Hendrickson Publishers, 1990), p. 45. Such an assumption is not necessary for a proper interpretation of this passage. See

William L. Lane, *Hebrews 1–8*, vol. 47a, Word Biblical Commentary, New Testament ed. Ralph P. Martin, gen. eds. David A. Hubbard and Glenn W. Barker (Dallas: Word Books, 1991), p. 47.

[3]The New International Version of Psalm 8:5 reads "heavenly beings" instead of "angels." The Hebrew word used here is *Elohim,* which is usually translated "God" but which can also mean "gods" or "heavenly beings." Thus some other English translations read "God" in Psalm 8:5 (see NRSV; NASB; but NASB margin reads "angels"). It is not normal, however, for the Old Testament to speak of human beings as being "a little lower than God." The Greek Old Testament which our author used properly translated *Elohim* as "angels" and thus enabled him to use this passage in his comparison between the Son and the angels. There is another feature of the Greek translation of this psalm which was helpful to the author of Hebrews. A comparison of versions will show that the phrase which the New International Version translates "a little lower than" in Hebrews 2:7 (quoting Ps. 8:5) is translated in many versions as "a little while lower than" (NASB; NRSV; REB). The Greek phrase can have either shade of meaning. While "a little lower than" is probably the original sense of the psalm, "a little while lower than" made it easy for the writer of Hebrews to apply this term to Jesus' incarnation, which lasted "a little while."

[4]Hughes, p. 84.

[5]"The subjection of 'everything' has ultimately to do with 'the world to come'" (Lane, p. 47).

[6]Bruce thinks that the pronouns in verse 8b refer to mankind (p. 75, note 35); Hughes, to Jesus (pp. 86–87).

[7]Bruce, p. 75, note 35.

[8]Lane, p. 48.

[9]Hughes, pp. 100–1; Paul Ellingworth, *The Epistle to the Hebrews,* The New International Greek Testament Commentary, eds. I. Howard Marshall and W. Ward Gasque (Grand Rapids, Michigan: Wm. B. Eerdmans Publishing Co., 1993), pp. 160–61.

[10]Bruce, p. 80.

[11]Some have understood "of one" (Heb. 2:11 NKJV) as a reference to Adam or as more general, such as the Revised English Bible's "of one stock." For an evaluation, see Lane, p. 58.

[12]James Luther Mays, *Psalms,* Interpretation: A Bible Commentary for Teaching and Preaching, Old Testament ed. Patrick D. Miller Jr., New Testament ed. Paul J. Achtemeier, gen. ed. James Luther Mays (Louisville: John Knox Press, 1994), p. 106.

[13]"Citing the first words of a text was, in the tradition of the time, a way of identifying an entire passage" (Mays, p. 105).

[14]Many commentators locate the Son's proclamation of Psalm 22:22 at the exaltation (Bruce, p. 82; Ellingworth, pp. 167–68; Lane, p. 59). Since the verbs of Psalm 22:22 are future tense, Lane thinks that the Son makes this declaration at His exaltation but that it looks forward to His second coming. Attridge thinks that the writer of Hebrews thinks of Christ as proclaiming these words at the Incarnation (Harold W. Attridge, *The Epistle to the Hebrews,* Hermeneia—A

Critical and Historical Commentary on the Bible, ed. Helmut Koester [Philadelphia: Fortress Press, 1989], p. 90). His position, however, neglects to take into consideration the use of the psalm by Jesus, the Gospel writers, and other early Christian tradition as described above.

[15]This translation is a slightly edited version of the translation found in *The Septuagint with Apocrypha: Greek and English* by Sir Lancelot C. L. Brenton (Peabody, Massachusetts: Hendrickson Publishers, 1995), p. 843. The Septuagint is the Greek version of the Old Testament, translated from the original Hebrew scrolls. It is often indicated by the Roman numerals LXX in accordance with the belief that it was translated by seventy scribes. The Apocrypha is the fourteen or fifteen books (or parts of books) that were considered by some to have been written during the time between the Old and New Testaments. In the sixteenth century, the Roman Catholic Church made these books part of their Canon (the sixty-six books considered to be God's authoritative written Word; the sacred Scriptures), but Protestants have never recognized the Apocrypha in any official way. During the development of the modern Protestant Bible, it was determined that these books did not fit the criteria to be included in the Canon. For instance, their apostolic authorship was questioned, as well as their authenticity, accuracy of information recorded, and agreement with the rest of the Scriptures. These books are still found in the Roman Catholic Bible and a few other versions.

[16]"I will put my trust in him" occurs three places in the Greek Old Testament: 2 Samuel 22:3; Isaiah 12:1-3; Isaiah 8:17. However, the fact that both the quotations in Hebrews 2:13 occur together in Isaiah 8:17-18 makes it very likely that Isaiah 8 is the source of both. Nevertheless, the context of 2 Samuel 22:3 would be well suited to the use Hebrews makes of the statement, "I will put my trust in him." In 2 Samuel 22:3, King David expresses his praise to God for delivering him from his enemies by saying, "I will put my trust in him." Thus this statement would make an admirable declaration of the exalted Son's deliverance from those who opposed Him and from the death He suffered at their hand. If the writer of Hebrews was thinking of 2 Samuel 22:3, it must have reminded him of Isaiah's words in Isaiah 8:17-18.

English readers will not find the words "I will put my trust in him" in 2 Samuel 22:3, because our English translations follow the Hebrew original and not the Greek translation used by the writer of Hebrews. Thus the New International Version reads, "My God, my rock, in whom I take refuge." An English translation of the Greek would be, "My God my Guard will be, I will put my trust in Him."

[17]For a helpful discussion of the use of Isaiah 8:17-18 in Hebrews 2:13, see Bruce, pp. 82–84.

[18]See section 9.46 in Johannes P. Louw and Eugene A. Nida, *Introduction and Domains*, vol. 1, Greek-English Lexicon of the New Testament Based on Semantic Domains (New York: United Bible Societies, 1988), p. 110.

[19]Hughes, pp. 117–19.

[20]Attridge, p. 94. The same word is used in Hebrews 8:9, quoting Jeremiah 31:32, of God's taking Israel's hand to lead them out of the land of Egypt (see Ellingworth, p. 176).

[21]Hughes, p. 120.

[22]Leon Morris, *The Apostolic Preaching of the Cross* (Grand Rapids, Michigan: Wm. B. Eerdmans Publishing Co., 1955), pp. 125–60; Lane, p. 66.

[23]It is probably true that the readers of Hebrews were familiar with Greek stories about a hero like Hercules who fought with and overcame death (Lane, pp. 61–63). Various Jewish sources depicted the Messiah as defeating demonic powers (Attridge, p. 92). While the language of verses 14 and 15 may be reflective of some of these traditions, the substance of the argument is very different. As noted above, the Son does not fight a battle with the Devil. Moreover, He overcomes by dying himself rather than by slaying His opponent. Attridge is very hesitant to see the Son's atonement for sin as the way He delivers from the fear of death. Yet Attridge can say, "His exaltation definitely confirms his victory and provides an access to God that renders death and the fear it inspires irrelevant" (pp. 93–94). But on what basis was Christ exalted and how did He provide this access to God? By making purification for our sins (1:3)!

OUR PIONEER IS FAITHFUL OVER GOD'S HOUSEHOLD AS A SON

Hebrews 3:1-6

The opening exhortation of this section of Hebrews (3:1) directs us to pay attention to the faithfulness of our Pioneer who has been described in 2:5-18. The writer compares the faithfulness of our Pioneer as the leader of God's household to the faithfulness of Moses (3:2), the greatest Old Testament leader of God's people. However, in His person and saving mission Christ our Pioneer is much greater than Moses (3:3-6a). Therefore, if we would continue to be a part of God's household which our Pioneer rules, we too must be faithful (3:6b). We must not be like the household of God which Moses led through the wilderness. The consequences of their disobedience are described in 3:7 through 4:11. Later in this sermon the preacher will balance the negative example of the wilderness generation with positive examples of the Old Testament faithful (11:1-40), followed by another call to keep our eyes on our faithful Pioneer (12:1-3).

Give attention to the way the preacher addresses his readers: **holy brothers, who share in the heavenly calling** (3:1). We have already seen that our Pioneer has declared God's people to be His **brothers** (2:11-12, 17). As Christians we are not only brothers and sisters of one another *in* Christ, we are brothers and sisters *of* Christ. If we are His brothers and sisters, it is necessary for us to be **holy.** Indeed, He is the One who makes us holy (2:10) through making atonement for our sin (2:17) so that we can **share in the heavenly calling.** This call comes to us from heaven and summons us to heaven. It is God's call to enter into His presence. The preacher understands the destination of our call as the heavenly most holy place that Christ has entered (9:23-25), the heavenly homeland (11:16), the "city with foundations" established by God (11:10), the "heavenly Jerusalem" (12:22). Although the complete fulfillment of this call is future, God speaks from heaven through the Son even now and invites us to participate in that call by enjoying His presence in our lives through faith (12:22-25).

Look how the One on whom we are to **fix** our **thoughts** is described (3:1). We are to focus our attention on **Jesus, the apostle and high priest whom we confess.** This is the only place in the New Testament where the term **apostle** is used to describe Jesus. An apostle is one sent with the authority of the sender. Thus, Jesus chose twelve disciples and sent them out as His apostles with His authority to represent Him. The Gospel of John often refers to the Son as being sent with the full authority of the Father (see John 3:17, 34; 5:36, 38; 6:29, 57; 7:29; 8:42; 10:36; 11:42; 17:3). In all of these references the Greek verb for "send" comes from the same root as the Greek noun translated "apostle." "Apostle" is thus another way of describing Jesus as the complete and final revelation of the Father. Within this context the preacher is also thinking of the authority of the Apostle to lead the people of God. Thus this term is an apt one to use when comparing Christ with Moses. Moses was the greatest mediator of God's revelation within the Old Testament (see Numbers 12:6-8) and the one God sent to lead His people into the Promised Land (see Exodus 3:8, 10). The term "apostle" joins the idea of the Son as the Revealer of God with that of the Pioneer who leads God's people into their heavenly homeland.

This One to whom we are to give our attention is, then, not only the ultimate revelation of God and the Leader of God's people, but also their **high priest** who atones for their sins (Heb. 3:1). The writer of Hebrews returns to the subject of Christ's High Priesthood in 4:14.

It is important to establish the relationship of the readers to this **apostle and high priest.** He is the One whom they, and we as Christians, **confess.** They believed in, and openly and publicly professed loyalty to, Jesus Christ as the Son of God. They had identified themselves with Him. The preacher is concerned that they not stray from their commitment.

In the Greek text the name **Jesus** is last: "the apostle and high priest whom we confess, Jesus." It is as if the preacher said, "Do not forget! No matter what else I say about this Person, He is Jesus. At a particular time and in a particular place He assumed our humanity." Most important of all, it was as Jesus, as a human being, that He was **faithful to** God the Father **who appointed him** High Priest, Apostle, and Pioneer of our salvation (3:2). Jesus lived as the faithful One here on earth, in the same circumstances in which we live, not in the ideal conditions of heaven.

The translation of the New Revised Standard Version makes it clear that it is this faithfulness to which, above all else, the preacher would direct our attention: "Consider that Jesus, the apostle and high priest of our confession, was faithful to the one who appointed him." It is also in regard to "faithfulness" that Jesus is compared to **Moses,** who was "faithful in all [God's] house," according to Numbers 12:7. In Numbers 12:6-8, God describes Moses as the one through whom He has revealed himself most directly and completely by speaking to him face-to-face. God's **house** is a term used to describe God's household, His people. Moses has been **faithful** to instruct the people of God's **house** in, and to lead them according to, this revelation. During His incarnation, Jesus demonstrated that He is now *the* faithful One through whom a revelation greater than that given to Moses has come.

In Hebrews 3:3, the preacher begins to contrast Jesus with Moses in order to demonstrate this superiority: **Jesus has been found worthy of greater honor than Moses.** The words **greater honor** are better rendered "more glory." Compare the New King James Version's "For this One has been counted worthy of more glory than Moses." We have seen above that the preacher alludes to Numbers 12:7. He will again allude to this passage in Hebrews 3:5. In Numbers 12:6-8, God rebukes Aaron and Miriam for not honoring Moses as the one through whom God had uniquely revealed himself. They should have deferred to Moses because he had seen the glory of the Lord (see Numbers 12:8).[1] The Son of God is "worthy of more glory" than the one who *saw* the glory of God because He *embodies* that glory (see John 1:14). God is the One who endowed Moses with more honor than all the other Old Testament figures by revealing himself directly to and through Moses. Therefore He expected Aaron, Miriam, and the rest of His people to honor Moses by submitting to and obeying the word God revealed through Moses. But the preacher points out that this God has now revealed himself finally and completely in His Son. Thus it behooves us to give the Son the greater honor that He deserves by an obedience more faithful and diligent than any ever shown to Moses.

Hebrews 3:3b shows us how much more we are to honor the Son our Pioneer than we are to honor Moses. In proportion, as **the builder of a house has greater honor than the house,** so we should give greater honor to the Son than to Moses. This proverb or general statement speaks about any house and any builder. We must not forget, however, that the preacher has already used the term **house** to describe God's people in 3:2. Thus, this statement would imply that the Son is in some way the founder of God's people while Moses is only one of those people. The Son is the One who establishes the people of God, because through His ministry as Pioneer and High Priest He enables them to be truly the people of God and to enter into God's presence.

When in 3:4 the preacher says, **God is the builder of everything,** he seems to be reminding us that, just as God has established His people through the Son (see 1:2), so He created the world through the Son. The Son is worthy of more honor than Moses to the degree that the Creator is worthy of more honor than what He has created.

This contrast between Moses and Christ is clarified and brought to a conclusion in 3:5-6. The chart below shows how the clauses of these two verses balance each other and set Moses and Christ in contrast:

Hebrews 3:5	Hebrews 3:6
Moses was faithful	**But Christ is faithful**
as a servant	**as a son**
in all God's house,	**over God's house.**
testifying to what would be said in the future.	**And we are his house, if we hold on to our courage and the hope of which we boast.**

The first clause in each verse is the basis of comparison between the two: **Moses was faithful . . .** (3:5); **But Christ is faithful . . .** (3:6). The **but,** however, implies that there will be a contrast. The New International Version reads **Moses was** but **Christ is.** Other versions use "was" in both places: "Moses was faithful. . . . Christ was faithful" (NASB; compare NKJV; NRSV). The preacher is primarily concerned about Christ's faithfulness as a human being when He was on earth. However, the One who was faithful on earth is now faithful in heaven to save us. Because of His faithful obedience while He was on earth, we can depend on Him to save us now.

The next phrases compare the positions of Moses and Christ in relation to God's **house.** Moses was a **servant.** The word the preacher uses for **servant** comes directly from the Greek translation of Numbers 12:7: ". . . Not true of my servant Moses; he is faithful in all my house." This same Greek word is often used to describe Moses as the servant of God (see Exodus 4:10; 14:31; Numbers 11:11; Deuteronomy 3:24). It could be translated "minister" or "steward" and puts Moses in a class by himself. There is no other servant like this servant. He is the great "steward," the servant in charge of God's household. Nevertheless, great as Moses is, Christ is far greater, for He is faithful **as a son.** His faithfulness is the kind of faithfulness that is appropriate to His sonship. We have already seen that as Son He is the complete and final revelation of God (see 1:1-3). Later in the letter we will learn that as Son He came into the world to perfectly and completely do the will of God (see 10:5-10). He is faithful as the One who completely reveals the Father by completely doing the Father's will.

Finally, the position of each is qualified by a prepositional phrase: Moses was faithful as a servant **in all God's house** (3:5); Christ as Son **over God's house** (3:6). A servant, no matter how high in responsibility, is merely part of the household. But the Son is **over** the household just as the Father is.

The final phrases in 3:5-6 are not parallel. The last phrase of verse 5 describes Moses' mission in God's plan of salvation. Much of the rest of Hebrews is dedicated to the description of Christ's role as Savior. As the steward of God's house, Moses is described as **testifying to what would be said in the future** (3:5). Moses bore witness to what God would reveal through His Son. Moses' witness is found in the first five books of the Bible. As the one who led God's people through the wilderness toward the Promised Land, Moses foreshadowed the Son as our Pioneer who brings us into the heavenly homeland. However, the preacher is probably thinking primarily of the priesthood that God established through Moses. Hebrews 7:14 refers to Moses as speaking of the priesthood. In Hebrews 4:14 through 10:18, the preacher is going to show us that the priesthood established by Moses and described in those books attributed to Moses was not an end in itself. Rather, it was a pointer, a witness to the complete and effective High Priesthood of Christ.

The preacher has much more to say about the faithfulness of the Son, but in 3:6b he makes immediate application to his hearers. In 3:2 and 3:5, it is clear that the **house** of God is a description of God's people. Because Christ is the faithful Son over God's household—the One Who perfectly reveals the Father by procuring redemption from our sin—it is all the more urgent to be a part of that household! The wonderful thing is, the preacher is convinced that his hearers are a part of that household over which the Son rules: **And we are his house . . .** (3:6b). The preacher, however, is anxious that his hearers remain a part of the people of God, so he adds: **if we hold on to our courage and the hope of which we boast.** The New American Standard Bible reads "if we hold fast our confidence," instead of **if we hold on to our courage.** The preacher is concerned about more than general discouragement. He is concerned that they not lose their "confidence" in the power of God to enable them to live victoriously in the present. He will show them that through Christ they have been authorized to enter God's presence so they can draw near to God with "confidence" (4:16) and receive His help. The preacher is also concerned that they hold onto the assured **hope** of living in God's presence forever. God's people are not ashamed of this future **hope.** On the contrary, they **boast** about it. It serves as the main focus of their lives. What are the main topics of their conversation or subjects of their thought? Not hobbies, amusements, or other interests. No, they focus their attention on their future hope of living directly in the presence of God with His people. This hope gives direction to their lives.

How easy it is for us who live in today's secular world to neglect the power of God in our daily lives. Instead of calling on Him for help, we try to fix things ourselves. How quickly we focus on the same goals that people around us have—comfort, amusement, financial security, retirement. We need the preacher's words to call us back to a sense of the divine power available through Christ for our daily lives! We need the preacher's vision to help us focus on the eternal hope that is our only true and lasting goal!

The example that the writer gives next in 3:7-19 shows a people who did lose confidence in God's power to do what He had promised—that is, to bring them into the Promised Land. Because they lost confidence in God's power to help them, they lost God's blessing for which they had hoped. The preacher does not want those whom he addresses to do the same. He addresses us today with the same message.

ENDNOTE

[1]"He has seen the glory of the Lord" is a translation of Numbers 12:8 according to the Greek translation, which the author of Hebrews probably used.

Our English versions translate the original Hebrew, "he sees the form of the LORD." The Greek term translated "Glory" and the Hebrew word translated "form" both refer to a revelation of the essential nature of God.

DON'T FOLLOW THE EXAMPLE OF GOD'S FAITHLESS HOUSEHOLD IN THE WILDERNESS

Hebrews 3:7–4:11

The writer, who has been thinking about the faithfulness of Moses in Hebrews 3:1-6, now turns to the unfaithfulness of the people Moses led. This was a natural transition for the writer as he meditated on the Old Testament Scripture. In Numbers 12:1-16, we read about Aaron and Miriam's challenging Moses. We know that the writer of Hebrews had been pondering this chapter because he cited Numbers 12:7 in Hebrews 3:2 and 3:5. We saw in Hebrews 3:1-6 how he compared our Pioneer with the faithfulness and unique position of Moses as described in this chapter from Numbers.

As he continued to read his Bible, the preacher came to Numbers 13 and 14. In Numbers 13:1 through 14:45, he found the account of how the people whom this faithful Moses led reached the climax of their unfaithfulness. Moses had led them through the wilderness. They had already failed to trust God and complained against Him a number of times (see Numbers 14). In these chapters they have come to Kadesh Barnea at the border of the Promised Land. Yet they rebelled against God by failing to trust Him to overcome their foes and refusing to enter the Promised Land. The great fortified cities and strong armies ahead intimidated them. They are often called the "wilderness generation" because they died in the wilderness without entering the land God had promised.

The preacher sees a close parallel in the lives of his hearers. They, too, faced opposition if they were going to continue to be faithful to God (see Hebrews 10:32-35; 12:3-4). The society around them was pressuring them to turn away from God's final revelation in His Son Jesus Christ (see commentary on 13:11-16). At least some of them had begun to wonder if faith in Christ was really worth the struggle. They were tempted to become slack in their Christian commitment. In 3:1-19, the preacher urges them not to follow the example of that unfaithful wilderness generation. In 4:1-11, he encourages them to enter God's blessing which the wilderness generation forfeited.

1. DON'T HARDEN YOUR HEARTS AS THEY DID 3:7-19

As noted above, Numbers 13:1 through 14:45 describes the climax of the unfaithfulness of God's people who were led by Moses. They did not trust God and obey His instructions to enter the Promised Land. The preacher, however, does not cite Numbers 13:1 through 14:45 in his description of the unfaithful wilderness generation. Instead, he quotes the words of Psalm 95. The writer of that psalm had already used the disobedient wilderness generation as a warning to the people of his own day. The **today** of the psalmist, quoted in Hebrews 3:7, becomes the **today** of those to whom the writer of Hebrews speaks. It is the **today** of God's people whenever they stand before a challenge to their faith. It is our **today,** the time for us to be faithful! The preacher is convinced that the **Holy Spirit** himself speaks directly through the words of the psalm to the people of his day (3:7). He addresses us **today** through the same psalm!

The preacher introduces this quotation from Psalm 95:7b-11 in a way that is appropriate to its context within the psalm. Both the preacher and the psalmist are concerned that God's people continue to be God's faithful people. Both address their words to the people of God. In Psalm 95:7a the psalmist has just said, "We are the people of his pasture, and the sheep of his hand." In Hebrews 3:6, the preacher said, "And we are his house." Then, both psalmist and preacher exhort, **Today, if you hear his voice, do not harden your hearts.**

The preacher quotes Psalm 95:7b-11 in Hebrews 3:7b-11 in support of his exhortation to faithfulness given in Hebrews 3:6. In 3:12-14, he applies the quotation to his hearers. In that application he expresses his concern that they listen to God's word **today** and **not harden** their **hearts.** The exhortation in 3:14 repeats and strengthens the initial exhortation in 3:6.

The writer summarizes his interpretation in 3:15 by quoting again from the psalm. This time he only cites Psalm 95:7b-8a so that his quotation ends with the word **rebellion.** In Hebrews 3:16-19, he clarifies the nature and consequences of the **rebellion** of the wilderness generation so that his hearers may avoid it.

Let us turn back to the quotation of Psalm 95:7b-11 in Hebrews 3:7b-11. By quoting Psalm 95:8 in Hebrews 3:8, the preacher introduces the idea that the sin of the wilderness generation was **rebellion** (Heb. 3:15) against God. Their sin was a faithless **testing** (3:8) of God's patience through distrust.

If we look at Psalm 95:8 in most English translations of the Old Testament, we will see that the words "rebellion" and "testing" do not appear. The writer of Hebrews is again quoting from the Greek translation of the Old Testament that was familiar to his readers. Our English Old Testaments represent the original Hebrew. The smooth translation of the New International Version makes comparison difficult. It will be easier to use the more literal translation of the New Revised Standard Version to clarify this difference.

First look at how the NRSV translates the Greek version of Psalm 95:8 as quoted in Hebrews 3:8: "Do not harden your hearts as *in the rebellion,* as on the day *of testing* in the wilderness" (my emphasis). Now observe how the New Revised Standard Version translates the Hebrew Old Testament version of Psalm 95:8: "Do not harden your hearts, as *at Meribah,* as on the day *at Massah* in the wilderness" (my emphasis). The words that differ are in italics. Instead of the Hebrew "at Meribah," the Greek has "in the rebellion"; instead of the Hebrew "at Massah," the Greek has "of testing."

"Meribah" and "Massah" were the names that Moses gave to the place at Rephidim where God's people rebelled against Moses and tested the Lord because they had no water to drink. This incident is recorded in Exodus 17:1-7. It happened before Israel even reached Sinai. Moses gave the names "Meribah" and "Massah" to this place because *meribah* means "quarrel," "contention" or "rebellion," and *massah* means "test." The people quarreled with Moses and tested God's patience because they did not trust God to give them water.[1] The Greek translation, then, only emphasizes the significance of these Hebrew place names. The location was not nearly so important as the fact that God's people had "quarreled," "contended," or "rebelled" against Him. They had "tested" Him because they did not trust Him to take care of them. What happened at Meribah/Massah was typical of the rebellion against God which characterized their time in the wilderness and reached a head when the wilderness generation arrived at Kadesh Barnea and refused to enter the Promised Land.

The preacher adds the words **that is why** at the beginning of Hebrews 3:10 right in the middle of this psalm quotation. (These words do not appear in the Hebrew or Greek texts of Psalm 95:7-11.) He wants to make it very clear that the rebellion of God's people was the reason why God was **angry** with them and did not allow them to enter His **rest** (Heb. 3:11; see commentary on 4:3-11 for a discussion of the term **rest**).

The preacher's interpretation of Psalm 95:7-11 in Hebrews 3:12-14 focuses on the first two lines of the quotation: **Today, if you hear his voice** and **do not harden your hearts.**

Hebrews 3:12-13 clarifies what it means to have a hardened heart. We can divide what is said about a hardened heart into three parts: (1) It is a **sinful, unbelieving heart;** (2) It is a heart that **turns away from the living God;** (3) It is a heart **hardened by sin's deceitfulness.** Let us examine in turn each of these three statements about a hardened heart.

The hardened heart is a **sinful, unbelieving heart** (3:12) or, more literally, "an evil heart of unbelief" (NKJV). It is an evil heart, a perverted heart, because it is characterized by "unbelief." The word here translated "unbelief" can also be translated "unfaithfulness." The heart of unbelief will not trust God. The heart of unfaithfulness cannot be trusted to obey God. Unbelief leads to unfaithfulness: Because a person with such a heart refuses to believe that God will keep His word, this person does not faithfully obey God.

Such unbelief and unfaithfulness were demonstrated by the wilderness generation. God's people in the wilderness refused to believe that God was powerful enough to overcome their enemies and give them the land He had promised them. This failure to believe God led them to the faithless disobedience of refusing to enter the Promised Land. This "evil heart of unbelief" is the opposite of the "sincere heart" which is characterized by the "full assurance of faith" in God's power and has been cleansed from sin through the faithful obedience of Christ (10:22). The whole purpose of the new covenant is that God's laws might be written on His people's hearts (8:10; 10:16) so that they might trust Him and walk in obedience.

The person with such an unbelieving heart **turns away from the living God** (3:12). What an awesome warning! If we persistently refuse to trust God with the kind of faith that leads to obedience, we are in danger. It is possible to come to the place where we have turned away from Him! To whom can a person turn when he turns away from **the living God,** the only God there is, the only source of life?

The wilderness generation was afraid of the people who lived in the Promised Land. Therefore they failed to trust God and refused to obey His command to enter the land. As a result they turned away from Him and lost the blessed rest which He had prepared for them.

The readers of Hebrews were facing opposition from other people (see 10:32-34; 12:3). Those outside the church looked down on them and persecuted them for being loyal to Christ. But God, through His Son, gave them the grace to endure. If they turned away from God's revelation in His Son, they turned away from the one and only true and living God.[2]

The unbelieving heart is a heart **hardened by sin's deceitfulness** (3:13). Sin deceives by causing people to see only the things of this world and not the possibilities made available through the power of God. Sin would convince us that the difficulties of this world are stronger than the power of God, and that the pleasures of this world are more satisfying than the eternal inheritance we have in His presence.

Again, God's people in the wilderness under Moses aptly demonstrated how this hardness works. The spies saw strong armies and fortified cities in the Promised Land. Those cities were more real to God's people than was the power of God to overthrow those cities (see Numbers 13:28-33). They preferred "to go back to Egypt and slavery" (Num. 14:3) rather than to enter the Promised Land that flowed "with milk and honey" (Num. 13:27).

If we let sin harden our hearts in this way, we will live only for what we can see. We will give in to the pressures that would turn us from Christ and begin to set our hearts on the fleeting pleasures of time, to the loss of the ever-satisfying joys of eternity. The modern world in which we live is ever intensifying its pressure to turn Christians away from complete loyalty to Christ. Unbelievers do not mind if we call ourselves Christians, so long as we do not take a stand for righteousness. The pleasures of the senses were never more available or more intense. The writer of Hebrews calls us to live by the unseen power of God in order to obtain the unending and fully satisfying joys of eternity.

The writer is anxious that his readers be concerned about their fellow Christians' hearts. After all, Christians are **brothers** (Heb. 3:12) and sisters in Christ and of Christ (see commentary on 2:11-12). We are to watch over, encourage, and exhort each other. We must exercise such care so that **none**

of us allows **a sinful, unbelieving heart** (3:12) to develop or is **hardened by** sin (3:13).

But how can we **encourage one another** (3:13) or, as the New King James Version says, "exhort one another"? We encourage one another by setting an example of faithful obedience and by reminding one another of the faithfulness of God. If we see a brother or sister lagging in faith, our encouragement may take the form of warning. The preacher is telling his hearers to do for each other what he is doing for all of them by sending them his sermon in the form of a letter!

The preacher emphasizes the word **daily** (3:13). Perseverance in faith is a **daily** business which we must continue as long as it is the **today** of God's speaking (3:7). The wilderness generation knew the **today** of God's speaking, but when they persisted in disobedience to the point of refusing to enter the Promised Land, their **today** ended. The people to whom Psalm 95 was addressed knew the **today** of God's speaking. All Christians, whether first-century or twenty-first-century, live in the **today** of God's final revelation in His Son. Even now God addresses us from heaven and calls us to himself (see Hebrews 3:1; 12:22-25). How important it is that we encourage one another until we reach that heavenly homeland, the rest that God has prepared for us in His presence. If lethargy leads us to persistent, deliberate disobedience, the time may come when our **today** of opportunity is no more (see 6:4-8; 10:26-31; 12:14-17).

The preacher has used the urgency of the psalm to prepare his hearers for a renewal, in intensified form, of the exhortation given in 3:6. Those of us who **have come to share in Christ** (3:14) are the same people as those who are God's "house" over which Christ rules faithfully "as a son" (3:6). Christ shared in our humanity in order that we might enjoy the "heavenly calling" (3:1) which invites us into God's presence. He became one of us to deliver us from sin and the fear of death (2:14-18) so that we, as his "brothers" (2:11-12, 17) and "children" (2:13-14), might share in the salvation He has provided.

The preacher is convinced that his hearers share in Christ and the salvation that Christ has provided, but he is intensely concerned that they continue in Christ, that they **hold firmly till the end the confidence they had at first** (3:14). **Confidence** is not the best translation for the underlying Greek word, although it is used by almost all English Bibles. Nowhere else does the word in question occur where it clearly means "confidence." It usually means something like "reality" and can, at times, be used for "determination" or "resolve." The preacher is either asking them to hold firmly to the "reality" of Christ which they experienced at the beginning of their Christian lives, or he is urging them to keep firmly to the "resolve" or determination to follow Christ which they had when they first became Christians. Thus could we paraphrase, "if we hold firmly to the reality that we experienced at the beginning of our Christian lives until the end" or "if we hold firm till the end the determination with which we began our Christian lives."[3] The wilderness generation did not hold firmly to the reality of God's power which they had experienced when He delivered them from Egypt and brought them through the wilderness. Neither did they maintain their determination to follow God, the resolve with which they came out of Egypt. This translation ("holding our determination") makes an apt contrast with turning **away from the living God** (3:12).

The words **if we hold,** used in both 3:6 and 3:14, translate the same Greek verb. However, the preacher intensifies his exhortation in verse 14 by adding **firmly** and **till the end. End** implies both termination and goal. This time of perseverance will have an end. It will terminate either at the believer's death or at the return of Christ (see 9:27-28). How important it is to hold firm until that time! However, this time of perseverance also has a goal. Those who **share in Christ** (3:14) will enter into the full enjoyment of the presence of the God whose reality they have already begun to experience (see 12:22-29).

The phrase **at first** (3:14) indicates that the hearers had determination to be faithful at the beginning of their Christian lives (see 10:32-35). The preacher wants them to end the way they began! How easy it sometimes is to let our first zeal for God grow cold (see Revelation 2:4-5).

The clause **As has just been said,** at the beginning of Hebrews 3:15, introduces a second quotation of Psalm 95:7b-8a: **Today, if you hear his voice, do not harden your hearts, as you did in the rebellion.** The repetition reminds readers that the writer's exhortation in Hebrews 3:11-14 has been based on this psalm. The repeated quotation of the psalm also introduces further explanation of the psalm in Hebrews 3:16-19.

The writer previously applied this quotation to his hearers in 3:12-14 by commenting on the **today** of the first clause and on the "hardening" of hearts from the second. He has explained that these words instruct Christians not to allow difficulties or persecutions to discourage them but to hold on to all they have in Christ until the end.

In 3:16-18, however, the preacher takes up the **hear** of the psalm quotation's first clause and the **rebellion** of the third clause. In these verses, he describes the wilderness generation in order to spell out the nature, greatness, and consequences of their sin so that his readers will avoid their example. This sin is described as **rebellion.** In 3:19 he gives his concluding description of their sin and its consequences.

The preacher focuses our attention in 3:16-18 with a series of questions. There is a pair of questions in verse 16, and another pair in verse 17, followed by a single focused question in verse 18. In each pair, the second question provides the answer for the first. The concluding single question in verse 18 implies its own answer. The first pair of questions focuses our attention on the enormity of the wilderness generation's sin. The second pair and the concluding question point out God's response to their sin.

The questions in 3:16 show how serious the wilderness generation's sin was by describing the great privileges which they had received. The New Revised Standard Version clarifies the sense of this verse by adding the word "yet" to the first question: "Now who were they who heard and yet were rebellious?" These were the privileged people who had heard God's word on Mount Sinai. They had often received the word of God through Moses after they had left Mount Sinai. Because they had heard God's word they were responsible; they should have obeyed. We can rebel only when we know the will of God. The sin of the wilderness generation can be rightly called "rebellion" because they deliberately "turned away from the Lord" (Num. 14:43 NKJV). They refused to follow the way God had directed them and purposefully turned to their own way.

The answering question in Hebrews 3:16b only emphasizes their responsibility. Those who rebelled were those **Moses led out of Egypt.** They had absolutely no excuse. They had not only heard God's word but they had experienced God's salvation. They had seen how God had delivered them from Egypt by sending ten great plagues, by bringing them through the Red Sea, and by drowning the Egyptian army. God had fed them in the wilderness and given them water to drink. He had led them with a pillar of cloud by day and a pillar of fire by night. God expresses this truth to Moses in words quoted in Numbers 14:22-23: ". . . not one of the men who saw my glory and the miraculous signs I performed in Egypt and in the desert but who disobeyed me and tested me ten times—not one of them will ever see the land I promised on oath to their forefathers. No one who has treated me with contempt will ever see it."

Their sin was rebellion because they deliberately rejected God despite the many ways He had blessed them. They had clearly heard the word of God. They experienced in a great way the salvation of God. They saw with their own eyes His mighty power in action. Yet they refused to trust His power and to obey Him. Instead they chose to follow their own way of life.

Hebrews 3:17-18 shows God's response to this sin of deliberate, informed, willful rebellion. Verse 17 prepares for verse 18. As the climax of His anger (3:17a), God excluded them from His Promised Land, His **rest** (3:18a).

God's forty-year anger with the wilderness generation described in 3:17a is an allusion to Psalm 95:9b-10a quoted above in Hebrews 3:9b-10a.[4] The suffering that they endured in the wilderness for forty years was an expression of God's anger at their sin. The answering question in Hebrews 3:17b makes it clear that those who suffered this anger were those who had **sinned** by rebelling against God. The Greek word here translated "sinned" is the same word used of their disobedience in the Greek translation of Numbers 14:43. The last part of Hebrews 3:17 shows how those forty years concluded: Their **bodies fell in the desert.** Their rebellion was such that their lives ended in tragedy rather than blessing.

There is a smooth transition from the end of 3:17 to 3:18. Obviously, those **whose bodies fell in the desert** were those who **would never enter his rest** in the Promised Land. Their rebellion was so serious that God swore that they **would never enter** the very place of blessing for which He had brought them out of Egypt. Those who received this terrible sentence of exclusion are now described as those who **disobeyed.** The Greek word here translated **disobeyed** is used in the Greek translation of Numbers 14:43 to describe the wilderness generation's refusal to enter the Promised Land. It is a particularly appropriate word to describe the sin of people who had clearly heard and understood the word of God but deliberately disobeyed it. It is also appropriate because, as a look at the New International Version marginal reading shows, it can also be translated "disbelieve."[5] As we have seen, theirs was a disobedience that sprang from disbelief. The readers of Hebrews have clearly heard the word of God (see Hebrews 2:1-4) and experienced God's power (see 6:1-6). The preacher does not want them to doubt God's power to help them and thus turn from Him in disobedience.

In 3:16-18, the writer has been describing the enormity of the sin of the wilderness generation and God's response to it. He wants to show his hearers how this sin's severity brought on the deadly punishment that the wilderness generation suffered. Verse 19 summarizes the sin, God's punishment of the sin, and the causal link between them in a powerful concluding sentence. The essence of their punishment was **they were not able to enter.** The writer does not tell us what they were prohibited from entering. Of course they did not enter the earthly Promised Land, but more was involved in their loss than earthly real estate. Those who persistently refuse to trust God are excluded from that ultimate **rest** which God has for His people (3:11).[6]

The essence of the sin of the wilderness generation is described as **unbelief.** The preacher uses the same word here that he did in 3:12 to describe the "evil heart of unbelief" (NKJV). As noted in reference to that verse, the word can mean either "unbelief" or "unfaithfulness." The primary significance here is "unbelief." God would not allow them to enter because they would not trust Him.

We can never know the rest of deep fellowship with Him unless we trust His love and His power. As noted above, however, "unbelief" leads to "unfaithfulness": refusal to trust God leads to disobedience. Thus both the word translated **disobeyed** in 3:18 and the word translated **unbelief** in 3:19 demonstrate the intimate connection between the failure to trust God and the resulting refusal to obey Him. The faith of the examples that the preacher will give in Hebrews 11:1-40 is the exact opposite of the wilderness generation's unbelief. The Hebrews 11 people of faith did believe and therefore obeyed.

At this point, the writer of Hebrews warns his hearers to avoid, at all cost, an **unbelief** like the unbelief of the wilderness generation, an unbelief that would prevent them from entering God's rest. In 4:1-11, he helps his readers understand what that rest really is and urges them most strongly to enter it.

2. ENTER THE REST THAT THEY FORFEITED 4:1-11

After warning his hearers in Hebrews 3:7-19 not to follow the example of the wilderness generation, in 4:1-11 the preacher urges them to enter into the **rest** that the wilderness generation forfeited. He exhorts his hearers to enter this **rest** in 4:1 and again, even more forcefully, in 4:11. In between these two exhortations he demonstrates, on the basis of Psalm 95 and supplemented by Genesis 2:2, that this rest is still accessible to those who believe. He also shows that this rest is God's own rest, of which the earthly Promised Land was no more than a type or picture.

The preacher's argument is tightly woven but can be divided into two sections: 4:1-5 and 4:6-11. Hebrews 4:1-5 cites Genesis 2:2 from the creation account, a time long before the wilderness generation. Hebrews 4:6-11 cites Psalm 95:7b-8a, written long after the wilderness generation.

In Hebrews 4:1, the preacher exhorts his hearers to enter the rest which the wilderness generation failed to enter. The first clause of 4:1 gives us the basis for his exhortation: **since the promise of entering his rest still stands.**[7] This phrase immediately suggests two questions: How do we know that the promise originally given the wilderness generation **still stands** for us? What kind of **rest** is this **rest** that is still available? The answers to these two questions are closely intertwined in the preacher's argument. It will help us to understand this passage if we address each question separately. Then we will examine the preacher's instructions on how to enter God's **rest.**

Is God's promised rest still available? How do we know that this **promise . . . still stands?** As always, the preacher answers by referring to Scripture. Verses 1 through 5 give the first two steps of his argument; verse 6, the third; and verses 7 and 8 the fourth and fifth.

He reminds us in verse 3 that God excluded the wilderness generation from the promised **rest.** He again cites Psalm 95:11 to prove his point—**They shall never enter my rest** (Heb. 4:5).

At the end of 4:3, he argues that this **rest** had been established since creation. He supports this statement in 4:4 by quoting Genesis 2:2: **And on the seventh day God rested from all his work.**

In Hebrews 4:6, the preacher begins a new paragraph by showing the significance of these first two points: Since God established this **rest** at the creation, it must still be in existence. Since the wilderness generation failed to enter it, it must still be available for somebody else. The next three steps of the preacher's argument clarify who this "somebody" is.

The preacher anticipates an objection from his readers: "True, the wilderness generation did not enter the **rest,** but their children did. After all, **Joshua** (4:8) brought them into the Promised Land. Didn't the children of the wilderness generation inherit God's **rest** by entering the earthly Promised Land?"

The preacher has an answer: "No, they did not." Psalm 95:7b-8a quoted again in Hebrews 4:7 shows that they did not enter God's **rest** by entering the earthly Promised Land. God spoke the words of this psalm through **David,** who lived several hundred years after Joshua. Thus **a long time** after Joshua had led the people into the earthly Promised Land God again invited them to enter His **rest.** Thus they must not have entered God's rest when they entered the earthly Promised Land (4:8).[8]

Finally, God addresses us **today** in Psalm 95:7-8 and invites us to enter His **rest** (see Hebrews 3:15; compare 4:9).

Let us summarize the preacher's argument with his Scriptural support. God established this **rest** at the creation (see Genesis 2:2). The wilderness generation did not enter it (see Psalm 95:11). Neither did the children of the wilderness generation whom Joshua led into the earthly Promised Land (see Hebrews 4:8, referring to Psalm 95:7b-8a). Therefore this **rest** is still available. God's **promise** (Heb. 4:1) of entering it found in Psalm 95 is for us **today!**

What is God's promised rest? What kind of **rest** is this **rest** that is still available? The above description of the preacher's argument helps us to answer this question. He has given us two arguments which explain the nature of this **rest.**

Joshua did not bring the people into this **rest** when he led them into the earthly Promised Land (Heb. 4:7-8; see Psalm 95:11). Thus it is something more than the earthly Promised Land.

God established this **rest** at the creation (Heb. 4:3-4; see Genesis 2:2). But God did not create this **rest** as part of His creation. According to Genesis 2:2 (cited in Heb. 4:4), this is the **rest** that God himself entered into on the seventh day after He had completed His creation. Since this seventh day is the great Sabbath on which the earthly Sabbath is patterned, the preacher calls this rest a **Sabbath-rest** in 4:9. This **rest** is beyond creation. It is God's own **rest,** the "kingdom that cannot be shaken" (12:28) when creation itself comes to an end (see 12:25-29). Yet believers are already "receiving" (12:28) this kingdom. God offers us this rest of blissful fellowship with himself.

Within the Old Testament the earthly Promised Land was called **rest** because it was the place where God's people would be at rest from the oppression of their enemies and from other hardships (see Deuteronomy 12:9-10). They would live in the **rest** of intimate fellowship with Him. Thus the earthly Promised Land was an appropriate type or picture of the eternal **rest** that God has for His people.

This eternal **rest** is the ultimate goal for God's people both before and after Christ. Both groups make up the household of God and are heirs of God's promise to Abraham (see commentary on 2:16; 3:1-6; 6:13-20; 12:22-24). Both have **had the gospel,** God's good news, **preached to** them (4:2). The wilderness generation received the **gospel** or the good news of deliverance from oppression and entrance into the Promised Land of fellowship with God. The preacher's hearers received the **gospel** of deliverance from sin, and entrance into intimate fellowship with God made available through Christ, God's Son and our High Priest. The **gospel** the wilderness generation received pointed forward to the **gospel** that we and the readers of Hebrews have received. If the unfaithful wilderness generation had been faithful, they ultimately would have entered into the blessings that are ours through faith (see commentary on 11:39-40). Thus, the most fundamental difference between the wilderness generation and Christians today is not a difference in the **gospel** preached to each group. The most fundamental difference is the difference between unbelief and faith. They did not believe and it is **we who have believed** who **enter that rest** (4:3).

The wilderness generation did not believe, but there were Old Testament people who did (see 11:1-40). During their lifetimes, these Old Testament faithful looked forward to God's eternal rest (11:13-16). **We,** however, **who have believed** after Christ's coming actually **enter that rest** (4:3). As our High Priest, Christ has provided for our hearts to be cleansed from sin (9:14), and thereby He has established a new covenant characterized by heart obedience (10:15-18). Thus, through the cleansing from sin and continual intercession of our heavenly High Priest, we have access into the heavenly most holy place, the very presence of God (4:14; 10:19-22).

Christ's atoning work has also opened the way for God's now-dead Old Testament people to participate more fully in God's rest. Through Jesus' blood they have entered into a fullness of rest in God's presence. They are "the spirits of righteous men made perfect" in the heavenly Jerusalem (12:23). Presumably, when Christians die they enter the same level of rest that these Old Testament saints now have. Both they and we look forward to the full enjoyment of this rest when Christ's returns (9:28) at the Judgment (12:25-29).

How can we enter God's promised rest? We must do the opposite of what the wilderness generation did. When we **hear his voice,** we must not **harden our hearts** as they did (4:7, quoting Psalm 95:7b-8a). We have seen that they could not enter because they "disobeyed" (Heb. 3:18) and because of their "unbelief" (3:19). We have noted above that the word translated "disobeyed" in 3:18 and the word translated "unbelief" in 3:19 reinforce one another. They both refer to a refusal to trust in God which leads to disobedience.

Hebrews 4:1-5 continues the theme of the wilderness generation's "unbelief" (3:19). They lost God's blessing **because those who heard did not combine it** [God's **message**] **with faith** (4:2).[9] The New Revised Standard Version offers a more accurate translation of this clause: "because they were not united by faith with those who listened." The following translation is also possible: "because they did not unite themselves by faith with those who listened" (see the New International Version's alternate reading). When God wanted to lead His people into the Promised Land, Joshua and Caleb listened. They believed God and were ready to enter the land in obedience (see Numbers 14:5-9, 30). The rest of the Israelites would not join Joshua and Caleb by believing. Of that generation, only Joshua and Caleb entered the land God had promised to give His people. It is urgent to join with those **who believe** and thus **enter that rest** (Heb. 4:3). The words **faith** (4:2) and **believe** (4:3) come from the same root as the word "unbelief" in 3:19.

Hebrews 4:6-11 picks up the theme of the wilderness generation's **disobedience** (4:6, 11) from 3:18. The word translated **disobedience** in these verses comes from the same root as "disobeyed" in that verse. The wilderness generation did not enter **God's rest** (4:3) **because of their disobedience** (4:6); neither will we enter if we follow **their example** (4:11). As noted above, none of them but Joshua and Caleb were willing to obey God's command to enter the earthly Promised Land because they did not trust God to give it to them.

The unbelief/belief/faith word group that characterizes 3:19 and 4:1-5 is closely related in meaning to the disobeyed/disobedience word group used in 3:18 and 4:6-11. Both refer to a lack of trust in God that leads to disobedience. They did not trust in God's *power* to bring them into the Promised Land nor in His *promise* that He would do so (see commentary on 11:6). They doubted God's ability and His character; therefore they would not obey.

Hebrews 4:10 gives further explanation of the faith and obedience necessary to enter **God's rest: for anyone who enters God's rest also rests from his own work, just as God did from his.** The New American Standard Bible brings out the significance of the tenses of the Greek verbs in this verse better than the New International Version: "For the one who has entered His [God's] rest has himself also rested from his works, as God did from His." This **rest** is the "Sabbath-rest" (4:9) which God entered on the seventh day after He completed creation (see 4:4). When God established this **rest,** He rested from the **work** of creation because it was perfect, completed just as He wanted it. When we enter His **rest,** however, we cease from the **work** of doing things our own way. We participate in deep fellowship with God and in His own blessedness by yielding to Him in faith and obedience.

The wilderness generation would not trust God, and so they took things into their own hands. First they were going to choose a leader and go back into Egypt (see Numbers 14:3-4). Then, after God had told them

He would not give them the Promised Land because of their disobedience, they got together and tried to enter the land on their own (see Numbers 14:39-45).

The preacher calls us to trust God with the kind of faith that turns from our own way to obedience. When we do so our Pioneer, by cleansing our hearts, brings us into this deep rest of fellowship with God, the promised land of His presence, the most holy place, the heavenly Jerusalem (see Hebrews 12:22-24). When we yield our own way completely to God's way, we enjoy the depths of this rest. We trust in His power to deliver us from sin and make us holy. This power is made available through our High Priest, Jesus Christ.

We also trust in His promise for the future. The **rest** we experience now is only a foretaste of the fullness of rest that will be ours at Christ's return (see 9:28; 12:25-29). Those who continue in God's rest now are assured of that fullness to come.

The exhortations at the beginning (4:1) and end (4:11) of this section demonstrate the urgency of the preacher. The phrase **let us be careful** (4:1) can be translated "let us fear" (NKJV; NASB). He wants his hearers to show a level of concern commensurate with the fear of losing and the hope of gaining God's ultimate **rest.** Many versions translate the clause **that none of you be found to have fallen short** (4:1) along the lines of the New Revised Standard Version: "that none of you should seem to have failed to reach it" (see NKJV; NASB). We must be concerned even if one of our fellow believers appears to be falling short of God's **rest.** The preacher wants his hearers to show a new level of concern for each other's spiritual and eternal welfare.

Hebrews 4:11 concludes this argument with an exhortation stronger than that of 4:1. Verse 1 instructed the readers to fear or be concerned lest any one of them even appear to be falling short of this rest. Verse 11 commands them to go further, to **make every effort** to enter the rest of full surrender to God now available through Christ, so that they will enter God's ultimate rest in heaven. The preacher still focuses on relationships among the people of God's household. All believers are to make every effort so that **no one** falls by following the example of **disobedience** set by the wilderness generation (4:11), but all will enter into this depth of relationship with God. The preacher would be no less urgent in exhorting us to experience the full privileges that are ours in Christ and to be concerned that our brothers and sisters experience the same. It is God's eternal **rest** that is at stake. Let's act like the stakes are high!

ENDNOTES

[1]In Numbers 20:2-13, another incident is recorded in which the people of Israel complained because they had no water. The water that they received from the rock is called "the waters of Meribah" because they had "quarreled" or "contended" with the Lord.

[2]We have seen in the introduction that the readers of Hebrews were Christians of Jewish heritage who were being pressured to give up their Christian distinctive and return to Judaism, perhaps by participating in certain ritual meals. However, once God has spoken His final revelation in the Son, there can be no turning back to the earlier and partial revelation. To refuse God's final and complete word is to turn away from Him!

[3]For discussion of the meaning of the word usually translated "confidence" in this verse, see William L. Lane, *Hebrews 1–8,* vol. 47a, Word Biblical Commentary, New Testament ed. Ralph P. Martin, gen. eds. David A. Hubbard and Glenn W. Barker (Dallas: Word Books, 1991), p. 82; Harold W. Attridge, *The Epistle to the Hebrews,* Hermeneia—A Critical and Historical Commentary on the Bible, ed. Helmut Koester (Philadelphia: Fortress Press, 1989), pp. 113, 118–19.

[4]As noted above, the writer of Hebrews inserted the words **that is why** between Psalm 95:9 and 95:10 when he quotes these verses in Hebrews 3:10. By inserting that phrase, he makes the phrase **for forty years** in Psalm 95:10 (Heb. 3:9) show the length of the time that the wilderness generation **saw what [God] did,** rather than the length of time that God **was angry with that generation** in Psalm 95:10 (Heb. 3:10). But here in Hebrews 3:17, the preacher says **with whom was he angry forty years,** showing that he knows the **forty years** also describes the period of God's anger, as the psalm had originally stated. Indeed, the wilderness generation both saw God's wonders and suffered His anger for forty years.

[5]The same verb is used in Hebrews 11:31, where again the New International Version translates it "disobedience" but gives a marginal alternative of "unbelieving." The noun related to this verb is translated "disobedience" in Hebrews 4:6 and 4:11 without an alternate reading in the margin. However, the King James Version translates this noun as "unbelief" in both of these places.

[6]The conduct of the wilderness generation subsequent to their rebellion at Kadesh Barnea does not seem to indicate true repentance (see Numbers 14:39-45; 16:1-50; 20:1-13). People who refuse to trust God do not enter eternal rest. The writer of Hebrews certainly uses the loss suffered by the unbelieving wilderness generation to warn his hearers against eternal loss. Indeed, the wilderness generation is his prime example of people who put themselves beyond God's grace by their apostasy (see commentary on Hebrews 6:4-8; 10:26-31). In Hebrews 11:13-16, we learn that the Old Testament faithful were seeking a heavenly, not an earthly, promised land. This truth would confirm that the promised land lost by the unfaithful in the Old Testament was also more than earthly.

[7]The New American Standard Bible and the New Revised Standard Version use the word "while" instead of **since:** "while a promise remains" (NASB). According to the New International Version, the continuing validity of God's

promise is the *reason* why we can and should enter God's rest; according to the NASB, God's promise gives the *opportunity* or occasion for us to enter, an opportunity that may pass. Although the Greek text of this verse can be translated in either way, the NIV expresses the main thrust of the preacher's concern. Because the **promise** remains, we can enter! In the following verses, he demonstrates that this promise does, indeed, remain for those who believe. However, he is keenly aware that the period of opportunity may pass if his readers reject the promise.

⁸The preacher has chosen his words with care. His words do not imply that the children of the wilderness generation were excluded from God's **rest.** Rather, **Joshua** did not give them **rest** *by bringing them into the Promised Land.* Exclusion from the Promised Land showed that the wilderness generation did not enter God's rest. However, the entrance of their children was no guarantee that those children had entered God's rest. The Promised Land was the symbol or type of God's rest. Exclusion from the type because of unbelief obviously meant exclusion from the reality to which the type pointed. However, entrance into the type was no guarantee of the perseverance in faith necessary to enter into the reality. As Hebrews 11:39-40 implies, none of the Old Testament faithful entered into this rest before Christ came. We can enter into it in this life in a way they could not because by His atoning work as High Priest our Pioneer brings us into the land of God's true rest.

⁹A literal translation of the Greek words behind **the message they heard** (4:2) is "the word of hearing." This **message** is God's "word" to be heard in such a way that it is obeyed. It **was of no value to** the wilderness generation because they did not "hear" it in this way. They did not truly believe it. Thus, they did not act upon it in obedience.

7

WE ARE ACCOUNTABLE BECAUSE GOD HAS SPOKEN TO US THROUGH HIS SON

Hebrews 4:12-13

Hebrews 4:12-13 concludes the first great section of the preacher's sermon, which includes Parts One (1:1–2:4) and Two (2:5–4:13) of our outline. In 1:1 through 2:4, the preacher focused on the Sinai Picture. The God who spoke on Sinai has spoken to us in His Son. How much more urgent it is for us to obey than it was for those who heard Him speak on Sinai! In 2:5 through 4:11, he focused on the Pilgrimage Picture. The wilderness generation refused to obey God's word spoken on Sinai and were excluded from the land of God's rest. We must obey God's word spoken in the Son by following our Pioneer into God's own rest, prepared from the creation. The proper response to God's word in the Son (1:1–2:4) is pilgrimage into God's rest (2:5–4:11).

Hebrews 4:12-13 is a fitting conclusion to the emphasis on accountability before God which is the theme of these chapters.

The word of God spoken in the Son (1:1-3) which we must obey (2:1-4)—which addresses us in the "Today, if you hear" of Psalm 95:7b-8a (see Hebrews 3:7–4:11)—is the **living and active** (4:12) word of God which holds us accountable before Him. Hebrews 4:12-13 especially emphasizes our accountability to the word of God spoken to us through this psalm "today." The "word they heard" (4:2 NASB; in the NIV it reads the "message they heard") is a word to which we are accountable. Verse 12 describes the **word of God** as penetrating and as exposing us for what we really are. Verse 13 portrays the resulting exposure before God.

It is easier to see the structure of 4:12 by following the more literal New American Standard Bible: "For the word of God is living and active and sharper than any two-edged sword, and piercing as far as the division of soul and spirit, of both joints and marrow, and able to judge the thoughts and intentions of the heart." In this verse, the preacher uses three adjectives (**living, active, sharper**), a participial phrase ("piercing as far as the division of soul and spirit, of both joints and marrow") and a final adjective ("able to judge" translates one Greek word) to describe the **word of God. Living** comes in the emphatic position at the beginning of the verse in Greek. Like God himself (see 3:12; 9:14; 10:31), His word is **living. Active** goes closely with and explains **living.** Because God's word is alive, it does things, it accomplishes God's purpose, it is effective. This is, of course, the word of God that created, that addressed God's people in the wilderness, and that now addresses His people through the Son. What God said in the wilderness came to pass. His word always does!

This verse emphasizes the effectiveness of God's word to penetrate and expose our inward beings. The next adjective and the words that go with it—**sharper than any double-edged sword,** and the following participial phrase, "piercing as far as the division of soul and spirit, of both joints and marrow" (NASB)—describe this penetrating exposure of God's word. God's word is so sharp that it can penetrate the impenetrable and separate the inseparable: **soul and spirit, joints and marrow.** The crucial reality, however, is now expressed without metaphor: It is able to judge **the thoughts and attitudes of the heart.** The phrase **thoughts and attitudes** or "thoughts and intentions" (NASB) is a comprehensive description of what goes on in our hearts. The word of God has not only the power, but also the right to judge the thoughts and intentions of the heart. It is the proper standard by which our internal lives, our real selves, are judged.

When God's word addresses us, it shows us how far the **thoughts and attitudes** or "intentions" of our hearts fall short of what God requires.

106

The hearts of the wilderness generation were the problem (see 3:8, 12-13, 15). It is hearts that are cleansed of their sinful propensity that are made obedient by the blood of Christ under the new covenant (see commentary on 9:14; 10:15-18).

Exposure to the word of God exposes us to God's own standard, His own holy character and, therefore, as 4:13 makes clear, to God himself. It is impossible to hide what we really are from Him because **nothing in all creation** is hidden from Him. No human being. No angel. No created thing at all. Absolutely nothing of any kind—material, mental or spiritual—is in the least hidden from Him. **Uncovered** and **laid bare** emphasize the thoroughness of this exposure right before the very **eyes** of the God **to whom we must give account.** The word here translated **account** is the same Greek term that is normally translated "word." The phrase could be more literally translated "to whom in relation to us a word must be given." The **word** or revelation of God (4:12) requires an answering "word" from us (see 4:13). Will it be a word of faith or disobedience?

Part Three

THE HIGH PRIEST PICTURE: DRAW NEAR TO GOD WITH A CLEANSED CONSCIENCE

Hebrews 4:14–10:31

ebrews 4:14 through 10:31 is the great central section of the book of Hebrews. God has revealed himself in the Son—that we know from 1:1-14. The preacher has made clear to his hearers how important it is to respond to God's revelation in His Son. They must respond with the kind of faith that results in obedience (see 2:1-4; 3:1–4:13). Only through such faith will they, and we, be able to enter the fullness of blessing that God has prepared for His own (see 4:1-11). But what has God revealed through His Son? What is the content of this great, final revelation of God? The central section of this "sermon" describes the content of this revelation in great detail as the salvation provided through the great High Priest of God's people.

Earlier chapters have alluded to "such a great salvation" (2:3). This salvation is the "purification for sins" that the Son provided before "he sat down at the right hand of the Majesty in heaven" (1:3). He made this salvation a reality when "by the grace of God" He tasted "death for everyone" (2:9). As our Pioneer and Champion, He provided this salvation when He opened the way for God's people to enter His "glory" (2:10). He opened the way for them when He delivered them from the fear of death by making atonement for their sin as their "merciful and faithful high priest" (2:17). In Hebrews 4:14, the preacher picks up the theme of priesthood from 2:17. Christ's High Priesthood is the subject of 4:14 through 10:31. By developing this theme, the preacher helps us gain a deeper knowledge of the Person and work of Christ. He encourages us to enter ever more deeply into the rich blessings Christ has provided.

The oath of God found in Psalm 110:4—"You are a priest forever in the order of Melchizedek"—establishes the High Priesthood of the eternal Son of God and does away with the ineffective Aaronic priesthood. From Psalm 110:1 (cited in Hebrews 1:13) we also know that this eternal High Priest is seated at the Father's right hand. In Hebrews 1:3, the preacher told us that He thus sat down "after he had provided purification for sin." Hebrews 7:27 tells us that He dealt with sin by sacrificing himself. It is time for the preacher to explain the nature of this sacrifice that effectively dealt with sin and thus enabled the Son to be a High Priest "who has been made perfect forever" (7:28) as our Savior.

Hebrews 8:1 through 10:18 provides an extended discussion of this sacrifice. Although Christ's sacrifice is the main theme of the section, it is interwoven with two other themes which help to explain its significance: the theme of sanctuary (or sphere of priestly ministry) and the theme of covenant. The preacher presents these three themes of sanctuary, sacrifice, and covenant in three stages. If we were to use a dramatic metaphor, we might call these three "acts"; or a symphonic metaphor, three "movements." The analogy with music is particularly appropriate because there is a certain balance, harmony, and resolution to the way the preacher develops these themes. We find the first movement in 8:1-13, the second in 9:1-22, and the third in 9:23 through 10:18. Each of these three movements begins by discussing the sanctuary or sphere of ministry (8:1-2; 9:1-10; 9:23-24) and ends by discussing the covenant (8:7-13; 9:16-22; 10:15-18). The central section of each demonstrates the uniqueness of Christ's sacrifice by relating it to these two themes (8:3-6; 9:11-15; 9:25–10:14). In each movement, the section on sacrifice occupies a larger and more predominant place than in the previous movement.

It is important to note the climactic progression of these three movements.

SANCTUARY, SACRIFICE & COVENANT
IN HEBREWS 8:1–10:18

Movement 1	Movement 2	Movement 3
A New Kind of Sacrifice	Christ's Own Blood	Christ's Perfect Obedience
Hebrews 8:1-13	Hebrews 9:1-22	Hebrews 9:23–10:18

SANCTUARY
Hebrews
9:23-24

SANCTUARY
Hebrews
9:1-10

SANCTUARY
Hebrews
8:1-2

SACRIFICE
Hebrews
8:3-6

SACRIFICE
Hebrews
9:11-15

SACRIFICE
Hebrews
9:25–10:14

COVENANT
Hebrews
8:7-13

COVENANT
Hebrews
9:16-22

COVENANT
Hebrews
10:15-18

Movement 1 (8:1-13) focuses on the facts: Christ ministers in a heavenly sanctuary; He mediates the new covenant; Jeremiah prophesied this covenant. These very facts, without further analysis of their quality, show that Christ's sacrifice must be different from and superior to the sacrifices of the Old Testament priesthood. This movement cites Exodus 25:40 in relation to the sanctuary (Heb. 8:5), and Jeremiah 31:31-34, the promise of the new covenant (Heb. 8:8-12).

Movement 2 (9:1-22) describes the old sanctuary and the establishment of the old covenant in considerable detail. It does this by extensive allusion to, but without direct quotation from, the Old Testament. This description shows the inadequacy of the old ways and the need for a blood sacrifice. Christ's blood is the sacrifice which truly atones for sin and establishes the new covenant.

Finally, movement 3 (9:23–10:18) focuses directly on the superior quality of Christ's sacrifice itself. Two facts demonstrate the adequacy of His sacrifice: He only had to offer it once for all and after He offered it He sat down at the Father's right hand. His sacrifice was made adequate, however, by His complete obedience. Only such obedience could deal with sin, bring Him into the heavenly sanctuary and thus establish the new covenant. This sacrifice makes our High Priest fully adequate as our Savior.

Thus, movement 1 is concerned with the fact that Christ ministers in the heavenly sanctuary and has established the new covenant. Movement 2 helps us to see the significance of Christ's sacrifice by comparing it to and demonstrating the inadequacy of the old sanctuary, sacrifice, and covenant. Movement 3 focuses directly on the adequacy of the new. The preacher moves from the fact that Christ's sanctuary and covenant are different, to the inadequacy of the old, to the sufficiency of the new. In movement 1, Christ's sacrifice is something different and better than the old; in movement 2, it is His own blood which atones for sin and establishes the new covenant; in movement 3, we discover that His "blood" is His human life of obedience climaxing in His death. It is His obedience that makes the difference. There is a progressively stronger emphasis on the failure of the old and the complete sufficiency of the new as we move from movement 1 through movement 2 to movement 3. The preceding chart pictures the proportions between the three movements and the three themes.

Consider several other important observations concerning Hebrews 8:1 through 10:18. First, it is important to note where the preacher cites Old Testament Scripture. In relation to themes 1 and 3, sanctuary and covenant, he cites Scripture in movement 1: Exodus 25:40 in relation to sanctuary, and Jeremiah 31:31-34 in relation to covenant. He uses these Scripture quotations to show that there is a difference between the new and the old. However, he quotes Scripture in relation to sacrifice, his central and most important theme, only at the climax of his argument in movement 3.   At that point, he quotes Psalm 40:6-8 to explain the qualitative superiority of Christ's sacrifice.   This arrangement of Old Testament quotations shows the importance of the sacrifice theme.   The climactic position of Psalm 40:6-8 demonstrates that it is the key to the preacher's argument.

Note also that the preacher explains Christ's sacrifice by analogy with three different kinds of Old Testament sacrifices.   He employs two of these analogies at the heart of movement 2, where he likens Christ's sacrifice to the Day of Atonement sacrifice (Heb. 9:11-14) and to a sacrifice of covenant inauguration (9:15).   In the third movement, 9:25 through 10:14, he compares Christ's sacrifice to the Old Testament sacrifice of priestly consecration.   The preacher already hints at this analogy in 7:28, when he says that the Son "has been made perfect forever" as our effective High Priest and Savior.

The key to understanding the preacher's vision of Christ's sacrificial death is His description of its significance in the third movement (9:25–10:14), especially in 10:5-10 at the heart of that movement.

8

OUR HIGH PRIEST HAS ENTERED HEAVEN FOR US

Hebrews 4:14-16

Because the preacher is vitally concerned for the spiritual welfare of his hearers, he begins (4:14-16) and ends (10:19-31) his discussion of the Son's High Priesthood by showing its relevance to their lives.

Hebrews 4:14-16 is in two parts—verse 14, and verses 15 and 16. The preacher begins each of these parts by telling his hearers something about the kind of high priest that **we** as Christians **have** (4:14). He concludes each by telling us what we can and should do because we have such a High Priest.

In 4:14, the preacher calls Jesus a **great high priest.** "Great priest" would be a literal translation of the Old Testament term that we usually translate "high priest." Thus to call Jesus a **great high priest** is the same as calling Him a "High, High Priest." The preacher forcefully emphasizes the unparalleled greatness of Jesus, the Christian's High Priest. He introduces his discussion of Christ's High Priesthood with this emphasis on how great a High Priest He is.

This High Priest is so great because He **has gone through the heavens,** He is **Jesus,** and He is **the Son of God** (4:14). Other high priests offered animal sacrifices and then passed through the first part of the Tabernacle and entered the Most Holy Place (9:1-10), the place which symbolized God's presence, but Jesus **has gone through the heavens.** After He had made purification for sin (1:3) by offering himself, He passed through the visible **heavens** of this created universe. He entered into that "heaven" that is the place where God dwells, and He sat down at God's right hand (1:3). The perfect tense of the Greek verb translated **has gone** implies that Jesus has entered God's presence and is still there. The benefits of His entrance into heaven are still available to His people. Moreover, it is not merely some angel or heavenly being who has gone through the heavens into the very presence of God. It is **Jesus** who has done this, the same **Jesus** who lived and died for us here on earth as a perfectly obedient human being. And yet He is also the One who from all eternity has been **the Son of God,** the Heir of all, the agent of creation, and the perfect revelation of the Father (1:1-3). In the following chapters, the preacher shows more fully why Jesus could enter God's presence and open the way for us to enter. He could only do this because He was the Son of God who became Jesus and lived a completely obedient human life. But for now He uses this description (**gone through the heavens, Jesus the Son of God**) to emphasize the greatness of this High Priest. There is no one who compares with Him.

Because there is no other high priest like this High Priest, the readers of Hebrews should **hold firmly to the faith** they **profess** (4:14). The word **faith** refers to the content of their faith, to what they believed about Jesus. They already believed that Jesus was the Son of God and they believed that He alone could save. The preacher wants to fortify them in these beliefs by explaining the High Priesthood of Jesus. He urges them to **hold firmly** to this belief in Jesus. He means more, however, than that they should continue to affirm certain ideas. The way they live their lives should demonstrate their belief that salvation comes only through the eternal Son of God, their High Priest. They must hold firm despite opposition. Endurance is essential!

Hebrews 4:14 emphasizes the transcendence of our High Priest. In 4:15, the author reminds his hearers of what it meant for this High Priest to be the earthly Jesus. This High Priest has stooped down to our level. He can reach us where we are! It is important that we understand both the words **sympathize** and **weaknesses** in the phrase **sympathize with our weaknesses.** To most modern speakers of English, the word *sympathize* denotes a mere feeling. However, the Greek word here translated **sympathize** means to actively help someone. Also, the **weaknesses** in question include sinfulness (see commentary on 5:2).

116

Human beings have a propensity to yield to temptation. This High Priest sympathizes with the **weaknesses** of His people by cleansing them from sin and enabling them to overcome temptation.

This ability to help is not based merely on the deity of the Son of God. His ability to deliver us from temptation results also from the sinless life He lived on earth as Jesus of Nazareth. He **has been tempted in every way, just as we are** (4:15). There is absolutely no difference between the way He was **tempted** or "tested" (NRSV) and the way we are tempted and tested. The scorn and abuse of the world pressured Him to abandon the road of trust and obedience. He was tempted by all of the kinds of temptations that Christians face. But the outcome of His temptation is what made the difference—He **was without sin.** The word used here for **without** is very strong. There was no difference in the way He was tempted, but there was a vast difference in the outcome of that temptation. He never yielded to temptation. This difference enables Him to help us overcome.[1] The phrase **has been tempted** translates a Greek verb in the perfect tense. The perfect tense here indicates that the results of His overcoming temptation when on earth are still available to us today!

Since He always resisted temptation in His earthly life and then went **through the heavens** into the Father's presence to sit at His right hand, **let us then approach the throne of grace with confidence** (4:16). (The term translated **approach** is also used in 7:25; 10:1, 22; 11:6; and 12:18, 22 to describe moving toward God in worship and prayer. Similar terms are used in 4:3 and 7:19.) We can come with true **confidence** or "boldness" (NRSV) because we know that our High Priest has opened the way for us (see 10:19-23). Through Him we are "authorized personnel" who have the privilege of entrance into the throne room. When we **approach the throne of grace,** we will be admitted and receive what we need to "hold firmly to the faith we profess" (4:14). Through the work of our High Priest, God's **throne** from which He judges evil has become a **throne of grace.** We will be given a gracious reception—not because our sinfulness or God's holiness are minimized (compare 4:12-13), but because of the surpassing work of our High Priest. We will receive **mercy** in the forgiveness of our sins and **grace to help us in our time of need** (4:16). We receive "timely grace." The readers are assured that they have access to God's grace whenever they face temptation.

The exhortation of 4:16, **Let us then approach the throne of grace with confidence,** parallels and supports the exhortation of 4:14b, **Let us hold firmly to the faith we profess.** How can we hold firmly to our faith in Jesus as God's Son and our Savior when the ridicule of others and the pressures of society try to make us give up that faith? By approaching **the throne of grace with confidence,** we receive the help we need. We modern Christians in this secular world need to remember this truth. We maintain our Christian walk only if we draw near to God in genuine public and private worship and in continual daily fellowship with Him.

The preacher has much more of profit to say about the significance of this great High Priest. Since he is convinced that the God who spoke in the Old Testament has now spoken through His Son, it is only natural that the preacher would begin his discussion of the Son's High Priesthood by comparing it with the Old Testament Aaronic priesthood. This was the priesthood revealed on Mount Sinai, the priesthood through which God's Old Testament people were to maintain their relationship with a Holy God. The preacher's comparison follows in Hebrews 5:1-10.

ENDNOTE

[1]"This sinlessness, it should be stressed, is not something passive, a mere state of being, but the achievement of Christ's active conquest of temptation. Indeed, it is entirely synonymous with the complete obedience learned by him through all he endured, by which his perfection was won and established, and which fitted him to become the source of our eternal salvation (Heb. 2:10; 5:8f . . .)" (Philip Edgcumbe Hughes, *A Commentary on the Epistle to the Hebrews* [Grand Rapids, Michigan: Wm. B. Eerdmans Publishing Co., 1977], p. 173).

9

THE NEW HIGH PRIEST AND THE OLD

Hebrews 5:1-10

ebrews 5:1-10 outlines the correspondence between the Old Testament high priest and Christ. This comparison, however, inevitably directs the reader's attention toward the superiority of the Son's High Priesthood. Hebrews 5:1-10 divides naturally into two smaller paragraphs, 5:1-4 and 5:5-10. The first describes the Aaronic high priest; the second portrays Christ as High Priest.

Each of these paragraphs begins and ends by referring to the high priest's call. Verse 1 tells how every high priest is **selected** and **appointed** to high priesthood by God. Verse 4 points out that no Aaronic high priest **takes** this honor upon himself but is **called** by God. The Greek word translated **selected** in verse 1 is the same word translated **takes** in verse 4.

In a similar way, verses 5 through 10 are framed by the appointment of Christ as High Priest. Christ **did not take** (5:5) the high priesthood upon himself but was called by God according to the order of Melchizedek. He received His call through the words of Psalm 110:4 quoted in Hebrews 5:6. He is **designated** by God as high priest of Melchizedek's order in 5:10.

The accompanying chart, "Two High Priesthoods Compared," diagrams the comparison/contrast between the Aaronic high priest and Christ in this passage. We will begin by examining the correspondence between the introductory and concluding verses: 5:1 and 5:10. Then we will go down the chart, looking at verses 2a and 9; 2b and 8; 3 and 7; and finally 4 and 5-6.

TWO HIGH PRIESTHOODS COMPARED
HEBREWS 5:1-10

THE HIGH PRIESTHOOD OF AARON	THE HIGH PRIESTHOOD OF THE SON
Every high priest is selected from among men and is appointed to represent them in matters related to God, to offer gifts and sacrificed for sins (5:1).	And was designated by God to be high priest in the order of Melchizedek (5:10).

THEIR HIGH PRIESTLY MINISTRIES	
He is able to deal gently with those who are ignorant and are going astray (5:2a).	And, once made perfect, he became the source of eternal salvation for all who obey him (5:9).

THEIR HUMANITY	
Since he himself is subject to weakness (5:2b).	Although he was a son, he learned obedience from what he suffered (5:8).

THEIR SACRIFICES	
This is why he has to offer sacrifices for his own sins, as well as for the sins of the people (5:3).	During the days of Jesus' life on earth, he offered up prayers and petitions with loud cries and tears to the one who could save him from death, and he was heard because of his reverent submission (5:7).

THEIR HIGH PRIESTLY CALL	
No one takes this honor upon himself; he must be called by God, just as Aaron was (5:4).	So Christ also did not take upon himself the glory of becoming a high priest. But God said to him, "You are my Son; today I have become your Father." And he says in another place, "You are a priest forever, in the order of Melchizedek" (5:5-6).

This comparison is introduced in 5:1 by a general description of high priesthood modeled on the Old Testament Aaronic high priest. Verse 1 gives the categories which are used to compare the high priesthood of Aaron and the Son: A high priest must (1) be human (**selected from among men**); (2) be God-appointed (**is appointed**), so that he can (3) have a ministry in which he represents other human beings before God (**to represent them in matters related to God**) and (4) offer sacrifices that deal with sin (**to offer gifts and sacrifices for sins**). The Aaronic high priest fully conforms to verse one's description of high priesthood. However, 5:10 concludes this comparison by proclaiming that the Son is High Priest **in the order of Melchizedek** and, therefore, transcends these Aaronic categories. The preacher will explain in greater detail the superiority of this new High Priest in 7:1 through 10:18.

5:1—**Every high priest is selected from among men and is appointed to represent them in matters related to God, to offer gifts and sacrifices for sins.**	5:10—**. . . and was designated by God to be high priest in the order of Melchizedek.**

The following verses compare and contrast the Aaronic high priest and Christ as High Priest according to each of the categories given in 5:1: in their sacrifices for sin (5:3, 7); in their humanity (5:2b, 8); in their ministry (5:2a, 9); and in their divine appointment (5:4-6). In a nutshell, the ministry of the Aaronic high priest (5:2a) was limited by his sinful humanity (5:2b). The sinfulness of his humanity was demonstrated by his need to offer sacrifice for himself (5:3). On the other hand, the Son's sacrifice of himself (5:7) was the fulfillment of His obedient humanity (5:8), and thus made His priestly ministry effective (5:9). As High Priest **in the order of Melchizedek** (5:10), Christ has perfectly fulfilled each of these aspects of High Priesthood. As the **source of eternal salvation** (5:9), He has been appointed to this eternal priesthood at God's right hand. (Hebrews 7:1-28 further explains this Melchizedekian priesthood.)

The benefit of the Aaronic high priest's ministry is described in 5:2a; that of Christ in 5:9.

5:2a—**He is able to deal gently with those who are ignorant and are going astray.**	5:9—**And, once made perfect, he became the source of eternal salvation for all who obey him.**

What kind of ministry did the Aaronic high priest have? He could **deal gently** with sinners. **Deal gently** means to restrain one's anger against or moderate one's emotions toward another person. The old high priest could not eliminate the sin problem; he could only restrain his anger against the sinner. Even the description of sinners here as **those who are ignorant and going astray** apparently softens their responsibility because of their ignorance of God's law. One could imagine the high priest saying, "I know it is hard not to sin; after all, you are **ignorant,** you don't know any better. We have offered a sacrifice for you. Go and do the best you can." The old high priest could not overcome sin; he had to tolerate sin. But, in reality, ignorance is no excuse. Ignorance often results from the chosen neglect of spiritual things. **Going astray** can lead to apostasy, the total rejection of God (see 3:10). In fact, the word here translated **going astray** is used for such apostasy in the Greek text of Deuteronomy 4:19; 11:28; 13:6; and 30:17.

We have already seen the significance of the fact that our High Priest Christ can "sympathize with our weaknesses" (4:15). He can actually deal with our sin; the old high priest could only put up with the sinner. Hebrews 5:9 describes Christ's glorious ministry, which corresponds to the picture of the Aaronic priest's ministry in 5:2a. Christ can truly help His people. He has been **made perfect** as their Savior and has thus become their **source of eternal salvation.** He was perfected as our Savior by His complete obedience up to and including His death (see commentary on 2:10; 7:28; 10:5-10). His fully obedient life, climaxing in an obedient death, serves as the sacrifice that atones for our sin and that makes Him a heavenly High Priest who can effectively meet our need. The Aaronic high priest put up with sin. This High Priest provides **eternal salvation** which provides forgiveness and cleansing from sin. Thus God's people can live eternally in the presence of God. This High Priest offers salvation to **all who obey him.** The present tense of the verb **obey** indicates that a continuous and purposeful obedience characterizes true faith. The preacher describes this salvation more fully in the extended discussion of the Son's High Priesthood found in Hebrews 7 through 10.

We have seen above that Christ was perfected as our Savior through His obedient human life. Verse 2b describes the humanity of the Aaronic high priest, verse 8 the humanity of the incarnate Son.

5:2b—**since he himself is subject to weakness**	5:8—**Although he was a son, he learned obedience from what he suffered**

The old high priest was a human being subject to sin like all human beings. Hebrews 5:3 makes it clear that **weakness** includes sin. Thus he could put up with the sins of others and be patient with them not only because he could do nothing about their sin, but also because he himself had sinned. His sinful humanity limited rather than facilitated his ability to deal with sin through his priestly ministry.

Although Christ was and is by nature the eternal **son,** He became a human being and **learned obedience** (5:8). It is no accident that Hebrews avoids saying that Christ is **subject to weakness** (5:2). We have seen above that **weakness** includes sinfulness. The Aaronic high priest's humanity was **subject to weakness** and thus sinful. Christ's humanity was characterized by the fact that **he learned obedience.** This phrase does not mean that He was once disobedient and then learned to be obedient. By becoming a human being, He learned what it was like to be obedient. **He learned obedience** by practicing faithful obedience to God in *every* concrete situation of His life, despite opposition, up to and including His suffering of death. He maintained the unity of His will with His Father's will. In 5:8, we see the crux of the difference between our High Priest and the Aaronic high priest; we are given the secret of Christ's effectiveness. Both high priests were human. But while the ministry of the Aaronic high priest was limited by his sin, Christ's obedience enabled His ministry. (Hebrews 10:5-10 discusses this obedience in more detail.) It is this learning of **obedience** that culminates in Christ's sacrifice (5:7; see below) and makes it effective.[1] By this obedience He has been perfected as the **source of eternal salvation** (5:9) and been designated a priest of Melchizedek's **order** (5:10).

In a nutshell, the old high priest's ministry was limited to putting up with sin because of his sinfulness; Christ's ministry brings eternal salvation because of His accomplished obedience.

Hebrews 5:3 and 5:7 compare the sacrifices of the old and new high priests.

5:3—**This is why he has to offer sacrifices for his own sins, as well as for the sins of the people.**	5:7—**During the days of Jesus' life on earth, he offered up prayers and petitions with loud cries and tears to the one who could save him from death, and he was heard because of his reverent submission.**

Hebrews 5:3 affirms that the sacrifice of the old high priest was proof of his sinfulness (described in 5:2b). Because he was guilty, he had a moral obligation to offer sacrifices **for his own sins** as well as for the sins of the people. Although there were several occasions when the high priest offered sacrifice for himself (see, for instance, Leviticus 9:7), this reference directs the reader's attention to the Day of Atonement in Leviticus 16:6-17. In Hebrews 9:11-14, the preacher compares Christ's sacrifice with that sacrifice. On the Day of Atonement, the high priest offered for himself first, then for the people. The preliminary offering for himself shows his own sinfulness. It demonstrates why his ministry was limited to being gentle with those who were sinning (see 5:2 and commentary above).

Hebrews 5:7 refers to the sacrifice of Christ, which was accomplished "in the days of his flesh" (KJV). While on earth, Christ experienced a human life as genuine as any ever lived. As we have seen, Jesus offered as His sacrifice not only His death but also the whole of His obedient life. His obedient humanity, which climaxed in His obediently submitting to death on the cross, was His sacrifice.

Christ's sacrifice is described as **prayers and petitions** (5:7), words often paired in first-century Judaism. They denote His continual dependence on God throughout His human life. The reality of the testing that He faced and the pain it cost Him are indicated by the fact that he offered these prayers **with loud cries and tears** (5:7). The extent of His dependence on God is shown by the phrase **the one who could save him from death. Loud cries and tears** certainly directs our minds to Christ's agonizing prayer in the Garden of Gethsemane just before His crucifixion. In that Garden prayer, "yet not my will but yours be done" (Luke 22:42), the consistent obedience of His life moved toward the climax of the cross.

The one who was able to save him from death describes God as the Ruler of life and death. It is probably better to understand this phrase as **the one who was able to save him [*out of*] death** (my emphasis). Jesus addressed His prayer to the God of resurrection.[2] This is the God who would raise Him from the dead, exalt Him to heaven, and seat Him at His right hand. This God not only would bring Christ out of death, but by so doing would validate the effectiveness of Christ's own self-sacrifice.

In the Greek text, the word translated **offered** (5:7) is put at the end of the first clause, very close to the word translated **he was heard.** God heard His prayer and accepted His sacrifice **because of his reverent**

submission. The two words **reverent submission** translate one Greek word, which the New King James Version translates as "godly fear," and the New American Standard Bible as "piety." Jesus completely submitted to God's will (see 10:5-10) that He bear the sin of the world on the cross. He did this because He fully trusted the Father to raise Him and validate His sacrifice. His faith, the very deepest, led to the fullest obedience.

But how was this High Priest able to live an obedient human life? What was the secret of his success? These questions are answered when we look at the nature of His call to or His establishment in high priesthood. His call reveals the power behind His High Priesthood. Thus, we look next at those verses in the center of our passage, verses 4 through 6, which compare the call of Aaron and of the Son.

5:4—No one takes this honor upon himself; he must be called by God, just as Aaron was.	**5:5-6—So Christ also did not take upon himself the glory of becoming a high priest. But God said to him, "You are my Son; today I have become your Father." And he says in another place, "You are a priest forever, in the order of Melchizedek."**

The first two clauses of 5:4 state how high priests do and do not receive their call. The writer then applies these ideas to Aaron at the end of 5:4 and to Christ in 5:5-6: **No one takes this honor** of high priesthood **upon himself,** but **he must be called by God.** For the preacher and his hearers, who were thoroughly grounded in the Old Testament, this truth was axiomatic. People could only approach God on God's own terms. Thus the high priest through whom they approach Him must be appointed by God. The Old Testament law made it clear that Aaron and Aaron's family alone were to be priests. Others who tried to usurp the priesthood were destroyed (see Numbers 16:1-35, especially 16:10).

Perhaps Hebrews' first readers wondered how the preacher could call Christ a High Priest. Had not God called and appointed Aaron and Aaron's family and them alone as priests? The preacher freely and firmly acknowledges Aaron's call. After all, the priesthood of Aaron pointed forward to the priesthood of the Son of God. However, he affirms that the call of Christ to High Priesthood is a call that surpasses all calls.

Christ did not assume for himself the **glory** of high priesthood, although the high priesthood He received was the most glorious. No, the God who announced Christ's Sonship is also the One who proclaimed Him High Priest. The preacher affirms this truth by citing Psalm 2:7 in Hebrews 5:5 and Psalm 110:4 in Hebrews 5:6. In Hebrews 1:5, the preacher already demonstrated that Psalm 2:7 is God's announcement of Christ's Sonship[3]: "You are my Son; today I have become your Father." He now affirms that in Psalm 110:4, God institutes Christ as Priest: **You are a priest forever, in the order of Melchizedek** (5:6).[4] By bringing these two Old Testament quotations together, the writer of Hebrews associates Christ's High Priesthood with His Sonship. His Sonship empowers His High Priesthood. Because He is God's Son He is an effective high priest (see Hebrews 7:1-28). Up until this point these two themes of Sonship and High Priesthood have been discussed separately: Sonship in Hebrews 1:1-14; High Priesthood in 2:16-18. In 4:14, the writer first mentions the two, side by side. He makes clear their association with the help of the two Scripture quotations in 5:5-6.

When did the divine proclamation of the Son's priesthood according to Melchizedek's **order** take place? Probably when Christ was exalted, when He sat down at the Father's right hand. As mentioned above (see commentary on Hebrews 1:13), Jesus and many early Christians understood Psalm 110:1 as the words God spoke to Jesus at the time of His exaltation to heavenly glory: "Sit at My right hand." The writer of Hebrews cited this verse as he concluded his exposition of Christ's Sonship (see Hebrews 1:5-14). The preacher alone, of all New Testament writers, drew the conclusion that if Psalm 110:1 was addressed to Jesus, then Psalm 110:4 must also be addressed to Him. The psalm that proclaimed Christ's exaltation at the Father's right hand also proclaimed His Priesthood. Thus it is likely that the preacher understood this proclamation as occurring at Christ's exaltation. Psalms 110:1 and 110:4 refer to the same moment in time. There is a sense in which Christ's earthly life was priestly. His perfect obedience unto death is His Priestly sacrifice (10:5-10). Nevertheless, it is this perfect obedience and sacrifice that enabled Him to become the effective High Priest after Melchizedek's order, at God's right hand. Thus He is now able to minister to our present need (8:1)! At the conclusion of Jesus' earthly ministry, God proclaimed Him both as High Priest (in the words of Psalm 110:4) and Son (in the words of Psalm 2:7, see commentary on Hebrews 1:5).

It is now quite evident why the author can describe Christ as one who can "sympathize with our weaknesses" (Heb. 4:15), while the Aaronic high priest can do no more than **deal gently with those who are ignorant and are going astray** (5:2). By living a completely obedient human life, climaxing in His obedient death, Christ offered an effective sacrifice for our sins. As a result of that sacrifice, He can deliver us from our sins. Through His obedience we can be obedient. The Aaronic high priest could only encourage his people to do better, to put up with their sin, because he also was sinful. He even had to offer a sacrifice for himself.

Who, then, is our **high priest in the order of Melchizedek** (5:10)? He is the eternal Son of God who offered His obedient human life and death as a sacrifice for our sins. Thus He is the One who now sits at the right hand of God and is able to help us.

Later in his letter, the preacher explains this priesthood more fully. However, he does not want to lead his hearers into speculations about this priesthood. Instead, he urgently desires that they enter into a deeper experience of its benefits. Therefore he postpones further discussion of these subjects until Hebrews 7:1. Before going further he wants to be sure that they are spiritually ready to hear what he has to say. Thus in 5:11 through 6:20 he challenges them to a deeper spiritual maturity.

ENDNOTES

[1]The obedience that Christ learned was obedience "to the call to suffer death in accordance with the revealed will of God" (William L. Lane, *Hebrews 1–8,* vol. 47a, Word Biblical Commentary, New Testament ed. Ralph P. Martin, gen. eds. David A. Hubbard and Glenn W. Barker (Dallas: Word Books, 1991), p. 121.

[2]Abraham believed in God's power to raise the dead (11:19; see also commentary on Hebrews 11:35).

[3]"The writer correctly interprets Psalm 2:7 as a declaration of appointment, not of parentage" (Lane, p. 118).

[4]The writer of Hebrews takes the word "priest" in Psalm 110:4 as the equivalent of "high priest." Since there is only one priest like Melchizedek, it is not necessary to distinguish between "priest" and "high priest." When the writer of Hebrews speaks of Christ's priesthood in relation to Melchizedek and Psalm 110:4, he often uses "priest," but when he compares or contrast's Christ's priesthood with the priesthood of Aaron, he uses "high priest."

10

PREPARE YOUR HEARTS TO RECEIVE THE TRUTH

Hebrews 5:11–6:20

There is a bond between obedience and spiritual understanding. Faithful obedience enables God's people to comprehend more clearly God's work in Christ that cleanses from sin and brings access to the Father's presence. In turn, this deeper comprehension is a source of power for faithful obedience.

The writer of Hebrews wants to explain the deeper things of Christ so that his hearers can be empowered for trust and obedience. He is concerned, however, that their present level of trust and obedience might prevent them from grasping the depths of Christ's High Priesthood. They appear to be negligent of spiritual truth, rather than diligent in their Christian walk. Thus he warns them against being satisfied with the beginning stages of Christian living (5:11–6:8) and challenges them to a more consistent faith (6:9-20). By these exhortations he prepares them for the theme of Christ's High Priesthood according to "the order of Melchizedek" (5:10), to which he returns in 6:20.

1. DON'T CONTINUE TO BE BABY CHRISTIANS 5:11–6:8

The preacher describes his hearers' potentially stunted state of Christian growth in Hebrews 5:11-14 and warns them of its possible results in 6:1-8;

5:11 states the problem clearly: **We have much to say about this, but it is hard to explain because you are slow to learn. About this** refers back to the High Priesthood of Christ, especially His High Priesthood after Melchizedek's order, and to all the blessings and benefits that are available through Christ's High Priesthood.

In order to render this verse clearly, the English translations have altered the structure of the sentence. The Greek uses a noun meaning "the word" instead of the verb, **to say.** A more literal but less clear translation of the first clause would read something like this: "The word we have about this is much." The Greek original is significant because the term translated "the word" is used elsewhere in Hebrews for God's "word" which addresses us and calls us to obedience (see 2:2; 4:12-13). The explanation about Christ's High Priesthood in the central portion of this book is the "word" of God that calls God's people to obedience.

This deeper spiritual truth about Christ's High Priesthood **is hard to explain** (5:11), but not primarily because it is challenging in itself. No, it's the spiritual situation of the hearers that causes the difficulty. Both the New King James Version and the New American Standard Bible read "dull of hearing" instead of **slow to learn.** The word translated "hearing" means the faculty of hearing or understanding. Words meaning "to hear," built on the same Greek root, are common in Hebrews (see 2:1-2; 3:7, 15-16; 4:2-7; 5:7-9) and are used to show that human beings should "hear" God's word in such a way that they obey it. Thus, the preacher has a "word" from God about Christ's High Priesthood. But he fears his hearers will not "hear" it in such a way that they will accept it and obey it. "Dull of hearing" means they have become slow to understand because they have become slow to obey. They bear responsibility for their dullness or sluggishness in hearing. The hearers shy away from understanding the truth more deeply because they fear the consequences of that understanding. They stumble at the radical obedience it will require.

There is a bit of irony in this description of the recipients of Hebrews as sluggish, dull, or slow to hear.[1] It goes beyond their actual condition, as 6:9-12 shows. Nevertheless, they showed signs that gave the preacher deep concern. He uses this description to challenge them to a deeper level of Christian living.

In 5:11, the preacher has stated the problem: He is afraid his hearers will not accept the deep spiritual truth they need because of their negligence. In 5:12-14, he urges them to a renewed diligence by describing this state of spiritual lethargy and its consequences.

Verse 12 describes their potentially "sluggish" state more fully. Many words in this verse emphasize the fact that this state is an unnatural one. The preacher had every reason to expect something much more from them. They were immature in an unhealthy sense. They were adults acting like babies. There is nothing wrong with a baby being a baby, but it is abnormal for an adult to act like a baby. That's a real problem. The first clause of 5:12 states forcefully what, by that time, they should have been: **though by this time you ought to be teachers.** In Greek the first word of the next clause is "again." They had been taught once, but "again need you have for" **someone to teach you** (5:12). The writer emphasizes the word **you** by its location in the Greek sentence. The phrase **elementary truths of God's word** is literally "the basic elements of the beginning of the words of God." Note that the Greek is "the words of God" (plural), not "the word of God." The people are described as being far from understanding the "word" of God (see 2:2; 4:12; 5:11, 13; 6:1; 13:7), the big picture of God's truth. They needed to be taught again the most elementary basic facts of the "words" of God, their spiritual ABCs, the rudiments of their catechism. Perhaps they needed to go as far back as the simplest truths found in the Old Testament.[2]

First-century writers often spoke of educational development, which included character formation, both in terms of athletic training and in terms of progress from infancy to maturity.[3] Philosophers might speak of those who were just beginning their studies as drinking milk and those more advanced as eating meat or solid food. Thus it seemed natural for the preacher to move from the language of education to the language of maturity: He has told his hearers that they should have been **teachers** but still needed to be taught. Now he tells them **you need milk, not solid food!** It was just as natural for him to add the analogy of athletic training at the end of 5:14.

The New American Standard Bible and New King James Version both translate **you need milk, not solid food** as "you have come to need milk and not solid food." The perfect tense of the Greek verb translated "you *have* come" (my emphasis) is again significant—they have entered into and continued in a state where they could take only milk. The significance of their needing milk is enhanced by the contrasting **not solid food.** They were sucking the spiritual bottle when they should have been eating the solid food of spiritual adults!

The following chart gives some of the preacher's terms in the first column, their meaning in first-century education philosophy in the second, and their significance for the hearers in the third:[4]

HEBREWS 5:12-14	USAGE IN EDUCATIONAL PHILOSOPHY	SIGNIFICANCE IN HEBREWS
infants	beginning learners	baby Christians
milk	elementary education	basic Christian doctrine
the mature	advanced learners	established Christians
solid food	ethical philosophy	the preacher's teaching, especially about Christ's High Priesthood

As we see below, however, there is a clear difference between becoming a "mature" or established Christian, in the way the word is used here, and becoming an advanced learner in one of the philosophical schools. The latter is a human achievement. The former is an entering into the privileges Christ has provided for us.

Hebrews 5:13 explains the significance of those who live **on milk,** and 5:14 of those who eat **solid food.** Verse 13 makes it clear that the milk they need refers to the **elementary truths** already mentioned. They are in danger of being like the person who remains a spiritual **infant** (5:13), toddling about, wanting to suck the spiritual equivalent of mother's milk (see 1 Corinthians 3:1-2; compare Ephesians 4:14). Such a person is **not acquainted with the teaching about righteousness** (Heb. 5:13). The New King James Version and the New Revised Standard Version read, "is unskilled in the word of righteousness." "Unskilled" hints at the athletic metaphor more fully developed in 5:14. They have not practiced following the "word of righteousness"; they do not know it in such a way as to be trained and formed by it. The **teaching about righteousness** or, more literally, the "word of righteousness" is God's "word" (see 2:2; 4:12-13), God's revelation. For the preacher and his hearers, the revelation of Christ's High Priesthood as found in 4:14 through 10:18 is probably to be included in this "word."

This revelation is a "word of "righteousness" because it calls God's people to "righteousness." This "righteousness" is the life of faith exemplified by the Old Testament faithful in Hebrews 10:38 through 11:40. Because of their faith they are called "righteous" (10:38; 11:4) or are said to have obtained "righteousness" (11:7). They are probably the ones the preacher calls "righteous" in 12:23. Those who are righteous have faith that God is real and that He rewards the faithful. They live in accord with this faith (see commentary on 11:1-6). Such righteousness is the basis for endurance. Thus, the "word of righteousness" is God's revelation which calls us to this kind of life and which enables us to endure in the face of pressure. Those who are still living on the milk-teaching are not skilled in living this life of faith because they have not practiced it.

Hebrews 5:14 describes the **mature.** They are ready for the **solid food** of advanced teaching about Christ's High Priesthood. They are the people who **by constant use have trained themselves to distinguish good from evil.** The desire for a smooth English translation has caused the New International Version translators to obscure the precise meaning of this clause. The translation of the New American Standard Bible is helpful: "who because of practice have their senses trained to discern good and evil." "Practice" evokes the athletic metaphor. An athlete improves his skill by practicing. So the **mature** are those who have practiced living by the truth that they have. The more they live by the faith that leads to obedience, the more fully they understand God's truth. The more fully they understand God's truth, the more they are enabled to live by faith. Thus they have "senses" that have been trained. "Senses" includes both discernment and choice. They have learned to distinguish what is **good** and appropriate (what pleases God) from what is **evil** (what does not please Him). Such knowledge has come because they have also consistently chosen the **good.**

Those who remain in or return to the immature life of babies do so because they fail to practice the life of faith. They are responsible for their lack of experience, for their lack of training. The preacher fears that his hearers have begun to show signs of such immaturity. He wants them to renew their faith and obedience so that they can digest solid food—the teaching about Christ's High Priesthood. He wants them to live in the full cleansing from sin and victory over temptation that this High Priesthood provides.

Hebrews' readers have not yet fallen back into this state of regression, but they are in danger of doing so. Thus in 6:1-8, the preacher urges them to **go on to maturity** (6:1). This exhortation concerning maturity is the central concern of 6:1-2. Of course if the hearers are going to enjoy Christian maturity, they must move beyond their fixation on **the elementary teachings about Christ.** These teachings are important, for they enable one's birth as a Christian. But believers must not continue to live as newborns. God offers so much more than what is revealed in these elementary teachings. Picture the person who again and again professes faith in Christ and then falls away. The only way to avoid such repeated falls is to go on to the deeper things of God.

What are these **elementary teachings** "of" (NKJV) or **about Christ?** They must be the teachings listed in the last part of 6:1 and in 6:2. Thus the preacher is not referring to what Christ taught nor to the Gospels'[5] teaching about the life of Christ. **About Christ** is another way of saying "Christian teaching." The preacher does not want his hearers to remain at the level of those elementary Christian teachings appropriate for people entering or newly entered into the Christian faith. (See below for a fuller description of those elementary Christian teachings.)

If the preacher's hearers will leave their preoccupation with these teachings and go on into the deeper truth of Christ's High Priesthood, they will be able to **go on to maturity.** It is necessary to carefully analyze this phrase. The word **maturity** here is used in a slightly different sense from the word "mature" in 5:14. In that verse, "the mature" are those who have grown in the Christian life by practicing faith and obedience. In these verses, **maturity** is something God has prepared for those who by means of faith and obedience show their sincere wish to move toward God's goal for them.

The Greek word translated **maturity** can also be translated "perfection." Indeed, that's how both the New King James Version and the New Revised Standard Version translate it in this verse. In related passages, this letter refers to both Christ and Christians as being "perfected." Christ, of course, is perfect in an absolute sense, without fault, from eternity; but He has been "perfected" as our Savior, become perfectly able to save us, by His obedience unto death, resurrection, and ascension to the Father's right hand (see 2:10; 5:9; 7:28). Thus He has become an effective High Priest able to cleanse us from our sins and bring us into God's presence. We will understand this cleansing from sin and access to God's presence more deeply as we study what the preacher says about Christ's High Priesthood in 7:1 through 10:18. When Hebrews says Christians are "perfected" it means that they have received this cleansing from sin and thus have the privilege of entering God's presence. They have received power to live a life of obedience like Christ's (see 10:14; 11:40; 12:23).

Thus this **maturity** or "perfection" results neither from human achievement or perfection of conduct. It is living in the full cleansing from sin, access to God, and victory over temptation provided by Christ. God has provided this cleansing and victory for those who are spiritually "mature." It is for those who have been growing through the practice of faith and obedience. The preacher urges his hearers to the maturity that comes from obedience so that they can fully experience this cleansing and access to God through Christ's High Priesthood. It is this High Priesthood which he expounds in 7:1 through 10:18.

We are called to live in faith and obedience. It is God, however, who enables us to live this life through the benefits of Christ's High Priesthood. The Greek verb translated **go** or **go on** emphasizes God's provision. This Greek word is normally translated "bear" or "carry." It is used here in the passive voice. William Lane correctly translates this verb as "let us . . . be carried forward."[6] The preposition translated **to** is often translated "in" or "upon." We might translate the verb as "Let us allow ourselves to be carried forward in." Christians are to trust and obey, but it is God who sustains them in the life of purity and victory over temptation. All this is provided for God's people by their High Priest. He is the One who enables them to continue living in this state of heart cleansing.

As noted above, 6:1b-2 describes the "elementary teachings" which the readers must go beyond. The **foundation** of the Christian life is obviously **repentance from acts that lead to death** and **faith in God.** One enters the Christian life through repentance and faith. All the rest of the Christian's walk is based on this repentance and continued trust in God. **Acts that lead to death** are those that come out of unbelief and disobedience. They are the acts of a person who depends on this world for security and satisfaction rather than one who believes in God's power and promises. **Faith in God** produces a different kind of life. The person who has **faith in God** believes in His existence and character. Such a person lives in the confidence that God's power is real and that God keeps His promises of future, eternal reward (see 11:6). **Faith** is described as **in God** rather than in Christ (6:1). However, the Christian who believes in God's power believes in Christ's High Priesthood. As High Priest, Christ is the "Perfecter" of His people's faith. He makes the power of God available so that His people can reach the goal of faith. But this foundation of **repentance** and **faith** has been laid. If the preacher's hearers stay at this foundational level too long they will never inhabit the house of the victorious Christian life.

Hebrews 6:2 continues with more "foundational" **instruction,** teaching appropriate for the new convert. **Baptisms** and **the laying on of hands** remind us of early church practice. The elders of the church laid their hands on those newly baptized and prayed for them (see Acts 8:17; 19:6). However, if the reference is to Christian baptism, it is rather unusual for the word **baptisms** to be plural. Perhaps the preacher is referring to teaching for new coverts that would explain the difference between Christian baptism and other washings. These other water-based rituals might have included the ceremonial washings of the Old Testament, the baptism practiced by John the Baptist, the washings non-Jews went through when they converted to Judaism, or the washings practiced by the people who wrote the Dead Sea Scrolls.[7]

The resurrection of the dead (6:2) was a fundamental teaching that distinguished both Judaism and Christianity from the surrounding pagan world. There is no Christianity without belief in the resurrection of Jesus, a belief which the writer of Hebrews mentions infrequently but assumes as foundational (see 13:20). He also assumes the resurrection of the righteous (see 11:19, 35). There is no reason to believe that he denied the resurrection of the wicked.

Every Christian convert heard much about his accountability before the coming **eternal judgment** (6:2; see 9:23-28; 12:25-29). The teaching that the preacher subsequently gives about Christ's High Priestly work makes this **eternal judgment** all the more awesome. This judgment is **eternal** because God himself carries it out; it is final, and its effects have no end.[8]

Jews also believed in **baptisms** or "washings," and sometimes practiced the laying on of hands. Some Jews believed in resurrection and judgment. However, new converts to Christ received distinctive teaching on each of these subjects. We have already suggested differences in regard to **baptisms.** For Christians, the **laying on of hands** represented the gift of the Holy Spirit given at Pentecost.[9] The resurrection of believers was guaranteed through Christ's resurrection. The results of the final judgment were determined by one's relationship to Christ.

Hebrews 6:1-3 is dominated by first person plural pronouns; these verses begin with **let *us*** and end with *we* **will do so** (my emphasis). The preacher includes himself with his hearers. Together they will move on to that **maturity** or "perfection" (6:1), cleansing from sin and victory over temptation through the saving work of Christ as High Priest. The preacher now moves on by explaining this deeper truth. He wants his readers to move on by living it. He urges them to be people of continued faith and obedience so that they can live in the full reality of this deep truth.

It is rather surprising that the preacher would say **God permitting** (6:3). This statement is certainly more than a respectful "if God wills." Why should God not permit them to go on to experience all the reality made available through Christ? By this phrase the preacher reminds his hearers and us that believers move on to perfection by God's grace and power.[10] This phrase also sets the stage for the finality of apostasy described in 6:4-8. If the hearers had entered this kind of apostasy, it would have been impossible for them to experience "perfection" through Christ. With 6:9 the preacher reassures them that they have not gone so far as to be excluded from God's grace.

Hebrews 6:4-6, then, give an important reason for moving on. Why does the preacher want his hearers to go beyond the elementary principles outlined in 6:1-3 and to live in the fullness of what our High Priest makes available? If they don't go on, they may fall back into apostasy. Verses 4 through 6 describe the terrible result of rejecting God.

The preacher placed the Greek word behind **impossible** at the beginning of 6:4 for emphasis. What is **impossible?** Being **brought back to repentance** (6:6). The New International Version text has four clauses that begin with the word **who**—three in 6:4 and one in 6:5. All four of these clauses refer to the same group of people and describe them as genuine Christians. The first clause of 6:6—**if they fall away**—implies that it is possible even for these genuine Christians to totally reject Christ. The last half of 6:6 shows why they cannot **be brought back to repentance** if they do fall away.

There can be no doubt that 6:4-5 describes people who have been converted and are genuine Christians. Although the preacher speaks here in a general manner, he implies that his hearers fit this description. The Greek verbs behind all four "who" clauses in 6:4-5 refer to the experience of Christians previous to any falling away or attempt at renewal. The word here translated **enlightened** (6:4) portrays spiritual enlightenment in John 1:9 and Ephesians 1:18. It probably refers to conversion. Second-century sources use this same term for baptism.[11] The combination of the word **once** with **enlightened** strengthens the emphasis on past experience.

The phrase **have tasted the heavenly gift** (Heb. 6:4) refers to the experience of salvation that these people continually enjoyed. The word **tasted** is used here with the sense of "fully experience."[12] Another New Testament passage which uses this word in a similar sense is 1 Peter 2:3 where "taste" is used for experiencing that the Lord is good. **The heavenly gift** refers to God's gift of salvation through Christ, the gift that comes from God in heaven and opens the way to heaven, to the presence of God (see Hebrews 3:1). The people whom the preacher describes enjoyed this gift.

The heavenly gift and the **Holy Spirit** (6:4) are closely related. Believers experience salvation only through the presence of the Holy Spirit. Hebrews 2:4 showed us that the hearers had received the Holy

Spirit at the time of their conversion. Thus, although the preacher does not emphasize the presence of the Holy Spirit in the life of the believer, he agrees with the rest of the New Testament that all true Christians experience His presence (see Romans 8:9).[13] In a closely related passage (Heb. 10:26-31), the preacher describes apostasy as an insult to the Holy Spirit (10:29). These Christians **have shared in the Holy Spirit** because they share in Christ and the salvation He has provided (6:4; see 3:14).

The preacher also describes Christians as having experienced **the powers of the coming age** (6:5). These **powers** remind us of the "various miracles" mentioned in 2:4. The same Greek word lies behind both **powers** and "miracles." This expression may indeed refer to the miraculous events which accompanied the hearers' conversion. This phrase also includes the transforming power of the gospel. The **coming age** has already begun. It was inaugurated by Christ's High Priestly ministry. Through that ministry God offers cleansing from sin and victory over temptation to all of God's people.

Those described have experienced the **goodness** (6:5), the appropriateness, the blessedness of God's word. The word of God that brought creation into existence (see 1:3; 11:3) has also revealed and effected God's gracious salvation in Christ. It is the source of all the blessings of this salvation which they have enjoyed.

All of the ways these people are described show that they have experienced the salvation brought by Christ. The similarities between this passage (5:11–6:8) and 2:1-4 make it clear that the recipients of Hebrews fit this description. They were genuine Christians who enjoyed these spiritual privileges. "God's salvation and presence are the unquestionable reality of their lives."[14]

If that is true, then the next words—**if they fall away** (6:6)—are introduced with shocking abruptness. The preacher is describing a decisive, definitive turning away from God in apostasy. A related verb, used in Galatians 5:4 and 2 Peter 3:17, pictures people falling away from God's grace. The noun that comes from the same root is used in Romans 5:15, 17, 18, 20 to refer to Adam's "trespass" through which he fell, and in Romans 11:11-12 of Israel's "fall" from God through unbelief. The Greek word translated **fall away** in itself does not necessarily indicate a definitive turning away from God from which there is no return. The preacher, however, is talking about just such an irrevocable turning away. He has already given us a paradigm of this apostasy: the Old Testament wilderness generation described in 3:7 through 4:11. The people of that generation repeatedly complained against God and then definitively refused to trust

God and believe His promises. They behaved in this way despite the fact that they had experienced His power like no one had ever experienced it (see Hebrews 3:16-18). This falling away from which there is no return results from the persistent rejection of the abundantly experienced grace of God. It culminates in a climactic definitive rejection of God and His ways. Esau is another who spurned grace in this way (see 12:14-17). Those who have fallen in this way cannot be brought back again to the **repentance** which is foundational to the Christian life (6:1).

The last half of 6:6 gives the reasons why those who have turned away in such apostasy cannot be brought back to repentance. Such definitive rejection results in their **crucifying the Son of God all over again.** They are "re-crucifying" the One who died for them. By their denial they have removed themselves from the benefits of His crucifixion. Their actions are such that they have exposed Him to the **public disgrace** of re-crucifixion: They have, by those actions, testified to the world that Christ's crucifixion is of no worth. Those who join Jesus' crucifiers cannot be renewed to repentance. They cannot lay again the foundation of Christ (see 6:1), since they have repudiated the only source of salvation, the only basis upon which repentance can be offered them. What they have done is to their own ultimate disadvantage and eternal loss. Their rebellion has reached the point of definitive rejection of God's grace. Their lives continue to bring **public disgrace** on Christ.[15]

The preacher's hearers, thank God, are far from such apostasy. However, the tendencies to slackness that they have evidenced and their slowness to take full advantage of the resources available in Christ could eventually lead them in that direction. Spiritual laxity and a refusal to receive offered grace may eventually lead one to turn away from Christ. Persistence and stubbornness in such rejection may lead to the place of no return.

The preacher does not direct his words to people who have sinned in this beyond-return way. An admonition to them would do no good, nor would they receive it. He is not trying to frighten people of tender conscience into thinking that they have committed such sin. Anyone who feels genuine sorrow and seeks to repent for sin has not committed this "unpardonable sin" (see Mark 3:29).[16] Rather the preacher is warning all Christians to avoid the danger of spiritual laxity.

Hebrews 6:7-8 illustrates the apostasy described in 6:4-6. The preacher compares two kinds of **land**—productive (6:7) and nonproductive (6:8). Those who have received and profited by God's grace are the productive **land** of verse 7. This verse looks forward to the preacher's positive description of the readers' spiritual condition in 6:9-12. Those who received but then rejected God's grace are the nonproductive **land** of verse 8. They illustrate the apostasy described in 6:4-6. The preacher warns his hearers by describing the terrible fate of this nonproductive **land.**

Both lands drink **in the rain often falling** (6:7) on them. This **rain** represents the abundant grace of God. The preacher rivets our attention on the fruit of the unproductive **land** (6:8): It **produces thorns and thistles** and therefore **is worthless** rather than **useful** (6:7). The **thorns and thistles** represent a refusal to live a life of faith and obedience. It is interesting to note that **thorns and thistles** were the result of the curse after the first sin (see Genesis 3:17-18), but here they portray the cause of the curse.

The phrases **blessing from God** and **in danger of being cursed** (6:7-8) remind us of how God spoke of His covenant in the Old Testament. Obedience to God's covenant brought His blessing, and disobedience His curse (see Deuteronomy 11:26-28). The good land **receives a blessing from God.** This is the blessing that God promised Abraham (see commentary on Hebrews 6:14) and the blessing that Esau lost because he had rejected God's grace (see commentary on 12:17). This is the blessing of living in the heavenly homeland of God's presence (see 11:13-16). The High Priesthood of the Son enables God's people to reach this blessing.

The **land** that represents people who refuse to believe and obey is **in danger of being cursed** (6:8). This translation is not strong enough because it sounds like the curse could be avoided. The New King James Version translation is more literal—"near to being cursed"; and the New Revised Standard Version most accurate—"on the verge of being cursed." The curse is inevitable because this land represents those for whom there is no opportunity for repentance.

After all, **in the end it will be burned** (6:8). The NRSV's translation shows how closely burning fits with the **land** metaphor: "Its end is to be burned over." Burning reflects a common biblical description of God's judgment. Sodom and Gomorrah were destroyed by fire (see Genesis 19:24). Moses used the destruction of those cities as a warning for God's people (see Deuteronomy 29:22-25). Judgment is the destiny of those who have truly experienced God's grace and then persistently and definitively reject it.

Worthless (Heb. 6:8) has significant biblical overtones. Every other time New Testament writers use the Greek word translated here as **worthless,** it refers to those who have turned away from God's grace (see Romans 1:28; 1 Corinthians 9:27; 2 Corinthians 13:5-7; 2 Timothy 3:8; Titus 1:16). The King James Version often translates this term as "reprobate." It is an appropriate word to use for those who have rejected God's grace. In might also suggest the idea of "not standing the test" at the final Judgment.[17] The preacher does not want his hearers to come under the category of those who are "reprobate."

Just as the preacher followed up his description of his hearers' potential spiritual laxity (5:11–6:3) with a description of those who fall away from the faith (6:4-8), so now he assures them that they have not fallen away (6:9-12), and affirms the certainty of God's promises by referring to faithful Abraham (6:13-20).

2. TRUST IN GOD'S PROMISES 6:9-20

The writer of Hebrews balances the warning of 5:11 through 6:8 with encouragement in 6:9-20. In 6:9-12, he gives his readers a true assessment of their present spiritual state. He encourages them in 6:9 by assuring them that he doesn't believe they have fallen away, despite his warnings. In 6:10, he gives the reason for his confidence in their present spiritual life. In 6:11-12, he explains why he has been warning them despite his confidence in them.

The present tense of the verb in the introductory clause, **Even though we speak like this,** is significant (6:9). The New American Standard Bible translation is helpful: "though we are speaking in this way." The author is not apologizing for his words of warning. The possibility of his hearers' falling away is real. He will continue to speak words of warning (note particularly 10:26-31). But it is time to encourage them by expressing his confidence in them.

The writer has carefully chosen and arranged the words of 6:9 to encourage his readers. In Greek the verse begins with the words translated **we are confident of better things in your case.** Only here in the whole book does the writer use the intimate term **dear friends** or "beloved" (NKJV; NASB; NRSV). He loves them because they are his brothers and sisters in God's household and because of his intimate acquaintance with them. The Greek verb translated **we are confident** is intensive. It is a powerful expression of the writer's assurance that the **better things ... that accompany salvation** which God has provided are for his readers. These **better things** include "the blessing of God" mentioned in 6:7, not the curse of 6:8. They take in all the benefits that come from Christ's High Priestly work, heart cleansing, access to God's presence, and the assurance of living in that presence forever. These **things** are **better** in the special sense in which the preacher uses the word

better. They really work, they are effective, they can be counted on. Only in these **better things** that Christ provides do we find true heart cleansing.

The writer states the basis for his confidence in 6:10. His confidence rests first of all in the character of God, then also on their conduct. The double negative in the statement **God is not unjust** is a very strong way of stating the dependability of God. He does sustain those who trust in Him. He will fulfill His promises of blessing to them. The preacher's hearers have shown evidence that they do trust God in this way. How does the preacher know this? Through their **work.** But what is this **work?** The New International Version's translation is very clear: It is **the love** that they **have shown** to God by serving and continuing to serve **his people.** The hearers display not only love, but also **hope** (6:11) and **faith** (6:12).

The New Testament often speaks of the Christian life in terms of faith, hope, and love (see 1 Thessalonians 1:3; 1 Corinthians 13:13; Colossians 1:4-5). The preacher connects these three virtues not only here (Heb. 6:10-12), but also in Hebrews 10:22-24. Faith and hope play a more prominent part in this sermon because of the situation of this letter's original hearers. Those believers were facing discouragement, ridicule, persecution, and possibly future martyrdom. The preacher focuses on the faith in God that is necessary to resist these pressures and endure until they receive what they hoped for. But the ultimate test is love for God demonstrated by ministering to the spiritual and physical needs of His people. No doubt this service included aid and encouragement for fellow Christians under persecution (see 10:33-34). It is important to note, however, that this love is not first of all service to others. It is first of all love for God which expresses itself in love for and service to others. These believers had fulfilled the words Jesus spoke: "By this all men will know that you are my disciples, if you love one another" (John 13:35).

Well, if his readers showed the distinguishing mark of love, why did the preacher address them in 6:1-8 with such a dire warning? Because he wants them to continue! This answer is given from two different perspectives, one in 6:11, another in 6:12. The first answer to this question is based on their own past conduct; the second draws their attention to the great examples of faith the preacher is going to introduce.

The first words of 6:11 express the depth of the preacher's concern. His concern is very intense. **We want** could be translated "We urgently desire."[18] His concern is individual and comprehensive: it is for **each** of his readers. He wants them to show the **diligence** that they have been showing, the diligence that has been evidenced by their loving service for one another, **to the very end** of their race. Only by persevering to the end will their **hope** be **sure.** Only by perseverance can they be certain to obtain the eternal blessings for which they hope.[19]

Verse 12 forms a natural transition to the example of faithful Abraham in verses 13 through 20, and looks forward to the many examples of faithfulness in 11:1-40. To **become lazy** or "sluggish" would be the opposite of the diligence commanded in 6:11.[20] The writer enjoins diligence, so his readers will not fall into negligence and thus run the danger of ultimately slipping away into apostasy. He lifts their sights above themselves by calling on them to **imitate** the great heroes of faith. The lives of these past saints were characterized by **faith** and **patience.** Hebrews 11, especially, will make it clear that the lifestyle of **faith** is a life of obedience that comes from trusting God's power and believing His promises. **Patience** is faith that keeps on keeping on, that continues to express itself in obedience, despite opposition. This continuity in faith is necessary to **inherit what has been promised** by God.

In 6:13-20, the preacher demonstrates that God's promise is certain. The promise Christians inherit is God's promise to Abraham confirmed by God's oath (6:13-14). This promise is sure because (1) **Abraham received** what was promised (6:15); (2) God **confirmed it with an oath** (6:16-18); and (3) **Jesus** guarantees it by entering God's presence (6:19-20). The importance of God's **oath** is the central concern of this paragraph.

This oath is announced in 6:13-14. **When God made his promise to Abraham** (6:13) refers to the time right after the offering of Isaac as a sacrifice. God speaks the words quoted in verses 13 and 14 while Abraham and Isaac are still on Mount Moriah. The angel of the Lord who commanded Abraham not to go through with the sacrifice of Isaac now speaks a second time (see Genesis 22:16-19). It is only at this point, after Abraham has obeyed God in the sacrifice of Isaac, that God **swore by himself** in order to confirm and renew His promise (Heb. 6:13). Previous to this point in the Genesis narrative there is no mention of God backing His promise with an oath. After this event Genesis speaks of God's oath to Abraham three times: 24:7 (Abraham speaking); 26:3 (God speaking to Isaac); and 50:24 (Joseph speaking). In the last of these, Joseph refers to the oath that God swore to Abraham, Isaac, and Jacob.

I will surely bless you and give you many descendants (6:14). The New International Version's translation of these words obscures the way in which the preacher has paraphrased Genesis 22:17. It says, "I will surely bless you and make *your descendants* as numerous as the stars in the sky and as the sand on the seashore" (my emphasis). However, the writer of Hebrews paraphrases, "I will surely bless you and multiply *you*" (6:14 NRSV, my emphasis). The preacher substitutes "multiply you" for "make your descendants . . . numerous." He does not alter the basic meaning of the text by this change. However, his focus on "you" rather than on "your descendants" prepares the way for him to show that the promise is fulfilled in Abraham's spiritual descendants. At one level, God promised Abraham descendants who would inherit the earthly Promised Land. However, the promise is truly fulfilled in Abraham's descendants by faith. They possess the heavenly homeland to which Abraham looked forward (see 11:9-10, 13-16), the great blessing God has prepared for His people.

But when was it that **Abraham received what was promised** (6:15)? After Abraham offered Isaac as a sacrifice, God not only reconfirmed His promise to Abraham with an oath, but He restored Isaac to him. Isaac, himself, was the fulfillment of the promise. He was the beginning of the many descendants, both physical and spiritual, who would come from Abraham. Through these descendants, the promise would reach its ultimate fulfillment. Abraham received this fulfillment only **after waiting patiently** (6:15). This translation (NIV) might give the idea that Abraham did nothing but sit and wait. The New King James Version helps us to understand the preacher's meaning a bit more clearly: "after he had patiently endured." Abraham trusted God and kept on obeying Him despite opposition, despite his inability to see how God would fulfill His promise. Picture Abraham puzzling over how God would fulfill His promise if he sacrificed Isaac, the one through whom the promise was to be fulfilled. But Abraham kept trusting and obeying God. Thus he stands as the primary example of "those who through faith and patience inherit what has been promised" (6:12). His example assures the readers of Hebrews that those who keep on keeping on in faithful obedience will receive what God has promised. God is faithful!

In 6:16-18, the preacher explains the significance of God's swearing this oath. According to 6:16, God swore this oath to accommodate himself to human understanding. Two points of human custom are important. First, **Men swear by someone greater than themselves.** This statement explains what has already been said in 6:13, that God swore by himself because there was no one greater by whom He could swear. The preacher draws attention here to the greatness of the Person who is swearing this oath. God's own unchanging character is the guarantee of this promise. Second, **the oath confirms what is said and puts an end to all argument.** The words translated **swear, confirms,** and **argument** are legal terms, all used to emphasize the power of an oath to confirm. **The oath** is the ultimate form of human confirmation. Thus 6:17 tells us that the greatest Person, **God,** accommodated himself by using the ultimate form of human confirmation, **an oath,** in order **to make the unchanging nature of his purpose** or "plan" absolutely **clear.** The New Revised Standard Version reads "unchangeable" instead of **unchanging.** God's **purpose** or "plan" is guaranteed by His own permanence and eternity. We are reminded of the Son's "inviolable" (my translation) priesthood (see 7:24). God's **purpose** or plan for our salvation cannot change. The preacher will deepen our understanding of God's plan by his upcoming description of the High Priesthood of Christ.

The word translated **confirm** comes from the same root as the word translated "mediator" in 8:6; 9:15; and 12:24. It can mean either "mediate" or "guarantee." Here it certainly means "guarantee." The oath is God's unconditional guarantee of the validity of His **purpose,** His plan of salvation. He puts this plan of salvation into effect in the "new covenant" which Christ mediates (see 8:6; 9:15; 12:24). In Hebrews 7:20-22, the preacher quotes God's oath to the Son (found in Psalm 110:4) which established Him as the "guarantor" of this new covenant. Thus God's oath to the Son confirms and fulfills His previous oath to Abraham. The second oath enables all people of faith to enter into the blessing promised in the first oath.

It is important to note that God seeks to certify himself to **the heirs of what was promised** (Heb. 6:17). He wants them to feel no doubt as to the permanence of His plan. Those who live the life of faith *are* the many descendants God promised to Abraham (see Genesis 22:17). They do inherit the blessings of God's promise. God encourages them to go on in the life of faith **by two unchangeable things** (6:18)—the promise of God and the oath of God which confirms that promise. Both of these are based on the integrity of a God for Whom **it is impossible . . . to lie.**

Verse 18 describes those who are inheriting the promise as **we who have fled to take hold of the hope offered to us.**[21] Instead of **fled,** the NASB has "fled for refuge." The term reminds us that we Christians are on a pilgrimage. We are fleeing to the "rest" God has prepared for us (see 4:1-11), to our heavenly homeland (11:13-16), to the blessing of and refuge in God's presence. This refuge is our **hope** (6:18). It is **offered to us,** "set before us" (NKJV), by God himself.[22] He has made it available. He has confirmed it to us by His promise and oath so that we might **be greatly encouraged** to persevere in faith and obedience.

He wants us to persevere until we have taken **hold** of the final fulfillment of that **hope** in God's presence.

Hebrews 6:19-20 documents how **Jesus** guarantees God's promise and oath by making available the promised blessings for which His people hope. Verse 19 is a wonderful statement of the **hope** that **we** Christians **have.** The preacher uses a metaphor (**anchor**), a pair of adjectives (**firm and secure**), and a statement (**It enters the inner sanctuary behind the curtain**) to describe the certainty and nature of this hope. This hope is like **an anchor** of the ship called **soul.** Just as an anchor keeps a ship safe and secure, so the reality of our final **hope** keeps our true selves—our inner reality that transcends death—secure and steadfast. **Firm and secure** interpret and reinforce each other. The last of these two words is one of the preacher's favorites for expressing the certainty of God's work (2:2; 3:6, 14; 9:17; see other words from the same root in 2:3; 6:16; 13:9). **Firm** may have the connotation of "safe." This hope is "safe and secure."

It may seem odd to say that this hope **enters the inner sanctuary behind the curtain.** The phrase translated **inner sanctuary behind the curtain** is always used in the Old Testament to describe the Most Holy Place where the ark of the covenant was located (see Exodus 26:33; Leviticus 16:2, 12-13, 15). It was the place where God "dwelt." The Christian's hope enters into the heavenly most holy place, the place where God dwells. The salvation that God has provided assures the ultimate entrance of the faithful into God's presence. It also provides for them to continually enter His presence now. The next verse makes it clear that our hope of entering is secured by Christ's having entered God's presence once-for-all.[23] The author is already thinking of the Day of Atonement sacrifice to which he compares Christ's sacrifice in Hebrews 9.

Hebrews 6:20 tells us why this assurance of present access and of final entrance into God's presence is so certain. **Jesus, who went before us, has entered on our behalf.** The phrase **who went before us** is one word, a noun in Greek, which most versions translate as "forerunner." This term reminds us that Jesus is our Pioneer (see 2:10; 12:2). A "forerunner" goes before other people go. It is assumed that others will follow. How does the writer of Hebrews know that Jesus has gone before? He remembers Psalm 110:1, which he quoted in Hebrews 1:13. In that verse the Father told the Son to sit down at His right hand. And **Jesus** has gone there **on our behalf,** so that we too might enter (see 2:9; 7:25; 9:12; 10:19-20).

A literal translation that reflects the Greek word order will help us understand the writer's emphases in this verse: "Where a forerunner for us has entered, Jesus; in the order of Melchizedek an high priest having become forever." The preacher placed "forerunner" at the beginning of this verse for emphasis. This "forerunner" is none other than the Son of God who lived a completely human life as **Jesus** of Nazareth. It is this human **Jesus** who has become the exalted **high priest . . . in the order of Melchizedek** (6:20). Since Psalm 110:4 applies to the same person as Psalm 110:1, the One whom the Father exalted to His right hand is also the One He proclaimed a priest in the order of Melchizedek (see 5:5-6). Thus our hope of entering God's presence, both now and finally in the future, is guaranteed by the High Priest **in the order of Melchizedek** (see Psalm 110:4), exalted to the Father's right hand (Ps. 110:1).

Thus Psalm 110:4, understood in the light of Psalm 110:1, is the Scriptural foundation for the High Priesthood of Christ. On the basis of this psalm, the preacher affirms that Christ has become an exalted (heavenly) High Priest who replaces the earthly Aaronic priests. It is important, then, that the preacher begin his explanation of Christ's High Priesthood by an exposition of Psalm 110:4. He must clarify what this psalm means by "a priest in the order of Melchizedek." He provides this explanation in Hebrews 7:1-25, which follows. He shows that the One who is a "a priest in the order of Melchizedek" is the eternal Son of God who is a priest "forever." In Greek, the last words of Hebrews 6:20 are a phrase translated into English as **forever.** With this **forever,** the preacher introduces the discussion to follow of the One who "remains a priest forever" (7:3).

After demonstrating that this exalted High Priest is the eternal Son of God in Hebrews 7:1-25, the preacher shows how His sacrifice enables Him to exercise an effective priestly ministry (see 8:1–10:18). Thus the whole discussion about Christ's High Priesthood in 7:1 through 10:18 assures our hope of entering God's presence by demonstrating how Christ our High Priest has gone before us and guarantees that hope.

ENDNOTES

[1]William L. Lane, *Hebrews 1–8,* vol. 47a, Word Biblical Commentary, New Testament ed. Ralph P. Martin, gen. eds. David A. Hubbard and Glenn W. Barker (Dallas: Word Books, 1991), pp. 136–37.

[2]See the term "words of God" in Romans 3:2 for God's revelations in the Old Testament.

[3]Lane, p. 137; Harold W. Attridge, *The Epistle to the Hebrews,* Hermeneia— A Critical and Historical Commentary on the Bible, ed. Helmut Koester (Philadelphia: Fortress Press, 1989), p. 159.

[4]This chart is adapted from Attridge, p. 162.

[5]The Gospels include the New Testament books of Matthew, Mark, Luke, and John.

[6]Lane, pp. 130–31.

[7]Philip Edgcumbe Hughes, *A Commentary on the Epistle to the Hebrews* (Grand Rapids, Michigan: Wm. B. Eerdmans Publishing Co., 1977), pp. 199–202.

[8]Paul Ellingworth, *The Epistle to the Hebrews,* The New International Greek Testament Commentary, eds. I. Howard Marshall and W. Ward Gasque (Grand Rapids, Michigan: Wm. B. Eerdmans Publishing Co., 1993), p. 316.

[9]In the New Testament, Pentecost primarily refers to the event when the Holy Spirit was given to the church; this occurred on the day of Pentecost. The Greek term *Pentecost* comes from means "fiftieth" or "the fiftieth day" and is literally the fiftieth day after the end of the Passover. It is also known as the Jewish Feast of Weeks; the day is part of the Jewish observances, and was the beginning of the offering of first fruits.

[10]Hughes, p. 206.

[11]Ellingworth, pp. 319–20.

[12]The word here translated **tasted** is often used in this way with reference to death (see Matthew 16:28; Mark 9:1; Luke 9:27; John 8:52; Hebrews 2:9).

[13]The Holy Spirit addresses us in Scripture (see 3:7; 9:8; 10:15) and empowers Christ's sacrifice of himself (9:14).

[14]Lane, p. 142.

[15]Hughes, p. 218, note 68.

[16]If the wilderness generation had truly repented, they would not have tried to enter the Promised Land on their own terms (see Numbers 14:39-45). Nor was Esau's repentance genuine. (See commentary on Hebrews 12:14-17.)

[17]Ellingworth, p. 328.

[18]Hughes, pp. 227–28.

[19]Several other translations interpret this verse in a different way. The New American Standard Bible, for instance, reads, "That each one of you show the same diligence so as to realize the full assurance of hope until the end." Instead of saying that we should be diligent so that in the end we will surely receive what we hope for, this translation says that we should be diligent to maintain our confidence in what we hope for until the end. Both the Greek grammar and the general context in which the preacher warns against apostasy favor the interpretation of the New International Version.

[20]The same word that is here translated **lazy** is translated "slow" in 5:11. In 5:11, it was followed by the words "to learn" and probably denoted active resistance to the message of the preacher. Here it denotes laziness, sluggishness, or neglect (Ellingworth, p. 333).

[21]In the New International Version, **to take hold of the hope offered to us**

gives the purpose for which we have fled. The New American Standard Bible translates "we who have fled for refuge in laying hold of the hope set before us" instead of **to take hold of the hope offered to us.** This makes the "hope" the means by which we have fled and something we have already taken hold of. It is the confidence and assurance of receiving God's promise that we already have. The translation of the NIV is a very natural rendering of the Greek grammar. It also fits well with the exhortation to endurance within this context. The New Revised Standard Version translates this phrase "to seize the hope set before us" and puts it with the word "encouraged" instead of with "fled." Whether one follows the NIV or NRSV understanding of the grammar of this verse, it is obvious that the preacher wants his readers to be greatly **encouraged** to take hold of the ultimate fulfillment of the hope God has prepared.

[22]The same word that is translated **offered** or "set before" (NKJV) is used of the joy "set before" Jesus in 12:2. This **hope** that has been set before Christians by God is the goal of the Christian pilgrimage just as the "joy set before" Jesus was the goal of His earthly life fulfilled by his exaltation to the Father's right hand. By entering into this "joy," He enables us to enter into this **hope,** God's presence in heaven.

[23]The aorist tense, which in this context denotes a definite past action, is used of Christ's entering God's presence in verse 20.

11

THE NEW HIGH PRIEST HAS AN ETERNAL PRIESTHOOD

Hebrews 7:1-28

We have seen the importance of Psalm 110:4: "You are a priest forever in the order of Melchizedek." This verse is the biblical basis for the High Priesthood of the Son. Through the Son's High Priesthood, God's faithful people enter God's presence. It is no surprise, then, that the writer of Hebrews would begin his more detailed explanation of Christ's High Priesthood by expounding Psalm 110:4.

But where would he find information to spell out the significance of being a priest of Melchizedek's order? He looked at what the Bible says about Melchizedek himself. Aside from Psalm 110, the only other Old Testament passage that mentions Melchizedek is Genesis 14:17-20. The preacher turns to that passage. There he finds Melchizedek meeting Abraham. The facts of this passage enable him to show the greatness of Melchizedek by comparing him with Abraham (see Hebrews 7:1-10). This comparison enables the preacher to demonstrate the superiority of the Priest in Melchizedek's order to the Levitical priests descended from Abraham (see Hebrews 7:11-19) and to describe the blessings that come from this superior Priest (7:20-25). Hebrews 7:26-28 summarizes this chapter and introduces themes to be discussed in following chapters.

1. MELCHIZEDEK 7:1-10

It is not merely the facts given in Genesis 14:17-20 which enable the writer of Hebrews to compare Melchizedek and Abraham and to show the superiority of the Priest in Melchizedek's order. The things the preacher would have expected Genesis to say but which are omitted are also important. There is no indication in Genesis of the origin or decease of Melchizedek, of his ancestors or descendants. This omission may not seem unusual to the modern reader, but it seemed very extraordinary to the preacher and, probably, to Christians of New Testament times in general. The Old Testament gives the genealogy of all of the great people of God. They are all part of the genealogy that goes from Adam to Abraham to Christ. It is the biblical way of showing how these people fit into God's plan of salvation which culminates in Christ.[1] Here, however, Genesis describes someone who is superior to Abraham, and yet there is no genealogy given for him!

In Hebrews 7:1-3, the preacher focuses on the person of Melchizedek as he is portrayed in Genesis 14:17-20. Hebrews 7:4-10 draws a comparison between Melchizedek and Abraham.

In 7:1-2a, the preacher begins this section by giving the name and titles of Melchizedek: His name is **Melchizedek** and he has two titles— **king of Salem** and **priest of God Most High.** The preacher also notes two events of importance that occurred when he met Abraham: Melchizedek **blessed** Abraham. Abraham **gave** Melchizedek a **tenth of everything.** In 7:2b-3, the preacher interprets the name and titles. Verses 4 through 10 explain the significance of the two events.

We need to be familiar with the background of these events: Four kings from Mesopotamia had come and defeated five kings from southern Canaan, including the king of Sodom, and carried them, their people, and their goods away. Along with those taken from Sodom was Lot, Abraham's nephew. Abraham and his allies pursued and defeated these kings. When Abraham returned from this victory Melchizedek met him. It was at this meeting that Melchizedek **blessed** Abraham, and Abraham **gave** Melchizedek **a tenth of everything.**

The interpretation of the names and titles? In 7:2b, the name **Melchizedek** is explained as meaning **king of righteousness.** This was a common interpretation of the name in New Testament times and was a natural one, for "Melch" represents the Hebrew word for "king," and "zedek" the word for "righteousness."[2] **Salem** is close to the Hebrew word for "peace," so it was also natural to interpret **king of Salem** as **king of peace.**³ Old Testament writers often used "righteousness" and "peace" when they described God's promised salvation.⁴ However, the preacher makes no further use of the meaning of the name or first title of Melchizedek.

Hebrews 7:3 appears to be an interpretation of Melchizedek's title as **priest of God Most High.** The whole point of the preacher's argument in this chapter is to show what kind of priest Melchizedek was so that he can clarify what kind of priest the priest of Melchizedek's order would be. Melchizedek is described as one who **remains a priest forever.** The preacher is obviously thinking of Psalm 110:4, which states that the priest in Melchizedek's order is "a priest forever."

Hebrews 7:3 makes it clear that the preacher was also reflecting on the fact that Genesis gives no list of Melchizedek's ancestors or descendants: **without father or mother, without genealogy.** By themselves, these terms can be understood to mean "without record of father, mother, or genealogy." The preacher explores the importance of Melchizedek's having no recorded genealogy in 7:5-6. But the next phrase goes beyond the fact that no genealogy is recorded for Melchizedek: **without beginning of days or end of life** (7:3). This description seems to describe One who is literally eternal, having neither beginning nor end. It is obvious that such a person cannot be an angel, for the writer has made it clear that the angels are created beings (see commentary on 1:6-7). Some have thought that the writer to the Hebrews thought that Melchizedek was an appearance of the eternal Son of God before the Son became a human being. It is more likely, however, that the preacher sees the way Melchizedek is described in Scripture as a *picture* of the eternal Son of God. The next phrase of 7:3, **like the Son of God,** can be translated "made like the Son of God" (NKJV; NASB) or "resembling the Son of God" (RSV; NRSV). The writer is already thinking of the "priest in the order of Melchizedek" more than of Melchizedek. That Priest **remains a priest forever** because He is the eternal Son of God.

These two lines, **without father or mother, without genealogy** and **without beginning of days or end of life,** are very important in the preacher's argument. He uses them to set two contrasts between Melchizedek and Abraham (7:5-6 and then 7:8). These contrasts, in turn, are crucial to the two major contrast between Christ and Aaron (7:11-14 and 7:15-19). The fact that the priest in Melchizedek's order is the eternal Son of God **without beginning of days or end of life** is the main point of Hebrews 7. The climax of this chapter's argument in verses 23 through 25 makes the significance of this truth clear. Because He is the eternal **Son of God he remains a priest forever** (7:3). His eternal being is the basis of His perpetual priesthood. This discussion was introduced in 6:20 and will be concluded in 7:28 by reference to that perpetual priesthood.

The preacher introduces the theme of 7:4-10 by his opening statement: **Just think how great** Melchizedek **was.** He demonstrates this greatness through the two contrasts between Melchizedek and Abraham noted above, the first in verses 5 and 6 and the second in verse 8. The first contrast is the most important within this paragraph, and the preacher's conclusion in verses 9 and 10 is based on it. The contrast in verse 8 lays an important foundation for the next paragraph, a comparison between the Levitical or Aaronic priests and the Son (see 7:11-19).

The fact that Melchizedek was **without father or mother, without genealogy** (7:3)—that is, without priestly genealogy—makes it very surprising that the **patriarch Abraham** would give **him a tenth** or tithe **of the plunder** (7:4). The preacher emphasized the word translated **patriarch** by placing it at the end of the Greek sentence. This word is indicative of Abraham's greatness and is particularly appropriate for a discussion in which genealogy is central. As **the patriarch,** Abraham was the progenitor of all of God's people. According to a requirement of **the** (subsequent) **law** of Moses **the descendants of Levi who become priests**[5] collect **a tenth from the** rest of God's **people—that is, their brothers,** who are also **descended from** the patriarch **Abraham** (7:5). The priests descended from Abraham collected tithes from the people descended from Abraham. Melchizedek, on the other hand, **did not trace his descent from Levi, yet he** [Melchizedek] **collected a tenth from Abraham,** who was both the father of the Levitical priests and of those from whom they collected tithes. This shows that Abraham, the patriarch, saw Melchizedek as superior to himself.

This greatness of Melchizedek is also demonstrated by the fact that he **blessed him who had the promises** (7:6). Abraham had received God's **promises** of blessing, those fulfilled in the salvation that Christ has provided, as 6:13-20 has demonstrated. This salvation enables us to be the people of God and to enter into God's presence. Melchizedek blessed the one who had received these promises! Melchizedek stands in a position above the promises of salvation! This indicates his greatness. Likewise, the Priest in Melchizedek's order does not receive those promises but puts them into effect.

Sometimes in the Bible, a person of lesser status is said to "bless" a greater.[6] Indeed people sometimes "bless" God (see Psalm 103:1-2, 20-22

[KJV; RSV] and many other psalms). When used in this way, the term "bless" is another way of saying that the person who blesses thanks or praises the one being blessed. However, Melchizedek's blessing is a priestly blessing (see Numbers 6:22-27). It is certainly the person of **lesser** status (Heb. 7:7) who receives a blessing from a priest.

Hebrews 7:8 introduces the second contrast. This time the contrast is not between Melchizedek and Abraham, but between Melchizedek and the priestly descendents of Abraham. The framework of this contrast is still the collecting of tithes: **In the one case, the tenth is collected . . . but in the other case. . . .** The crucial contrast, however, is between **men who die** and **him who is declared to be living.** For that last phrase, most English translations read "he lives." Where is it declared that "he lives"? The preacher sees such a declaration in the silences or omissions of Genesis 14:17-20, understood in the light of Psalm 110:4. That is why he described Melchizedek in Hebrews 7:3 as **without beginning of days or end of life. Who is declared to be living** (7:8) means more than that he continues to live or "he lives on" (NASB). The Levitical priests all died. The preacher is already thinking about the Priest of Melchizedek's order who always has lived and always will live (see 7:15-19).

This paragraph (7:4-10) concludes with an inference drawn from the contrast in 7:5-6. As their physical and spiritual forefather, Abraham's actions were representative of his descendants. Thus when Abraham paid tithes to Melchizedek, **Levi, who collects the tenth, paid the tenth through Abraham.** At the time this event occurred, **Levi** could not act independently because he **was still in the body of his ancestor** Abraham. The unstated implications are clear: Since Levi, in principle, paid tithe to Melchizedek, then the priest in Melchizedek's order must be superior to the priest descended from Levi.

2. THE PRIEST LIKE MELCHIZEDEK 7:11-19

The writer of Hebrews has given needed background to the meaning of God's declaration of the priest "in the order of Melchizedek." The preacher did this by clarifying the relationship between Melchizedek and Abraham/Levi in Genesis 14:17-20. He has indicated the consequences of this comparison for both the priest in Melchizedek's order and the Levitical priests. In Hebrews 7:11-19, he turns from Genesis 14:17-20 back to Psalm 110:4; from comparing Melchizedek and Abraham to comparing the priest "in the order of Melchizedek" with the priest "in the order of Aaron" who descended from Levi.

The preacher's argument progresses in two stages. In 7:11-14, he argues on the basis of the scriptural prophecy itself without reference to its fulfillment in Christ. The very existence of a prophecy of a priesthood other than Levitical implied that the new priest would be "without father or mother, without [Levitical] genealogy" (7:3). The priest **in the order of Melchizedek** is therefore **not in the order of Aaron** (7:11). In 7:15-19, the preacher argues on the basis of the fulfillment of that prophecy in Christ. He is "without beginning of days or end of life" (7:3). Therefore He is **like Melchizedek** (7:15) in that He is empowered by **the power of an indestructible life** (7:16).

It is profitable to look at 7:11-14 in greater detail. The very fact that Psalm 110:4 prophesied a different priest meant that the Aaronic priesthood would be changed. The **perfection**[7] that consisted in true cleansing from sins and access to God could not have been **attained** through the sacrifices of **the Levitical priesthood.** If it could have, God in the Scripture need not have declared that a new priest would come **in the order of Melchizedek** rather than **in the order of Aaron** (7:11). It is clear that this Melchizedekian priest is "without [Levitical] genealogy" (7:3) because the prophecy pertains to someone from a **different tribe** (7:13). The writer of Hebrews probably sensed that Psalm 110 was a royal psalm which looked forward to the promised Messiah-King (note the references to "scepter" and "rule" in Psalm 110:2). This king would be of David's line and therefore from the tribe of Judah, not Levi. The "different tribe" aspect of this priesthood is confirmed when we begin to look at the fulfillment of this prophecy in Christ. He was **descended from Judah,** the tribe of David (Heb. 7:14). But, **in regard to that tribe Moses** in the law **said nothing about priests.** Thus if Christ is a priest, he must be of a line altogether different from the traditional line of Levi. The preacher here refers to Christ as **our Lord.** This reminds us that Psalm 110:1 begins, "The LORD [God the Father] says to my *Lord*" [God the Son, my emphasis].

The apparently parenthetical phrase, **for on the basis of it the law was given to the people** (Heb. 7:11), is important. There are several different ways to understand the phrase **on the basis of it.** The New American Standard Bible supports the interpretation of the New International Version. The New King James Version and Revised Standard Version read "under it" (compare the NRSV). The point is, however, that there is an intimate and inseparable connection between the Levitical or Aaronic priesthood and the Law given by God through Moses on Mount Sinai. This priesthood was prescribed by that Law. Only through this priesthood could that Law be carried out. Thus 7:12 makes perfect sense: **For when there is a change of the priesthood, there must also be a change of the law.** The very prophecy of another priest in Psalm 110:4 means that the entire **law,** the whole system of approaching God that this law represented, the whole "old covenant," would be changed. Even before fulfillment in Christ, the very prophecy of a new priesthood in Psalm 110:4 implied this momentous change.

The totality of this change becomes **even more clear** (Heb. 7:15) when the prophecy is fulfilled in Christ. Hebrews 7:15-19 describes the fulfillment of Psalm 110's prophecy in the time when Christ actually **appears** as **another priest like Melchizedek.** Note that **a priest in the order of Melchizedek** means a **priest like Melchizedek** in that He has "no beginning of days or end of life" (7:3, 11, 15). This is not an **order** like the Aaronic priestly **order.** In the Aaronic **order** a person became **a priest . . . on the basis of a regulation as to his ancestry** (7:16): He had to be descended from Aaron. The NKJV is more literal: "according to the law of a fleshly commandment." "Fleshly commandment" does, of course, refer to **a regulation as to his ancestry,** to the requirement that he be a descendent of Aaron. But the word translated "fleshly" also implies human weakness. Although this Aaronic priesthood was established by God, it was ineffective because it depended on weak, sinful human beings.

The priesthood, however, of the **priest like Melchizedek** (7:15), who was "without beginning of days or end of life" (7:3), is based on **the power of an indestructible life** (7:16). Only God's life is indestructible. This Priest is also the eternal Son of God (see 5:5-6) who shares in God's life. Only in this way could He be **a priest forever** (7:17).

Hebrews 7:18-19 concludes this discussion. The Priesthood of the new Priest is based on the eternal life of God and not human weakness. Thus the quality of the new Priest shows clearly that **the former regulation** of priesthood based on Aaronic descent and the whole covenant dependent on it are **set aside.** That priesthood and covenant were never intended to be anything more than "former" or "preliminary." The word here translated **is set aside** is much stronger than the words translated "change" in 7:12. The quality of this new Priest is clear; therefore it is evident that the old priesthood is "abolished." The NRSV speaks of the "abrogation" of the old commandment. It was **weak** because it was based on frail, sinful humanity (7:18; see 4:15; 5:2; commentary on 7:28) **and useless** in that it could not deal with sin. When the preacher says that the old Law **made nothing perfect,** he means that it could not cleanse God's people from sin and thus enable them to come into the presence of God. Compare what Christ can do, as described in 10:14.

Christians do not have a new "law" but a **better hope** (7:19). The old law was **weak and useless,** but this **hope** is **better,** in Hebrews' special sense of this word "better."[8] Backed by God's own power, it really works! Through this hope we are truly cleansed from sin so that we can **draw near to God** (7:19). This is the "hope" spoken of in 6:19-20 that assures us of entrance into God's presence through our Forerunner and High Priest.

3. THIS PRIEST PROVIDES FULL SALVATION 7:20-25

The prophecy of a new priesthood showed that the Aaronic priesthood would pass away (see 7:11-14). The actual fulfillment of that prophecy by the eternal Priesthood of Christ demonstrated that the Aaronic priesthood had passed away (see 7:15-19). The eternal quality of Christ's Priesthood, empowered by the "indestructible life" of God, demonstrates the total inadequacy of the former priesthood. Because His Priesthood is of this quality, it provides cleansing from sin and access to God. In 7:20-25, the writer elaborates the benefits of this priesthood more fully. Verses 20 through 22 draw on the fact that God's declaration of Psalm 110:4 is an oath: **The Lord has sworn** (Heb. 7:21). Verses 23 through 25 focus on the content of this oath, the eternal nature of the Son's Priesthood declared in Psalm 110:4.

Verses 20 through 22 take us back to the theme of 6:13-20: God has supported His promise of salvation with an oath. That promise and supporting oath were made to Abraham and are inherited by Christians, who are Abraham's spiritual children. Hebrews 6:20 affirmed that Jesus assured the fulfillment of God's sworn promise of salvation by entering God's presence as our Forerunner. A second oath of God now supports Christ's entry and ministry as our High Priest. This oath is of course the oath of Psalm 110:4, quoted in Hebrews 7:21: **The Lord has sworn and will not change his mind.**

The double negative, **not without an oath** (Heb. 7:20), strongly affirms that Christ was made a priest by the oath of God in Psalm 110:4. God established the Levitical or Aaronic priesthood, but He did not guarantee its perpetuity and effectiveness with any **oath.** Thus Christ's Priesthood is qualitatively different from that priesthood.

Hebrews 7:22 shows the significance of the fact that Christ's Priesthood was established by the oath of God and the Aaronic priesthood was not: God's **oath** is the reason why **Jesus has become the guarantee of a better covenant.** Every word of this statement is important. The perfect tense of the Greek verb translated **has become** indicates that He has become and still is this **guarantee.** Jesus is not just the "mediator," but the **guarantee** or the "guarantor" of this **better covenant.** The old covenant had a mediator, Moses. God revealed that old covenant and established it through him. On the basis of the old covenant the human priests served as mediators between God and the people. But no one could guarantee the effectiveness of the old covenant. No one could ensure that access to God was available through that covenant. Jesus, on the other hand, guarantees the **new covenant.** He makes it effective! He insures that cleansing from sin and access to God are available through this covenant. We can be sure that He guarantees it because He has been made an eternal Priest by the unchanging oath of God. Thus when the word "mediator" is used of Jesus in 9:15 and 12:24, the writer can expect us to remember that Jesus is a "mediator" who *guarantees* what He mediates.

The biblical writers use the word **covenant** to designate the way God has arranged for people to live in fellowship with himself. This word **covenant** does not describe an agreement which God and humanity have mutually negotiated. God offers it and human beings can accept or reject it. The preacher often uses words like "law" (7:11) or "regulation" (7:18) to refer to the old covenant or way of approaching God established through Moses. God based the new **covenant** on the oath-secured High Priesthood of Jesus. Therefore this new covenant is **better** (7:22). It brings true cleansing from sin and enables people to actually come into the presence of and have fellowship with the living God.

In Greek, the name **Jesus** appears as the last word of this verse (7:22). By using **Jesus** instead of "Christ" or "Son of God" the preacher emphasizes that this Guarantor lived a fully earthly life as a human being. We can be sure that Jesus is the Guarantor of the new covenant because His Priesthood was established by the oath of God. But we also see that the new covenant has been made effective by His perfect obedience as a human being on earth (see 10:5-10).

As noted above, 7:23-25 explains more fully the significance of the content of the oath found in Psalm 110:4. This oath declared that Christ's priesthood was "forever." He is a Priest "on the basis of the power of an indestructible life" (7:16) who is "without beginning of days or end of life" (7:3). Again the preacher contrasts the Aaronic priests, described in 7:23, with Christ, described in 7:24. Verse 25 summarizes the benefits that accrue to God's people because of the eternity of their High Priest, the very point highlighted by this paragraph's contrast.

The preacher emphasizes the word **many** in the Greek text both by its location near the beginning of the sentence and by its form (7:23). It is, literally, "more" rather than "many." This verse could be literally translated "On the one hand the more have become priests because by death they were prevented from continuing on." There were both "more" or **many** priests at any one time as well as **many** in the long succession of priests throughout the history of God's people. In several cases through this letter, multiplicity is a sign of imperfection (see commentary on 1:1; 9:24–10:4; and 10:11-15). The old system required many priests because none could effectively do the job that needed to be done.

But, on the other hand, according to 7:24, **because Jesus lives forever, he has a permanent priesthood.**[9] The word that the New International Version translates **lives** and the New American Standard Bible, "abides" can also be translated "remains." The preacher uses it in 7:3 to indicate that the one who is "without beginning of days or end of life" also *"remains"* as "a priest forever" (my emphasis). He also uses the same word to describe the *permanence* of the "better possessions" that God's faithful people have (10:34), the "enduring city" (13:14) that is their final home, and what remains for God's people after all of this visible created world is shaken and removed by the final judgment of God (12:27). A strengthened form of this word is used in 1:11 (quoting Psalm 102:26) to describe the eternity of God. This Priest **lives** or "abides" eternally because He is the eternal Son "without beginning of days or end of life" (7:3) who participates in the **indestructible life** (7:16) of God. Thus, because of His eternal nature, He has a permanent priesthood. This Priest has a priesthood which is permanent, "unchangeable" (ASV), "inviolable," and "indefectible." This Priesthood is final and absolute.

In 7:25, the preacher comes to the point of the contrast given in 7:23-24. Because Christ has such a Priesthood, **he is able to save completely those who come to God through him.** Instead of **completely,** the NASB reads "forever," and the NRSV, "for all time." The Greek word involved can denote degree, "completely"; or time, "forever." At first it might seem like the temporal significance would better fit the context of Hebrews. Christ "lives" forever so He can save forever. This certainly is true. But a major point throughout this letter is that the Priesthood of the new High Priest is empowered by His eternal life, by the fact that He partakes of the very life of God. Thus His Priesthood has a different quality. Because of this quality the new High Priest can *really* save where the old could not. Thus the qualitative translation of the New International Version, **completely,** is the best translation of this verse. (Compare the King James Version's translation: "to the uttermost.") Because this Priest is empowered by God's Own eternal life, He is able to save God's people **completely** from sin so that they can truly come into God's presence. Of course the temporal idea is also included. Because He can *truly* save from sin, He can save *for all time*. He can enable us to endure to the end.

Those who are being saved are described as **those who come to God through him.** The language of drawing near to or of approaching God fits well with the language of priesthood (see 4:16; 10:22). In the Old Testament, God's people came near to worship Him in the Tabernacle or Temple through the priests. The phrase **those who come to God through him** describes the Christian life as the practice of worship made possible through the High Priestly work of Christ. Christians live in the most holy place, in the presence of God, on "holy ground" separate from the world. As the preacher continues to describe the High Priesthood of Christ in more detail, he continues to develop this image of the Christian life as worship.

What the preacher has said in 7:24 about this Priest's living "forever" and having a "permanent priesthood," he reinforces by his next phrase: **because he always lives to intercede for them** (7:25). He is High Priest by "the power of an indestructible life" (7:16). He is the one Melchizedek foreshadowed, the One who truly "lives" (7:8 NKJV) and is truly "without beginning of days or end of life" (7:3). He is the eternal Son who shares the life of "the living God" (3:12; 9:14; 10:31; 12:22).

The phrase **to intercede for** (7:25) fits well with the priestly imagery of the writer of Hebrews. As our High Priest, Christ offered himself for our sins once for all in the past. The preacher will explain this sacrifice in Hebrews 8 through 10. By His intercession, He makes the benefits of that sacrifice available to God's people in the present. Thus, through His interceding they enjoy cleansing from sin, victory over temptation, and access to the very presence of God.

It is true that the word **intercede** usually means to petition someone on behalf of someone else. We must not, however, think of the Son as begging the Father to save His people. The preacher makes clear that the Father has received the Son. The Son is thus sitting at the Father's right hand (see 1:13; 10:11-15). The preacher uses this word **intercede** in a more general way. The Son is able to "help" those who approach God through Him. He is able to cleanse and to give them continual victory over temptation so that they have access to God.

The preacher's explanation of the declaration of Christ's Priesthood in

Psalm 110:4 reaches its climax in Hebrews 7:23-25. Because this Priest is the eternal Son of God empowered by the life of God, He can save God's people **completely.** He can completely cleanse them from sin, give them victory when they are tempted, and thus bring them into the presence of God. He can do this daily and continually until they reach that deeper participation in the presence of God which is the final and eternal destiny of God's people.

4. THIS PRIEST IS JUST THE PRIEST WE NEED 7:26-28

Hebrews 7:26-28 serves as a bridge passage: It summarizes the preceding picture of this High Priest who **meets our need** (7:26). It prepares readers for the description of this High Priest's sacrifice in the following chapters. In these verses the preacher praises God for providing such a High Priest. At the same time he instructs us about the nature of His Priesthood. Verse 26 describes the character and sphere of ministry of this High Priest. Verse 27 describes the sacrifice of this High Priest by contrasting it with the sacrifice of the Aaronic high priests. This idea of sacrifice introduces the discussion that follows in 8:1 through 10:18. Hebrews 7:28 summarizes the whole by integrating the teaching of 7:26-27 with what the preacher has said in 7:1-25.

Such a high priest—the one the preacher has spoken of and the one he describes in these verses—**meets our need** of cleansing from sin and access into the very presence of God. Every part of the description of this High Priest (see 7:26-28) shows how He is qualified to meet **our need.**

As noted above, 7:26 describes His character and the sphere of His priestly ministry. He is **holy, blameless, pure.** These three words each have a different nuance, but together they emphasize that our **high priest** has been completely obedient to the Father and that His character is untouched by sin. Only a sinless one could meet our need because only such a one could deal with our sin.

Set apart from sinners comes between the preceding description of the High Priest's sinlessness and the following declaration of His exaltation into the Father's presence. Although He once lived an obedient and therefore sinless life among **sinners** on this earth, He is now **set apart** from them because He has been **exalted above the** visible **heavens** into that place where God dwells. **Exalted above the heavens** is rendered more literally in the New King James Version as "has become higher than the heavens." The perfect tense of the Greek verbs translated as **set apart** and **exalted above** denotes the continuing result of a past act. This Priest was set apart and exalted at a particular time in the past, but He continues in that set apart and exalted state today in the Father's presence. He is in the place of authority, in the presence of God, where He can truly help us.

Hebrews 7:27 describes this High Priest's sacrifice by showing how it is unlike the sacrifice of the Aaronic high priests. They had to offer first for their own sins, and then for the sins of the people and they had to do it repeatedly, day after day. Christ, however, sacrificed himself for the sins of the people, and He did it once for all. In 8:1 through 10:18, the preacher will discuss the issues raised by this contrast between the new and the old sacrifices.

Hebrews 5:3 has already shown that the Aaronic priests' need to offer sacrifice for their own sin marked them as sinful and therefore unable to deal with the sin of others. But the One who was holy, blameless, pure (7:26) certainly would have no need to sacrifice for himself. Hebrews 9:11-17, 26 and 10:5-10 explain the significance of His offering himself. He offered His own perfectly obedient human life, culminating in His obedient death, for our sins.

By the phrase day after day, the preacher expresses the repetitiveness of these sacrifices. The Old Testament high priest did not have to make the double sacrifice for his own sins and for the sins of the people every day. He did offer these sacrifices regularly, especially on the annual Day of Atonement to which the preacher will refer in 9:7-8 and 9:11-14. Hebrews 9:24 through 10:4 and 10:11-14 explain the significance of Christ's sacrifice being once for all. The fact that His sacrifice was once for all shows that it truly dealt with sin and therefore needs no repetition.

The preacher summarizes the argument of this chapter by a concluding contrast in 7:28. There are three aspects of this contrast: (1) The old high priests were established by the law, the new by the oath of God in Psalm 110:4; (2) The old were men (mere human beings), the new, God's Son; and (3) The old were weak, the new made perfect forever. The first of these contrasts reminds us again that the old law did not do the job. It could not establish an effective priesthood (see 7:11-19). The oath takes us back to the argument of 7:20-22. The second of these contrasts directs our minds back to the eternal quality of the new Priest, as developed in 7:11-19 (particularly 7:15-17) and in 7:23-25. In the latter block (7:23-25), the preacher contrasted the human mortality of the old priests with the eternity of the new Priest, the Son. These first two aspects of the contrast emphasize (just as 7:1-25 did) both the eternity and the finality of the new High Priest.

The third aspect of this contrast relates to the obedience and sacrifice of the new High Priest, as described in Hebrews 7:26-27. This idea reaches back to such passages as 2:10-18 and 5:1-10. The problem with the Aaronic high priests was that they were **weak.** A literal translation would be "human beings having weakness." They are characterized by a "weakness" that implies "sinfulness" (see commentary on 5:3). By contrast, the new High Priest **has been made perfect forever.** (For a discussion of Christ being **made perfect,** see commentary on 2:10 and 5:9.) He is the perfect Son of God from all eternity, but He became **perfect** as our Savior, perfectly able to save us. He became perfect by completely obeying the Father throughout His earthly life, climaxing in His obedient death on the cross (see also 10:5-10). In this sense He is **holy, blameless, pure** (7:26). Through this obedience and sacrifice of himself, He has been exalted. The perfect tense of the Greek verb behind **has been made perfect** indicates both that He became perfectly able to save us at His exaltation and that He *continues* perfectly able to save us **forever.** His ability to save us will not change (see 13:8). A literal rendering of this verse's last Greek words would read, "a Son forever having been made perfect." The preacher highlights both the eternal being and the earthly obedience of the Son in one concentrated phrase. This phrase summarizes the effectiveness of His High Priesthood.

In 7:1-25, the preacher has discussed the High Priest's being "Son." In 8:1 through 10:18, he will discuss how this "Son" was perfected as our Savior by obediently offering himself for our sin.

ENDNOTES

[1]The Gospels of Matthew (Matt. 1:1-17) and Luke (Luke 3:23-38) give genealogies of Jesus to show that He is the fulfillment of God's plan of salvation.

[2]"Melchizedek" was understood as "king of righteousness" by the first-century Jewish historian Josephus (*Jewish Antiquities* 1.180), by the Jewish philosopher Philo (*Allegorical Interpretation* 3:79-82), and by several ancient translations of Genesis into the Aramaic language, which was the common language of Jews living in Palestine.

[3]Philo also interpreted "king of Salem" as "king of peace." See the reference given in the previous footnote.

[4]See Isaiah 9:6-7; 32:17; Jeremiah 23:5-6; 33:15; Zechariah 9:9-10; Micah 5:4-5; Malachi 4:2.

[5]Levi was one of the twelve sons of Jacob, a great-grandson of Abraham. The sons or descendants of Levi were in charge of caring for the Tabernacle and later the Temple, but only the sons of Aaron, the brother of Moses and a Levite, could offer sacrifices and function as priests and high priests (see Numbers 3:5-10). Thus only a part of the Levites could serve as priests. The writer of Hebrews is

aware that only the sons of Aaron and not all Levites were priests (see 5:4; 7:11). Nevertheless it was acceptable to refer to Levi as the ancestor of the priests and to the priesthood as "Levitical" (see 7:11), and it was particularly appropriate in this context. First of all, the comparison with Abraham makes reference to Levi, a great-grandson of Abraham and the progenitor of one of the tribes of Israel, more natural than a reference to Aaron. Second, the context of tithing the people makes reference to Levi appropriate. All the Levites received tithes from the people. Then the priests, the sons of Aaron, received a tithe from the Levites. The preacher is aware of these details but they are not important for his argument. Thus he condenses the process by saying, **The descendants of Levi who become priests . . . collect a tenth from the people** (7:4).

⁶For instance, in 1 Kings 1:47 David's servants "blessed" him because his son Solomon succeeded him on the throne. The word used here is the one normally translated "bless," and the New American Standard Bible so translates it. The New International Version, however, correctly interprets the word in this context as "congratulate." David's servants congratulated him because his son had become king.

⁷See commentary on Hebrews 2:10; 5:9; 7:28.

⁸The Greek word translated "better" is used in Hebrews to describe the "new" that Christ has brought (see 11:40). Christ's priestly ministry is "better" (8:6), the covenant He mediates is "better" (7:22; 8:6), and it is based on "better" promises (8:6) and established by His "better" sacrifice (9:23). "Better" means the new is reality, is the fulfillment—the old was a copy; the new is heavenly, eternal, established, certain, leading to God, not "former" or "transitory." The "better" brings "perfection," actual access to God. To this access the old only looked forward.

⁹The name "Jesus" does not occur in the Greek text of this verse (Heb. 7:24). The New International Version has supplied "Jesus" in order to make it clear about whom the verse is speaking. The insertion of the name blurs the striking way in which this verse opens: "But He, on the other hand, because He abides forever" (NASB).

12

THE NEW HIGH PRIEST'S SACRIFICE: A DIFFERENT DIMENSION

Hebrews 8:1-13

Hebrews 8:1-6 addresses the relationship between sanctuary (or sphere of high priestly ministry) and sacrifice. Since Christ exercises His High Priesthood in the heavenly sanctuary (see 8:1-2), His sacrifice differs from and surpasses Old Testament sacrifices which were offered in the earthly sanctuary (8:3-6). His sacrifice also surpasses the Old Testament sacrifices because it is based on the **better promises** founded in Jeremiah 31:31-34 and quoted in Hebrews 8:7-13 (see Hebrews 8:6). Hebrews 8 is the first "movement" in the writer's extended discussion of Christ's sacrifice.

1. A HEAVENLY SANCTUARY 8:1-2

Verse 1 introduces this entire main section (8:1–10:18). The preacher's main **point** is that **we do have such a high priest, who sat down at the right hand of the throne of the Majesty in heaven.** Again, it is Psalm 110:1 and 110:4 which lie behind this assertion. Psalm 110:4 assures us that our High Priest replaces the Aaronic high priest, as

Hebrews 7:1-25 has so clearly shown. Psalm 110:1 assures us that this superior High Priest has **sat down at the right hand** of the Father. The rest of 8:1 through 10:18 shows the significance of His being at the right hand and the adequacy of the sacrifice which enables Him to be there. These chapters demonstrate that, because of His sacrifice and heavenly position, He administers a covenant far superior to the old covenant.

The phrase **We do have** is important (see 4:14-16). The preacher is not engaging in speculation. He describes the greatness of the High Priest that Christians **have** so that his hearers will fully enter into the privileges that are theirs. The whole section from 8:1 through 10:18 focuses on Christ's sacrifice. The preacher is interested in Christ's sacrifice because through it Christ has become the effective High Priest that we now **have.** His past sacrifice enables Him to help us today.

The immediate interest of the preacher in 8:1-2 is in the "location" or sphere of Christ's High Priestly ministry. According to Psalm 110:1, God invited Him to sit at His right hand. The first allusion to this verse in Hebrews 1:3 described God's right hand as "the right hand of the Majesty in heaven." The description in 8:1 is even stronger: **the right hand of the throne of the Majesty in heaven.** By the additional words, the preacher emphasizes even more strongly the significance of this place of Christ's ministry. He underlines the sovereign authority and glory of God the Father in whose presence Christ ministers. Can there be any doubt that this is **the sanctuary, the true tabernacle set up by the Lord, not by man** (8:2)?

Most English translations follow the Greek text by putting "and" between **sanctuary** and **the true tabernacle;** for example, "a minister in the sanctuary and the true tent" (8:2 RSV). Some interpreters believe the writer of Hebrews thinks that heaven has two parts of which the two parts of the earthly Tabernacle are a copy. The outer section of the earthly Tabernacle which Moses constructed was the Holy Place where the priests normally ministered. A second or inner section of this Tabernacle was the Most Holy Place where in some sense God's Presence dwelt (see 9:1-10). If the preacher believes in a two-part heavenly tabernacle then the **sanctuary** of this verse designates the inner of those two parts, the heavenly most holy place where God actually dwells. If so, then the **true tabernacle** could be the outer of those two parts, the heavenly holy place through which one must pass to enter the most holy place. Or the **true tabernacle** could be a reference to the entire heavenly tabernacle encompassing both holy place and most holy place.

The New International Version is correct, however, in taking **the sanctuary, the true tabernacle** as one single reality. Heaven does not have two compartments. When Christ sat down at the Father's right hand He entered "heaven itself" (9:24). As we shall see, the fact that the earthly Tabernacle had two compartments was an indication that access to God was not open under the old covenant (see 9:6-10). None but the high priest could ever go beyond the first compartment. But now, since Christ has opened the way for all, there would be no point in an "outer compartment" in heaven.

This heavenly **sanctuary** (8:2) is the place where God dwells, the reality pictured by the Most Holy Place of the earthly Tabernacle. The earthly Tabernacle was only a copy; therefore the preacher never calls it the **true tabernacle.** The heavenly **sanctuary** is the place where God really dwells. Its reality is demonstrated by the fact that it was **set up by the Lord** himself without the agency of **man.** It is, indeed, equivalent to the God-established permanent city (see 11:9-10) or heavenly homeland (11:13-16; 12:22-24). There God's people find true eternal "rest" in His presence (4:1-11). In more contemporary terms, we might say that Christ's sacrifice belongs to a different dimension, to the dimension of the eternal, not the temporal.

2. THE UNIQUE SACRIFICE 8:3-6

So, what does the fact of Christ's High Priestly ministry in this heavenly sanctuary say about His sacrifice? Hebrews 8:3-5 begins to answer this question. If a person is a **high priest** at all, he has been **appointed** by God **to offer both gifts and sacrifices.** The phrase **gifts and sacrifices** is a comprehensive term that includes the various kinds of Old Testament sacrifices. Offering sacrifice describes, by definition, what it means to be a high priest (see commentary on 5:1). This basic understanding of high priesthood is not changed by the fact that Christ ministers in the heavenly sanctuary or sphere. If He is a High Priest, and He is, then it is logically **necessary** for Him, too, to offer **something** (8:3).

But what is this "something"? The preacher does not yet tell us, but he prepares us for the answer that he gives in 9:12-15 and 10:5-10. At this point he does make plain that this "something" Christ offers is not the same kind of sacrifice that the Aaronic priests offered! This truth is implied by 8:4: **If he were on earth,** instead of in heaven, **he would not be a priest** of the Aaronic order at all, much less a high priest, **for there are already** those **who offer the gifts prescribed by the** Mosaic **law.** His kind of High Priesthood has a sacrifice, but it is a very different kind of sacrifice from that of the Aaronic high priest in the earthly sanctuary.

The necessary difference between their sacrifice and His becomes clearer when we look at the place where the earthly priests serve and its relationship to the heavenly sanctuary of Christ's service. Note especially 8:5: **They serve at a sanctuary that is a copy and shadow of what is in heaven.** The New International Version has added the word **sanctuary** for clarity, but the Greek text is more accurately rendered by the New American Standard Bible: "who serve a copy and shadow of the heavenly things." The preacher did not even call their location a "sanctuary" at all, but only a "copy and shadow." The writer does not imply that every piece of furniture and every detail of the earthly Tabernacle was a copy of something in heaven. He is not affirming exact correspondence between the two, but the inferiority of the earthly. The earthly Tabernacle Moses established mirrored the true approach to God in heaven, but only in a shadowy way. It was *only* a copy. Obviously Christ's sacrifice must be something of a vastly different quality than the sacrifices appropriate for this "copy and shadow."

How does the preacher know that the earthly Tabernacle was merely a copy? Again he finds support for this assertion in Scripture. In Exodus 25:40, God says to Moses, **See to it that you make everything according to the pattern shown you on the mountain** (Heb. 8:5). Thus the preacher asserts that God himself, in Scripture, at the very time when the earthly Tabernacle was being built, affirmed that it was a copy. God authorized the making of this copy but also indicated its inferiority to the heavenly original by referring to it as a **copy** (8:5).

At this point, the preacher does not tell his readers any more about the nature of Christ's sacrifice. He has merely demonstrated that it is something very different from the sacrifices of the Aaronic high priests. It is of a different quality and pertains to a different order. The sacrifice which Christ has offered is appropriate for the heavenly sphere in which His continuing High Priestly **ministry** (8:6) takes place.

The location of Christ's ministry in the heavenly sanctuary is not the only support the preacher offers to document the superiority of Christ's **ministry** and the sacrifice on which it is based. The preacher also notes that **the covenant of which he** [Christ] **is mediator is superior to the old one** (8:6). We have already seen that a "covenant" is a way that God establishes for people to approach Him (see commentary on 7:20-22). By His sacrifice and priestly ministry, Christ is the **mediator** of the new covenant. The superiority of this new covenant offers further proof for the superiority of Christ's sacrifice. This covenant is **founded on better promises.**

170

The preacher does not elaborate on *how* the promises underlying the new covenant are **better.** However, he quotes, without interpretive comment, Jeremiah 31:31-34, the passage where he finds these **better promises,** in Hebrews 8:8-12 below. In 10:15-18, at the end of his discussion of Christ's sacrifice, he will show how he believes these promises are better by citing the crucial parts of the same Jeremiah passage again. There he points out that they are **better** because they promise true forgiveness of sins. See 8:12 below: "For I will forgive their wickedness and will remember their sins no more." They are **better** because they promise that God will cleanse and change people's hearts. See 8:10 below: "I will put my laws in their minds and write them on their hearts." As a result, God's people will have true access to and fellowship with Him: "I will be their God, and they will be my people" (8:10; see also 8:11). This last statement describes the purpose and goal of the old covenant which God has now achieved in the new (see Exodus 19:5-6). These qualities of the new covenant become clearer in the later stages of the preacher's argument. At this point he merely looks forward to them by his use of the term **better promises** (Heb. 8:6) and by quoting the new covenant promise from Jeremiah 31:31-34.

3. AN APPROPRIATE COVENANT 8:7-13

In Hebrews 8:7, the preacher turns his attention to the covenant theme. At this point he does not base his argument on the qualities of the new covenant. It is enough that God *promised* a new covenant. The very fact that God made such a promise in Scripture meant that something was **wrong with that first covenant.** It was not "faultless" (NKJV; NASB; NRSV). The preacher's argument is similar to the argument he used in 7:11-14. In that passage, he argued that the very prediction of a different kind of priest (see Psalm 110:4) meant the old was insufficient.

No place would have been sought for another may seem like a strange statement. What does the preacher mean? Who sought a **place** for another covenant? Where do we find the record of their seeking? The passive tense of the verb **have been sought** probably implies that God is the Seeker. God himself sought an occasion to establish another covenant. Jeremiah 31:31-34, quoted in Hebrews 8:8-12, describes that seeking. The promises God gave in this passage from Jeremiah show His intention and plan to establish another covenant. Thus it was **God** himself who **found fault** with the first covenant by promising the new.

We might expect the beginning of 8:8 to say, "But God found fault with the first covenant." Instead we read, **But God found fault with the people.**[1] After all, it is the first covenant that was not "faultless" (see 8:7 NKJV; NASB; NRSV). Some scholars have proposed, on the basis of an alternate reading found in some trustworthy Greek manuscripts, that the verse might be translated, "God finds fault when he says to them."[2] However, according to Jeremiah 31:31-34, God finds fault with the first covenant by finding fault with the behavior of the people under that covenant: **. . . They did not remain faithful to my covenant . . .** (Heb. 8:9; see Jeremiah 31:32). This problem points to the great strength of the new covenant: under the new covenant God's grace enables His people to be faithful to Him and His covenant. The preacher wants his hearers to know that God offers grace to enable them to live in faithful obedience!

The statement in 8:13 with which the preacher concludes his Jeremiah quotation is very important. There he points out that God not only promises a second covenant, but He calls this second covenant **new.** Thus He indicates that the old has become **obsolete.** What is obsolete has no further use because people have something so much better. The old covenant has not become obsolete because of some development in human technology, nor has it become obsolete simply because it has been worn out by use. It has become obsolete because of God's own gracious action in establishing a better covenant that truly meets the need of the sinful human heart.

The phrase **will *soon* disappear** (my emphasis) does not mean that the old has not yet disappeared. It was *soon* to **disappear** from the point of view of Jeremiah 31:31-34. Now that Christ has come, the **soon** of the future has become the "now" of the present.

Thus the preacher has laid a solid scriptural foundation for his discussion of the **new covenant** (Heb. 7:8). The very fact that God promised a second covenant in Jeremiah 31:31-34 meant that the first covenant had **fault** (Heb. 8:8). The fact that he called **this covenant "new"** meant that **the first one** was old and **obsolete** (8:13).

To summarize, this first movement of the preacher's argument in 8:1 through 10:18 has given us reasons to believe that the sacrifice of Christ is something much better than the sacrifice of the earthly high priests. Christ's sacrifice is appropriate for the heavenly sanctuary where He sits at the Father's right hand, rather than for the inferior copy made by Moses. God's own words show us that Christ is in that sanctuary (see Psalm 110:1, 4) and that the earthly is an inferior copy (Exodus 25:40). Christ's sacrifice is one that is appropriate for the new covenant, the covenant which God promised in Jeremiah 31:31-34, the covenant which made the old obsolete.

ENDNOTES

[1]The Greek text reads "them" instead of "people." The New International Version has supplied "people" for clarity. Compare the New Revised Standard Version: "God finds fault with them."

[2]William L. Lane, *Hebrews 1–8,* vol. 47a, Word Biblical Commentary, New Testament ed. Ralph P. Martin, gen. eds. David A. Hubbard and Glenn W. Barker (Dallas: Word Books, 1991), p. 202s.

THE NEW HIGH PRIEST'S SACRIFICE: HIS BLOOD

Hebrews 9:1-22

W e have seen that Hebrews 8:1-13 concentrated on the facts: Christ served in the heavenly, not the earthly, sanctuary; He mediated the new, not the old, covenant; and therefore His sacrifice was of a different order than the old sacrifices. This first "movement" also introduced the Old Testament quotations necessary to support the difference between the heavenly and the earthly sanctuaries (see Exodus 25:40) and to affirm the new covenant (see Jeremiah 31:31-34).

The preacher's second movement in discussing Christ's sacrifice (Heb. 9:1-22) gives extensive description of the old sanctuary (9:1-10) and old covenant (9:16-22) to help the readers understand more deeply the nature of Christ's superior sacrifice (9:11-15). The preacher details the old system so he can highlight the significance of blood sacrifices in both the old sanctuary's worship and in the establishing of the old covenant. This background provides the understanding of Christ's sacrifice as **his own blood** (9:12) and emphasizes the ineffectiveness of the old, especially in the case of the earthly sanctuary in 9:1-10.

1. THE EARTHLY SANCTUARY 9:1-10

In Hebrews 9:1-10, the preacher turns from his discussion of the new covenant (see 8:7-13) to a description of the **regulations for worship** (9:1) and **earthly sanctuary** established by the **first covenant.** Both the New King James Version and the New American Standard Bible read "the" rather than *an* **earthly sanctuary** (my emphasis). The old covenant's sanctuary is **earthly** in character, but it is not just an earthly sanctuary. It is the particular sanctuary God established through Moses. Thus, although it may have been ineffective as an avenue of approach to God, it did point forward to what would be effective.

The **regulations for worship** under consideration are the rituals performed in that **earthly sanctuary.** The preacher portrays these rituals in 9:6-10 after setting the stage for them by describing the **earthly sanctuary** in 9:2-5. His description highlights the inadequacy of the old sacrifice. After all, Aaronic priests offered their sacrifices in an **earthly sanctuary** and the rituals they followed were mere **external regulations** (9:10). Yet they bear some analogy to what God would accomplish in Christ. The blood sacrifices required by the rituals in the ancient earthly sanctuary pointed forward to His sacrifice of His own blood, as 9:11-14 shows.[1]

Exodus 25:1-31; 36:2 through 39:43; and 40:1-38 describe the arrangement of the furniture in the Old Testament Tabernacle. These passages locate the **lampstand** (Heb. 9:2) and the **table** (on which **the consecrated bread** was put) in the outer part of the Tabernacle, **the Holy Place,** just as Hebrews does. They both also locate **the gold-covered ark of the covenant** (9:4) containing **the tablets of the covenant** on which the Ten Commandments were written, within the Most Holy Place.

This **ark** was a box about four and one-half feet long, two and one-half feet wide, and two and one-half feet high. Its cover was **the atonement cover** (9:5). On either end were the images of **the** winged **cherubim of the Glory** who overshadowed that cover. **The Glory** refers to the presence of God. The **atonement cover** was His throne, and the **cherubim** were His attendants. It was on this **atonement cover** that the High Priest sprinkled the blood of the sacrifice on the Day of Atonement (see Leviticus 16:14-15).

Hebrews, however, seems to disagree at two points with the Old Testament on the location of articles within the Tabernacle. The Old Testament says that the **jar of manna** (9:4; see Exodus 16:33-34) and **Aaron's staff that had budded** (see Numbers 17:1-10) were in the

Most Holy Place, but it does not say that they were in the ark. This does not preclude the possibility that they might have been in the ark. In the time of Solomon, long after Moses, the Scripture says that nothing was in the ark but the stone tablets (see 1 Kings 8:9; 2 Chronicles 5:10). This is said, however, in a way that might imply something more had once been in the ark.

More serious is the fact that Hebrews appears to locate the **golden altar of incense**[2] in the Most Holy Place (Heb. 9:4) while the Old Testament locates it in the Holy Place (see Exodus 30:6). This seems strange because the preacher knows that the high priest entered the Most Holy Place only on one day of the year (see Hebrews 9:7). How, then, could this **altar of incense,** which was used by the priests every day (see Exodus 30:7-8), be in the Most Holy Place? Several Old Testament passages associate this altar closely with the Most Holy Place. Exodus 30:6 locates it "in front of the curtain that is before the ark of the Testimony—before the atonement cover that is over the Testimony— where I will meet with you" (see 40:26). Exodus 40:5 situates it "in front of the ark of the Testimony." First Kings 6:22 refers to this altar as "the altar that belonged to the inner sanctuary" of Solomon's Temple. This altar was situated right before the veil or "curtain" that separated the outer or Holy Place from the inner or Most Holy Place which represented the dwelling place of God. This altar was the place where priests offered incense, which represented the prayers of the people. It was the place where they made intercession. We might call it the "gateway" to the Most Holy Place. It was the place priests held communion with God. Thus, while it would not have been proper to say that the **altar of incense** was "in" the Most Holy Place, it was not totally misleading to say that the Most Holy Place **had the golden altar of incense** (Heb. 9:4). The Most Holy Place represented the dwelling place of God, while the altar represented the priests' regular communion with and close approach to God.[3]

Why did the writer describe these furnishings of the Tabernacle if he **cannot discuss** them **in detail** (9:5)? He certainly did not include these furniture items so that his readers could find hidden meaning in them. He listed them to emphasize the "earthly" nature of the Mosaic Tabernacle. The material nature of the Tabernacle and its contents provides a basis for his conclusion (see 9:10) that the rituals of the Tabernacle pertained only to outward, ritual cleansing.

The phrase **when everything had been arranged like this** introduces 9:6-7. These verses describe the ritual ministry of the priests and high priest in the first and second rooms of the Tabernacle, as the preacher has described them in 9:2-5. Verses 8 through 10 will describe the significance of this ritual ministry.

It is important to note that both the **priests** (9:6) and the **high priest** (9:7) **entered** key Tabernacle areas—the priests the **outer room,** the high priest the **inner room.** Old Testament writers and the preacher following them understood priestly ministry as approach to God. The work of a priest was to come into God's presence and to enable others to approach Him. However, in the Tabernacle both the priests and the high priest were very limited in their ability to approach God. How could they help others approach Him?

The priests entered **regularly** or, better, "continually" (NASB; NRSV). It is as if they repeatedly tried to approach God without complete success. They entered only the **outer room,** not the inner area which represented God's presence (9:6). Also, they repeatedly carried out a **ministry** that included only "ritual duties" (NRSV). The repetitiveness of their actions points toward the ineffectiveness of those actions.

The function of the **high priest** confirms and demonstrates even more clearly this limitation of approach (9:7). True, he could enter **the inner room,** but **only** he could enter, and **only once a year**—that is, on one day in the year, the Day of Atonement (described in Leviticus 16:1-28). Thus even his access to God's presence was severely limited. The preacher goes on to explain another restriction on his entrance: He could **never** enter **without** the **blood** from a sacrifice. On the Day of Atonement he first entered the Most Holy Place with the blood from the sacrifice of a bull **for himself** and his household (see Leviticus 16:11-14). Then he entered a second time that same day with the blood from the sacrifice of a goat **for the sins** of the people (see Leviticus 16:15-19).

The old high priest had to offer these blood sacrifices because of sin. His own and his people's sinfulness blocked access to God's presence. Moreover, his sacrifices did not adequately deal with sin. On the Day of Atonement, the priest offered sacrifice only for the sins **the people had committed in ignorance** (Heb. 9:7). The Old Testament usually speaks of the sacrifices as atoning for unintentional sin (Leviticus 6:1-6 is an exception). There were no sacrifices for some sins, such as murder, adultery, and idolatry. The Day of Atonement sacrifices never professed to deal with all sin. The preacher affirms that the Old Testament sacrifices in themselves never effectively atoned for *any* sin (see Hebrews 10:4). If they had, the people would have been able to come into God's presence. But he firmly believes that Christ's sacrifice covered *all* sin, with the single exception of apostasy, for apostasy is the complete denial of Christ's sacrifice and its effectiveness (see 6:1-8; 10:26-31).

The Holy Spirit (9:8) inspired Scripture and now speaks through it. He had a purpose in directing the writers of Scripture to record all of these features of the old priesthood and its duties in the earthly Tabernacle. **By this** description He **was showing . . . that the way into the Most Holy Place had not yet been disclosed** while this **first tabernacle was still standing** (9:8).

Interpreters are divided over the meaning of **first tabernacle.** Should it be translated **first tabernacle** (as in the NIV) or "outer tabernacle" (NASB; compare the NEB's "earlier tent"). The New International Version's translation understands the word **first** in the sense of "former" and the word **tabernacle** as a reference to the whole Old Testament Tabernacle. The second interpretation takes the word **first** to mean "the first part that one comes to"—that is, the "outer"; and the word **tabernacle** as referring to only one part of the Tabernacle, the Holy Place.[4] It is true that the writer has used the word "first" in 9:2 to refer to the "outer" part of the Tabernacle. Nevertheless, the understanding of **first** as former and **tabernacle** as the whole Old Testament Tabernacle better suits this verse. The NIV translators appear to have followed this interpretation. The *whole* Tabernacle and its ritual together demonstrate the fact that God had not yet made known **the way into the Most Holy Place.** The fact that this **tabernacle** had two parts emphasizes the inaccessibility of God. Both the ministry of the priests in the outer part of the Tabernacle and the limited access of the high priest into the inner part demonstrate that the way of entrance into God's presence was not yet **disclosed.** If the priests and high priest could not enter, certainly the common people were excluded. By His sacrifice Christ has both opened and disclosed **the way into the Most Holy Place.**

What is the meaning of **still standing** (9:8)? Is the writer referring to the literal existence of the Old Testament Tabernacle or to the continuation of its ritual in the Temple? He is probably not referring to either of these options.

Certainly he does not refer to the first possibility, for the Jerusalem Temple had replaced the previous Tabernacle a thousand years before the preacher wrote. It would make no sense for him to say that the way into God's presence had not been disclosed until a thousand years before Christ came. Christ himself had disclosed that way!

Nor does **still standing** mean "as long as the Tabernacle ritual was being carried on in the Temple." The preacher never says that the destruction of the Temple brought the old covenant order to an end. Indeed, the Temple was probably still standing when he wrote.[5] No, the coming of Christ our High Priest demonstrated the end of the old system.

The Greek translated **still standing** can easily mean "still having validity."[6] As long as the Mosaic Tabernacle with its priestly ritual had validity or standing, the fully effective way to enter God's presence had not yet been revealed.

Some interpreters have thought that **the present time** was a reference to the time of the old Tabernacle and sacrifice—"the time then present." They understand the **first tabernacle** (9:8) and its worship (described in 9:6-7) as **an illustration for** or "symbol of" (NRSV) the time before Christ. Since the priests and high priest could not freely enter God's presence in that Tabernacle, it demonstrated that **the gifts and sacrifices** then **being offered were not able to clear the conscience of the worshiper.**

However, it is probably most natural to understand **the present time** as the age of salvation inaugurated by Christ in which we live. The Revised English Bible's translation of 9:9 is very helpful: "All this is symbolic, pointing to the present time." The "first tabernacle" and its worship were not **an illustration** or symbol *of* Christ's ministry but a symbol that pointed forward *to* **the present time** of His heavenly High Priestly ministry. How did the Tabernacle worship point forward to **the present time?** First, by demonstrating its own inadequacy, it indicated that something better was to come. The description of the old ways (in 9:6-7) has demonstrated that the worship of the old Tabernacle did not reveal the way into God's presence (see 9:8). The inability of the priests and high priest to freely approach God demonstrated that the **gifts and sacrifices** that were offered **were not able to clear the conscience of the worshiper** (9:9). Thus the whole old system demonstrated the inadequacy of the old sacrifice to deal with sin and pointed forward to the sacrifice of Christ (to be discussed in 9:11-15). Second, the old system also looked forward to the new in a positive way. It demonstrated that a sacrifice was necessary for sin, a **blood** sacrifice (9:7), thus pointing to the kind of sacrifice that Christ would make.

Consider more closely the inadequacy of the sacrifices of the old covenant. The phrase **not able to clear the conscience** (9:9) is a weak translation of the preacher's original words. The New American Standard Bible does better: "which cannot make the worshiper perfect in conscience." No animal sacrifice could make the priests, high priests, or the worshipers they represented "perfect in conscience." The preacher uses the term **conscience** in a broader way than we usually use it. For him **conscience** includes everything we might indicate by use of the word "heart." The **conscience** "embraces the whole person in his relation to God (9:9, 14; 10:2, 22; 13:18)."[7]

Christ "has been perfected" as our Savior by His life of complete obedience, climaxing in His obedient sacrifice on the cross (see commentary on 5:9; 7:28). He now "perfects" those who come to Him (10:14) by forgiving their sin, cleansing sin from their hearts, and by enabling them to live lives of obedience that mirror His life of obedience. That is, He makes the provisions of the new covenant a reality in their lives (see 10:15-18). By contrast, the old sacrifices could not deal with the inner reality of the human heart in relationship to God. They pertained **only** to **food and drink and various ceremonial washings** (9:10), only to **external regulations,** to ceremonial things, and not to the inner reality of the "conscience." Obviously they applied only **until the time of the new order** of salvation—the new way of approaching God, the new covenant—that has now been established by the sacrifice of Christ.

So, the old Tabernacle and its sacrificial ritual pointed toward the sacrifice of Christ, both by showing that its own sacrifices were not adequate and by establishing a pattern of the true sacrifice that would come, the "blood" sacrifice of a pure victim. In verses 11 through 15 the preacher turns to that effective sacrifice, to the sacrifice of Christ.

2. THE SACRIFICE OF CHRIST'S BLOOD 9:11-15

Hebrews 9:11-14 relates Christ's sacrifice to what has been said about the sacrifices in the old earthly sanctuary in 9:1-10; 9:15 relates His sacrifice to what 9:16-22 will say about the establishing of the old covenant.

Verse 11 gives the sanctuary or sphere of Christ's priesthood. This sanctuary differs sharply from the Tabernacle of the Aaronic high priest (as described in 9:1-5). Verse 12 contrasts the sacrifice which brought Christ's entrance into the sphere of His priesthood with the sacrifice of the old high priest in the earthly sanctuary. (That old priestly ministry was described in 9:6-10.) Verses 13 and 14 develop this contrast in order to show the finality and superiority of Christ's sacrifice.

The New Revised Standard Version makes the contrast between Christ and what has been said about the old in 9:1-10 quite clear: *"But* when Christ" (my emphasis). **When Christ came as high priest** (9:11), refers to more than Christ's coming to earth. He **came** as High Priest when He had completed His earthly life of obedience, obediently offered up His life, and sat down at the Father's right hand. He **came** into His own only at the Father's right.

The term **good** was used in the Old Testament to describe the Promised Land (see Exodus 3:8; Numbers 14:7; Deuteronomy 1:25). In Hebrews 9:11, the phrase **good things** refers to the blessings of the new covenant, forgiveness of sin, cleansing from sin, and fellowship with God. These **good things . . . are already here.**[8] They "have come" (NRSV) because they have been made a reality through **Christ,** the **High Priest.** Yet they find their ultimate fulfillment in the heavenly "promised land" which God has prepared for His people (11:9-10, 13-16).

In 9:11-14, the preacher contrasts Christ's sacrifice of himself with the sacrifice the Old Testament high priest offered on the Day of Atonement (as described in 9:7). On that day, the old high priest entered through the Tabernacle into the Most Holy Place. Christ, however, **went through the greater and more perfect tabernacle that is not man-made, that is to say, not a part of this creation.** This "tabernacle" is **greater and more perfect** because it is the *true* dwelling place of God, as contrasted with the **man-made** Mosaic Tabernacle. Exodus 36:1 through 39:43 describes how all of the parts of that Tabernacle were made. Exodus 40:1-33 shows Moses putting all the parts together to complete the Tabernacle. But God himself established **the greater and more perfect tabernacle** in which He truly dwells. He established it beyond **creation** as the place of His "rest" and the place where His people would truly fellowship with Him (see 4:1-11).

What kind of sacrifice was necessary for Christ to enter this heavenly sphere, to come into the very presence of God? **He did not enter by means of the blood of goats and calves** (9:12). The sacrifices that provided annual entrance to the earthly Most Holy Place on the Day of Atonement (see 9:7) were not adequate here. He entered the true **Most Holy Place,** the heavenly dwelling place of God, **by his own blood.** He entered this presence of God **once for all,** not repeatedly or annually, **having obtained eternal redemption.** The New Revised Standard Version better catches the sense of this last phrase: "thus obtaining eternal redemption." It was the sacrifice of **his own blood** that enabled Him to obtain this **eternal redemption.** This **redemption** provides true cleansing from sin, as described at the end of 9:14. Those who experience this redemption are "liberated" from sin. This **redemption** is **eternal** because it is effected by the power of the eternal God (see 7:16). Thus it truly liberates from sin and brings God's people into His presence. It provides grace for them to live *forever* in fellowship with Him.

Hebrews 9:13 describes what the sacrifices of the old covenant will do; 9:14, what the **blood of Christ** will do. **The blood of goats and bulls** (9:13) reminds us of the Day of Atonement sacrifice, in which the high priest first offered a bull from himself and his family and then a goat for the sins of the people. By this phrase, the preacher probably intended to refer more comprehensively to the Old Testament animal sacrifices in general. The preacher adds a reference to **the ashes of a heifer.** As related in Numbers 19:1-10, God told Moses to have Eleazar, the son of Aaron who succeeded his father as high priest, slaughter a "red heifer" outside the camp of Israel. He was to sprinkle some of its blood before the Tabernacle and then burn the rest of the body, including the blood. The ashes from this red heifer were to be kept and mixed with water when needed. God makes the general statement that this water was to be used "for purification from sin" (Num. 19:9). However, God gave only one specific example of how this water should be used: when someone had touched something dead, the water-ashes mix should be sprinkled on that person, in order to make him ritually clean (see Numbers 19:11-22). Thus this water was used for ceremonial cleansing. The preacher probably refers to this ritual because it was closely related to the sacrifices, was performed by Eleazar the high priest, and clearly portrayed the outward, ceremonial nature of the sanctifying or cleansing ability of the old covenant sacrifices and rituals. Those rituals could only make the **ceremonially unclean . . . outwardly clean** (Heb. 9:13).

The phrase **sanctify them so that they are outwardly clean** clearly expresses the preacher's meaning, but the New American Standard Bible more closely follows the Greek construction: "sanctify for the cleansing of the flesh." Outward cleansing is "cleansing of the flesh." "Flesh" has the connotation of "weakness and uselessness" (see commentary on 7:16). The blood of the old system offers human, not divine, cleansing.

The writer has admitted that Old Testament sacrifices and rituals provided ritual or outward cleansing, for what it was worth. **How much more** (9:14) certain it is that **the blood of Christ** will provide true inner cleansing. His offering was not based on mere "flesh," mere human power. He made His offering **through the eternal Spirit.** This term may refer to the Holy Spirit. It may also refer to Christ's Own eternal Spirit, to the "indestructible life" (7:16) that was His because He was and is the eternal Son of God (1:1-3). Because He was the eternal Son of God, He could do what no one else had ever done, offer **himself unblemished to**

God. The word translated **unblemished** was one used to describe Old Testament sacrifices as without physical defect (see Numbers 6:14; 19:2). In Hebrews 10:5-10, the preacher explains this phrase in relation to Christ: He was morally pure in that He lived a completely obedient human life. Thus, the old sacrifices could **sanctify** the **ceremonially unclean** from outward or ritual impurity, but Christ's sacrifice can **cleanse** or purify our **consciences.** We have already seen that "conscience" in Hebrews refers to our true inner selves, our "hearts," our whole person turned toward God. He can cleanse our inner beings from the **acts that lead to** eternal **death** because they separate us from the **living God,** the God who is alive, who involves himself with us, who is the source of all life.

Freed from this impediment of sin we can **serve** this living God! The word translated **serve** is the verb form of the word translated **worshiper** in 9:9. The preacher envisions Christians transformed through the atoning sacrifice of Christ, offering their whole lives as true worship of God.

So, the sacrifice of Christ provides true inner cleansing from both the guilt and power of sin and thus enables us truly to come into God's presence. Christ has provided a *new* and truly *effective* way of approaching God. And that is exactly what a covenant is. It is a God-ordained way in which human beings can approach Him and have fellowship with Him. Thus Christ's sacrifice has established the new covenant Jeremiah predicted (see Jeremiah 31:31-34; quoted in Hebrews 8:7-13). This truth is exactly what Hebrews 9:15 affirms: **For this reason,** because Christ has offered a sacrifice that truly provides inner cleansing (as 9:14 describes), He **is the Mediator of the new covenant,** a new way of approaching God. Because of the effectiveness of Christ's sacrifice He guarantees the effectiveness of this covenant (see commentary on 7:20-22). The phrase **those who are called** refers to all of God's people. Only because God has invited (**called**) us are we able to live for Him now and be with Him in heaven (see 3:1). Through Christ **the promised eternal inheritance,** that "rest" of God (4:1-11), that eternal city (11:10, 13-16; 12:22-24) which God promised Abraham as a gift for his descendents (6:13-20), is actually made available to all God's people. God opens the door both to the faithful who lived before and to the faithful who come after Christ (see commentary on 11:39-40; 12:23).

Christ offered His sacrificial death as **a ransom to set [his people] free** from their sin. The word **sins** in this verse (9:15) is better translated "transgressions" (NKJV; NASB; NRSV). The word "transgressions" describes violations of God's **covenant.** This term refers to violations of the revealed will of God. Those who transgress God's covenant live under His curse (see Deuteronomy 11:26-28). By His death Christ took that curse on himself. Thus He set free those who approach God through Him.

Hebrews 9:15 helps us to clarify the relationship between the old and new covenants. There have been two ways that God ordained for approaching Him: the **first** or "former **covenant** and the "new covenant." The **first covenant** revealed the will of God but did not provide effective deliverance from sin, from the "transgressions" that people committed. It did, however, point forward to the "new covenant," which abundantly provided that needed deliverance. Indeed, the **first covenant**['s] inability to deal with sin made it a clear pointer toward the new covenant.

The people of faith in the Old Testament who lived after Moses (see 11:23-40) may have lived under the **first** or old **covenant,** but they also lived by faith in God's promises. These promises would be fulfilled in the new covenant to which the old looked forward. Because they lived by faith in God's promises, they were accepted by God. However, if we deny the fulfillment of those promises in Christ, then we deny the faith by which they lived. Those who deny the promises live under God's condemnation for the "transgressions" or **sins committed under** and revealed by **the first covenant.**

3. THE OLD COVENANT 9:16-22

Because Christ's death adequately dealt with sin, it established the new covenant. In Hebrews 9:16-22, the preacher confirms the covenant-establishing aspect of Christ's death. He compares the inauguration of the new covenant with the way covenants were established in the Old Testament. Old Testament covenants were always established on the basis of sacrificial death.

It is helpful before going further to discuss two Greek words that are sometimes translated "covenant." The first is *suntheke,* the second, *diatheke.* Ancient writers used *suntheke* to represent an agreement mutually negotiated and agreed on by two or more parties. *Diatheke,* however, described a disposition or potential agreement that one person gave to other people which they could accept or reject but could not negotiate or change. Secular Greek writers often used *suntheke* for covenants or agreements among people. However, the translators of the Greek Old Testament used *diatheke* to portray God's "covenant" with His people. New Testament writers followed the practice of the Greek Old Testament. God's people could reject the covenant He offered them, but they could not negotiate or alter its stipulations. Since, however, *diatheke* referred to a potential contract that one person gave to another, which the recipient could not alter or change, Greek speakers often used it to mean a "will" by which a person disposed of his inheritance. Most English versions translate *diatheke* as **will** (NIV; NRSV) or "testament" (NKJV) in Hebrews 9:16-17, although they translate it as "covenant" everywhere else. However, the New American Standard Bible translates *diatheke* as "covenant" in 9:16-17, as well as in the other places where it is used.

Several scholars have presented a convincing case that *diatheke* should be translated "covenant" throughout these verses.[9] The preacher wrote verses 16 and 17 to show that all Old Testament covenants were established by blood sacrifices. Verses 18 through 22, then, show specifically how the Mosaic **covenant** was established by blood sacrifice.

The sacrifice that inaugurated a covenant in the Old Testament represented the death of the one or ones making the covenant. A sacrificial animal was slaughtered and cut in two. The one making a covenant passed between the halves of the animal, signifying that if he did not keep the covenant he was making, he would die as the animal had died. Genesis 15:7-21 offers the best example of this type of covenant. In the incident that passage describes, Abraham killed the animals and divided them in two, but "a smoking fire pot with a flaming torch" (Gen. 15:17) representing God himself passed between the pieces. By that act, "the Lord made a covenant with Abram" (Gen. 15:18).

In the case of a will, it is necessary to prove the death of the one who made it (Heb. 9:16). The Greek word here translated **to prove** seldom has this meaning elsewhere. It is a passive form of a verb meaning "bear," "carry," or "bring." This word is closely related to another word often used for "bringing" or "offering" a sacrifice. Thus we could translate this sentence, "In the case of a covenant, it is necessary for the death of the one who made it to be offered." A covenant-maker did not literally die, but his death was symbolized by the covenant sacrifice.

Hebrews 9:17 offers a similar meaning. The New International Version reads, **because a will is in force only when somebody has died.** However, in the first century a will was valid as soon as it was signed and could be put into effect by the maker before his death.[10] The Greek original behind **only when somebody has died** is, literally, "on the basis of deaths." This phrase could mean "on the basis of the deaths of sacrificial animals" or "on the basis of sacrifices." We could translate the entire sentence, "Because a covenant is in force only on the basis of sacrifices."

Thus, 9:16-17a could be translated "In the case of a covenant, it is necessary for the death of the one who made it to be offered, because a covenant is in force only on the basis of sacrifices." Verse 17b reads, **it never takes effect while the one who made it is living,** or "it does not take effect until the maker's death has been symbolically enacted by the sacrifice." In the case of Christ, however, the death was not symbolic but real![11]

In 9:18-22, the preacher turns to the Mosaic covenant, that definitive example of a covenant established or inaugurated by blood sacrifice. Since every ancient covenant was ratified by a blood sacrifice, certainly the **first covenant,** which God made at Sinai when He formed His people into a nation, **was not put into effect without blood** (9:18). The double negative strongly states that the Mosaic covenant was put into effect with blood sacrifices.

The preacher's mind immediately turns to Exodus 24:3-8, which records Moses' inaugurating the covenant with blood sacrifices. Hebrews 9:19 gives us the setting: **When Moses had proclaimed every commandment of the law to all the people.** God had given the stipulations of the covenant. The people clearly understood that they were entering into a covenant with God. Moses first "told the people all the Lord's words and laws" (Exod. 24:3), then "wrote down everything the Lord had said" (Exod. 24:4), and finally read the "Book of the Covenant" to the people (Exod. 24:7). The people affirmed their commitment to obey (see Exodus 24:3, 7). Moses sealed the validity of this covenant between God and the people by taking **the blood of** the **calves** that had been sacrificed and sprinkling **the scroll** (the "Book of the Covenant" in which he had written the God-given stipulations of the covenant) and **all the people.** God did not make this covenant in private, just with Moses, or just with the leaders; He offered it to **all the people.** The **scroll,** representing God, and **all the people** were bound together by the blood of the covenant. Exodus 24:3-8 actually says that Moses put the blood on "the altar" and "the people" not "the scroll" and the "people." The "scroll" or "Book of the Covenant" may have been laying on the altar when Moses poured the blood on the altar. The preacher speaks of **the scroll** (Heb. 9:19) because it contained the stipulations of the covenant. By saying that Moses bound the people to **the scroll** with the blood, he emphasizes the need for God's people to obey. The definitive statement with which Moses concluded the establishment of the old covenant shows the importance of blood: **This is the blood of the covenant, which God has commanded you to keep** (9:20). The preacher has slightly paraphrased this statement of Moses found in Exodus 24:8 in a way that does not change its essential meaning but which emphasizes the fact that God gave the stipulations of the covenant. Violation of the covenant meant desecration of the blood by which it was established. In 10:26-31, the preacher shows that apostasy desecrates the sacrifice of Christ.

Exodus 20:3-8 does not say that Moses used **water, scarlet wool and branches of hyssop** (Heb. 9:19) along with blood when he established the old covenant. Nevertheless, the use of these elements elsewhere made it natural to associate them with the blood on this occasion (see Leviticus 14:4-9; Numbers 19:6-10; Psalm 51:7; and John 19:29). By saying that Moses **sprinkled with the blood both the tabernacle and everything used in its ceremonies** (Heb. 9:21), the preacher affirms that the old covenant was carried out as well as inaugurated by blood sacrifices. Although the Old Testament says that the Tabernacle was consecrated by being anointed with oil (see Exodus 40:9-11; Leviticus 8:10-11), the first-century Jewish historian Josephus also refers to the Tabernacle as being purified by blood at its anointing.[12] The Old Testament records blood being used in the consecration of the priests and of various articles of the furniture in the Tabernacle (see Exodus 29:10-12, 15-16, 19-20; Leviticus 8:30).

Hebrews 9:22 generalizes from what the preacher has already said. He has made clear that the old high priest only entered the Most Holy Place with blood (see 9:7), that all covenants were inaugurated with blood sacrifices (9:16-17), and that the Mosaic covenant was inaugurated by blood and carried out by using the blood of sacrifices to bring purification (9:18-21). **In fact, the law**—that is, the old covenant—**requires that nearly everything be cleansed with blood.** The word **nearly** is the preacher's admission that a few things were not purified under the old covenant with blood. But **without the shedding of blood there is** *absolutely* **no forgiveness.** The New Revised Standard Version adds the words "of sins," "no forgiveness of sins," for clarity, but the preacher uses the word **forgiveness** here without qualification. The writer may have stopped short of adding "of sins" because he did not want to imply that the blood of those old-covenant sacrifices could actually bring true, definitive forgiveness of sins. Also, he may have used the Greek word that lies behind the English word **forgiveness** to include more than forgiveness. The New King James Version reads, "there is no remission." There is no "release." Under the new covenant sins are forgiven and people are cleansed from sin. They are enabled to live in victory over sin (see commentary on 4:14-16; 8:7-13; 10:15-18). Sin has been dealt with decisively.

Thus within the Tabernacle ritual, especially the Day of Atonement sacrifice (see 9:1-10), and the inauguration of the old covenant (9:16-21), blood sacrifice was necessary. The preacher argues, by analogy, that only by means of Christ's blood could God inaugurate His new covenant, which offered true cleansing from sin and empowerment to obey Him (9:11-15).

ENDNOTES

[1]The main point behind the description of the earthly sanctuary or **tabernacle . . . set up** by Moses was its possession of a **first room . . . called the Holy Place** (Heb. 9:2) and a **second . . . room called the Most Holy Place** (9:3). God's presence dwelt in **the Most Holy Place.** Various English translations use different words to designate the Tabernacle and its two main sections in these verses. The New International Version's translation expresses the meaning of the preacher clearly, but the New Revised Standard Version is more literal. It may help you to see these two translations in parallel columns:

NEW INTERNATIONAL VERSION	NEW REVISED STANDARD VERSION
9:2—A *tabernacle* **was set up. In its** *first room* **were the lampstand, the table and the consecrated bread; this was called the Holy Place.** 9:3—**Behind the second curtain was a** *room* **called the Most Holy Place.**	9:2—For a *tent* was constructed, the *first one,* in which were the lampstand, the table, and the bread of the Presence; this is called the Holy Place. 9:3—Behind the second curtain was a *tent* called the Holy of Holies.

Note the italicized words. The NIV words **tabernacle . . . first room . . . room** are equivalent to the NRSV's "tent . . . first one . . . tent." The NIV translates the same Greek word as **tabernacle** in 9:2 and as **room** in 9:3. The NRSV translates this word as "tent" in both places. This same Greek word is implied behind the NIV's **first room** and the NRSV's "first one" in 9:2. Thus the writer uses the same word for the whole **tabernacle** *and* for each of its two sections—the first or outer **Holy Place** and the second or inner **Most Holy Place.** Some feel that the preacher was thinking of two different tents. This assumption is unnecessary, for the two are divided by a **curtain** and the writer refers to the whole structure as the **tabernacle** or "tent" at the beginning of 9:2. His mode of expression, however, does emphasize their difference and the separation between them. This separation of the **tabernacle** into two parts is important for the preacher's demonstration of the inadequacy of the old system in 9:6-10.

[2]The New King James Version reads "golden censer" instead of **golden altar of incense.** The few times when the word involved appears in the Greek Old

Testament, it does refer to "censers" and not to the altar of incense. However, it was used by other writers from the time in which Hebrews was written to refer to the golden altar of incense. It certainly refers to that altar in this context. Otherwise the writer of Hebrews omits a very important part of the Tabernacle furnishings.

[3]See the discussion in *A Commentary on the Epistle to the Hebrews* by Philip Edgcombe Hughes (Grand Rapids, Michigan: Wm. B. Eerdmans Publishing Co., 1977), pp. 312–13.

[4]The word the preacher uses here for **tabernacle** is the same word that he uses in 9:2-3 to refer both to the Old Testament Tabernacle as a whole and to each of its parts individually.

[5]See the section in the introduction titled "When Was Hebrews Written?"

[6]See Donald G. Guthrie, *The Letter to the Hebrews,* The Tyndale New Testament Commentaries, ed. Leon Morris (Grand Rapids, Michigan: Wm. B. Eerdmans Publishing Co., 1989), p. 183; Hughes, p. 322, note 71.

[7]William L. Lane, *Hebrews 9–13,* vol. 47b, Word Biblical Commentary, New Testament ed. Ralph P. Martin, gen. eds. David A. Hubbard and Glenn W. Barker (Dallas: Word Books, 1991), p. 225.

[8]The New King James Version and New American Standard Bible read "good things to come." This difference among translations is due to a variation among the Greek manuscripts of Hebrews. The reading that affirms the present reality of these good things, the reading followed by the New International Version, is probably the correct one. If, however, the author wrote "good things to come," he probably meant that they were "to come" from the point of view of the old covenant. He certainly believes that they are a present reality in Christ.

[9]Lane, p. 231.

[10]Ibid.

[11]Thus the preacher's thought flows more smoothly from verse 15 to verse 18 if we understand *diatheke* as "covenant" instead of "will" in verses 16 and 17. Otherwise these verses fit only awkwardly within their context. The translation "will" makes the preacher's argument disjointed and ad hoc.

[12]*The Antiquities of the Jews,* iii. 206.

14

THE NEW HIGH PRIEST'S SACRIFICE: PERFECT OBEDIENCE

Hebrews 9:23–10:18

I n Hebrews 9:23 through 10:18, we come to the third, and greatest, movement in which the preacher explains the significance of the sacrificial death of Jesus. Just as in the first two movements (8:1-13; 9:1-22), the preacher explains the significance of Jesus' sacrifice in the light of the sanctuary or sphere to which it pertains and the covenant it establishes. This movement does much more than summarize the preacher's previous argument. It is his fullest and clearest explanation of the significance of Christ's High Priestly sacrifice. The sections that deal with the sanctuary (9:23-24) and the covenant (10:15-18) are shorter than the parallel sections in the previous movements, though they are not insignificant. The bulk of this passage focuses directly on the sacrificial death (9:25–10:14), expanding and adding to what the preacher has said on these subjects in 9:11-15, the central section of the previous movement.

The central section of this movement, which focuses on Christ's sacrifice, can also be divided into three parts: 9:25–10:4; 10:5-10; and 10:11-14. (See the chart below, and compare the earlier chart, "Sanctuary, Sacrifice, and Covenant in Hebrews 8:1–10:18," from the introduction to part 3 of the commentary.) The second of these three parts, 10:5-10, is the heart of this entire movement and the key to a clear understanding of all the preacher says about Christ's sacrificial death. We might think of 9:25

through 10:14 as a sandwich: 9:25–10:4 and 10:11-14 are the bread; 10:5-10 is the meat between the bread.

The top piece of bread, 9:25 through 10:4, picks up the theme of the once-for-all character of the sacrifice of Christ from 9:12. The bottom piece of bread, 10:11-14, explains the significance of the fact that Christ "sat down" at the right hand of God after offering His sacrifice. Both of

Movement 3: Christ's Perfect Obedience
Hebrews 9:23–10:18

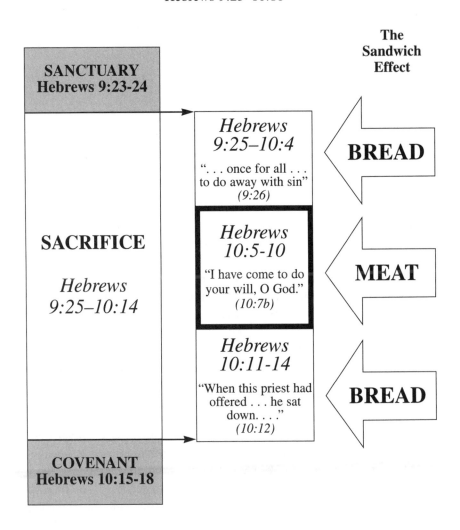

these themes are based on Psalm 110:1, alluded to in Hebrews 1:3 and 8:1, and quoted in 1:13. The sandwich effect of 9:25–10:4 and 10:11-14 is enhanced by the fact that the author moves from new to old in 9:25 through 10:4, and then from old to new in 10:11-14. Christ entered once-for-all (9:25-28), but the old priests entered continually (10:1-4). The old priests stood (10:11), but Christ "has sat down" (10:12-14).

The second part (10:5-10), which is sandwiched between or framed by the other two, expands the explanation of Christ's sacrifice presented in the last movement: In 9:14, the preacher said that Christ "offered himself unblemished to God"; in 10:5-10, we learn that offering "himself" means that He offered His entire human life culminating in His death. This offering was "unblemished" because throughout this life He was completely obedient to the Father's **will** (10:7, 9-10). The fact that His sacrifice was once-for-all and that He "sat down" at the Father's right hand may offer *evidence* that His sacrifice was effective, but the *reason* behind its effectiveness was Christ's complete obedience to the Father's will! Christ's obedience is the "meat" of the preacher's argument.

1. A SANCTUARY THAT IS HEAVEN ITSELF 9:23-24

The heavenly sanctuary into which Christ has entered required a sacrifice of a different order from the sacrifice necessary for the earthly sanctuary. The writer of Hebrews has shown that **it was necessary** (9:23) for **the copies of the heavenly things,** the earthly Tabernacle and its rituals described in 9:1-10, **to be purified** with those blood **sacrifices** described in 9:16-22, especially verse 21. The Tabernacle and its rituals were only **copies.** The New Revised Standard Version reads, "sketches." The original word admits a correspondence between the earthly and the heavenly, but the preacher uses it here to emphasize the inferiority of the earthly. Thus the **heavenly things themselves,** the true reality, obviously required **better sacrifices.** The preacher uses the plural, **sacrifices,** because he is following the pattern he set earlier in the verse, when he spoke of **these sacrifices,** the ones that purified the earthly **copies.** **Better sacrifices** refers to the once-for-all single sacrifice of Christ, which is of a different order, of a different dimension, than the animal sacrifices that pertained to the earthly copy.

It may seem odd for the preacher to say that **the heavenly things** must be **purified.** It is easy to understand how our consciences need to be purified or cleansed (9:14), but why should heaven need purification? The preacher is merely making a comparison, drawing an analogy, with the old covenant. In 9:21, he said that Moses sprinkled the Tabernacle and all the things used in it with blood when he established it and then immediately, in 9:22, he said that nearly everything related to the old covenant was "cleansed" with blood. The word translated "cleansed" in 9:22 is the same translated **purified** here. He is probably using that word here in the sense of "inaugurate" or "establish for use." Just as Moses' inauguration of the old Tabernacle involved blood purification, so the inauguration of the heavenly sanctuary is spoken of as purification by Christ's blood. Yet there may be another reason why the preacher says that **the heavenly things** must be **purified.** This way of speaking reminds us that our sin is a barrier between us and God. Entrance to God's presence in heaven was blocked by the pollution of our sins.

Hebrews 9:24 strengthens the assertion of 9:23 that **better sacrifices** were necessary for **the heavenly things** by clarifying what those **heavenly things** are. Remember that the earthly Tabernacle was **man-made,** its parts constructed by skilled craftsmen and assembled by Moses. The adjective **man-made** implies a contrast with a sanctuary directly established by God and sustained by His power. The **man-made sanctuary** was not a false sanctuary, but it was **only a copy** of the **true** sanctuary that God himself established. The author now clearly states the identity of this God-made sanctuary: It is **heaven itself.** The preacher uses the word **heaven** here for the place of the very presence of God. By entering this sanctuary Christ has appeared **in God's presence** on our behalf, in order to enable our entrance. The words **enter** and **appear** set the stage for the discussion of Christ's once-for-all entrance in the next section, 9:25 through 10:4.

2. "ONCE FOR ALL . . . TO DO AWAY WITH SIN"[1] 9:25–10:4

Hebrews 9:23-24 has spoken about Christ's entering God's presence in heaven after He offered His sacrifice. This is the appearance implied by Psalm 110:1, "sit at my right hand." Hebrews 9:25-26 focuses on another "appearance" of Christ, His "appearance" on earth to offer that adequate sacrifice for humanity's sin. Verses 27 and 28 describe a third "appearance," Christ's second coming when He will bring the full blessings of salvation to the faithful.

In 9:25-26, the preacher focuses on the "once-for-all" definitive character of Christ's earthly sacrifice. Verses 23 and 24 imply the "once-for-all" character of this sacrifice as they describe Christ's leaving earth (never to be sacrificed again) to "appear" in God's presence.

The preacher, however, has added a reference (9:27-28) to the subsequent "appearance" of Christ at His second coming for several reasons. First, although Christ's coming to earth the first time was "once-for-all" in that it dealt completely and definitively with the human sin problem, it did not preclude Christ's second coming to bring final salvation to the faithful. The preacher does not want his hearers to think he is denying Christ's second coming by his emphasis on the "once-for-all" character of the first. Second, his reminder of Christ's second coming offers his hearers implicit encouragement to remain faithful in order to receive the promised blessing.

The reference to Christ's second coming in 9:27-28 also completes the analogy with the Aaronic high priest on the Day of Atonement. On that day, the high priest first offered sacrifice (see Leviticus 16:15). This offering was the equivalent of Christ's coming to earth and offering himself once-for-all (Hebrews 9:25-26). Then the high priest entered the earthly Most Holy Place (Leviticus 16:15), the equivalent of Christ's entering God's presence in heaven for us (Hebrews 9:23-24). Finally, the high priest returned to the waiting people (Leviticus 16:17), the equivalent of Christ's second coming with the fullness of the promised blessings for God's own (Hebrews 9:27-28).[2]

The definitiveness of Christ's sacrifice by which He entered heaven is demonstrated by the fact that it was not repeated.[3] Thus He was not like the Aaronic **high priest** who did offer sacrifices every year before he could enter **the** earthly **Most Holy Place.** We are reminded that the Aaronic high priest was limited because he came with blood **not his own.** His own blood was not worthy to be offered because of his sin.

Hebrews 9:26 makes it clear how ridiculous it would be for Christ to repeatedly sacrifice himself. It is historical fact that He suffered and died only once. If He had had to offer repeated sacrifices then He **would have had to suffer many times since the creation of the world.** By contrast, He **appeared** on earth as a human being **once for all . . . to do away with sin.** The phrase **to do away with sin** is a strong expression. The Revised English Bible translates this phrase "to abolish sin." Christ's work includes grace for forgiveness, true heart cleansing, and empowerment to live in victory over temptation. This appearance came **at the end** or the "consummation" (NASB) **of the ages.** Although occurring in the middle of our earth's history, the Incarnation was the climax and the high point that completed God's plan to deliver people from sin and bring them into His own presence. Christ's appearance **once for all . . . to do away with sin** clarifies the meaning of God's earlier revelation and makes clear the true nature of God's promised eternal blessings. Christ's work offers the basis for the full experience of life in God's presence which will be ours at His return.

This definitive removal of sin is accomplished by nothing other than **the sacrifice of himself** (9:26). Contrast what was said of the Aaronic high priest in 9:25, "with blood that is not his own." The preacher further clarifies the significance of this phrase (**the sacrifice of himself**) in 10:5-10.

Hebrews 9:27 describes human experience, human need. Verse 28 shows how Christ's sacrifice for sin at His first coming and the completion of **salvation** at His second correspond to that human need.

Verse 27 reminds us of the human predicament described in 2:14-18. According to those verses, human beings are sinful and therefore afraid of death because it leads to judgment for their sins. Here (9:27) the preacher picks up those themes, saying that all human beings are inevitably **destined to die once.** After death they all **face** God's **judgment** for their sins. There is no reason to think that the preacher is limiting this judgment to a judgment that immediately follows death. Whatever judgment immediately follows death, his primary focus is on what happens at Christ's return, as 9:28 shows. This is the final judgment which he describes in 12:25-29.

Christ's experience mirrors and remedies this human predicament. Human beings die once. Likewise Christ died once. Human beings face judgment for sin. Christ removes that problem. Hear the preacher: **Christ was sacrificed once to take away** or "bear" (NASB; NKJV; REB; NRSV) **the sins of many people,** literally, "of many" (NASB; NKJV; NRSV). This expression does not mean that some are necessarily excluded from Christ's atonement regardless of what they do. The preacher wrote the word "many" to contrast with the "once" of the sacrifice. The sacrifice was "once," but its effectiveness was multiple; it was effective for "the many." The Revised English Bible brings out the preacher's intent by translating **many people** or "the many" as "mankind." Christ "bore" the curse of the covenant that fell on those who "transgressed" the covenant. He took on himself the judgment that was due us as sinners who have violated God's covenant.

Thus, when **he will appear a second time** He will not have "to deal with sin" (NRSV) because He has already provided the only adequate sin sacrifice. We **who are waiting for him** in faithful obedience (see commentary on 10:35-39) will receive **salvation** rather than condemnation at the "judgment." This **salvation** is "final salvation." It is the fullness of the "rest" that God's people now experience (see 4:1-11).

We already participate in the fellowship of the heavenly city (12:22-24), but we will then enter into it in the final and fullest way (12:25-29).

The fact that Christ has offered His sacrifice "once-for-all" demonstrates that it has completely, finally, and definitively dealt with the human sin problem (9:25-28). In 10:1-3, the preacher brings this truth into even clearer focus. Here he shows the significance of the repetition of the old sacrifices. This repetition demonstrates their ineffectiveness in dealing with sin and points to the need for the sacrifice of Christ.

Hebrews 9:23 showed that the "earthly things" pertaining to the old priesthood were only "copies" or "sketches" (NRSV) of the heavenly realities. The "man-made" earthly Tabernacle was only a "copy" of the "true" sanctuary, "heaven itself" (9:24). In 10:1 the preacher repeats and reinforces this same pattern of thought. **The law** (a term broadly describing the old covenant) was **only a shadow** of the **good things** that did not come until Christ brought in the new covenant. With the phrase **good things,** the preacher may have been hinting at the way the Old Testament writers described the blessings of the Promised Land (see Exodus 3:8; Numbers 14:7; Deuteronomy 1:25). Here it refers to the blessings of the heavenly promised land (see Hebrews 11:13-16), **the realities** of Christ's atoning work and the cleansing and fellowship with God that come from it.

Because the old covenant (**the law**) was **only a shadow,** a witness to the true reality, it could **never** by repeated annual **sacrifices** make **perfect** those who approached God. The preacher uses the word **perfect** in a special way.[4] He does not mean that God makes human beings absolutely perfect in any sense. By **made perfect,** he means that God's people are cleansed from sin within, given a new heart that knows and obeys God's law, and thus enabled by God to live in obedience. Those old repeated **sacrifices** could never truly help people forward. Their repetition proves they could not. If they could have, they would **have stopped being offered** (10:2). If they had been truly effective, those who worshiped God on the basis of these sacrifices **would have been cleansed** from sin. The perfect tense of the Greek verb translated **have been cleansed** denotes entering into *and remaining in* a state of being cleansed. They would have been cleansed of sin in such a way that they would have been able to remain in that cleansing and so not needed another sacrifice. Thus they **would no longer have felt guilty for their sins.** It might be more accurate to say that they would no longer have had any "consciousness" (NKJV; NASB; NRSV) or "sense" (REB) of sin. More than guilt is involved. They would have been free from the guilt *and* the pollution and power of sin. God's grace would have freed them from sin to live for God, victorious over temptation.

But obviously the repetition of the sacrifices showed that God's Old Testament people did have a continuing "consciousness" of sin. They did continue to feel guilty and to sense the power of sin in their lives. What did their sacrifices accomplish? They served as **an annual reminder of sins** (10:3) and thus pointed to the coming sacrifice of Christ which would effectively deal with sin. In this way they were a "shadow" of Christ's sacrifice to come. Paul argued that the demand of the moral law exposed human sin (see Romans 7:7-12). Hebrews approaches the issue from another direction: The repeated sacrifices of the ceremonial law remind God's people that human beings are sinful unless they have been cleansed through Christ's sacrifice.

The statement **because it is impossible for the blood of bulls and goats to take away sins** (Heb. 10:4) forms a transition. It bridges the discussion of the repetitive old sacrifices (see 10:1-3) and the description of why Christ's sacrifice is effective in the key central section of 10:5-10.

The New International Version links 10:4 too closely with 10:3. The New American Standard Bible, New Revised Standard Version, and New King James Version all put a period, instead of a comma, after 10:3. Verse 4 does not give the reason why the old sacrifices were "an annual reminder of sin" (10:3). It tells why they could "never . . . make perfect those who draw near to worship" (10:2). The repetition of those sacrifices was the symptom, not the disease. It demonstrated their impotency, but did not cause it. Why could they not cleanse from sin? The problem was in the quality of the sacrifices themselves; they were merely **the blood of bulls and goats.** How could animal blood **take away** human **sin?** There's no way that such blood could really cleanse human hearts of sin and enable people to live above temptation.

In 9:11-14, the preacher demonstrated the qualitative difference in Christ's sacrifice by comparing Christ's "own blood" (9:12), the blood of Him "who through the eternal Spirit offered himself unblemished to God" (9:14), with the blood of animal sacrifices. In 10:5-10, the preacher shows clearly the significance of the phrases: Christ's "own blood" and "through the eternal Spirit offered himself unblemished to God." The preacher does not contrast the chemical constituency of Christ's blood verses that of animal blood. No, he focuses on the complete, intentional obedience of the Son, obedience that came from the Son's heart. The preacher contrasts the shed blood of animals (see 10:4) with the obedience of Christ (10:5-10).

3. "HERE I AM, I HAVE COME TO DO YOUR WILL"[5] 10:5-10

Hebrews 9:25 through 10:4 and 10:11 through 10:14 are the bread of the sandwich, but 10:5-10 is the meat. These verses are the "meat" of the preacher's argument because they show us why Christ's sacrifice is superior. They are the key to understanding the significance of "the blood of Christ" (9:14). The "blood of Christ" represents the complete obedience of Christ in becoming human, living an obedient human life, and dying for sin. It is this complete obedience that makes His sacrifice different from any other. What enabled His obedience? He offered himself "through the eternal Spirit" (9:14). That is, He could be perfectly obedient only because He was the Son of God. No mere human being ever did or could obey as He did. His effective sacrifice of obedience required both His full deity and His full humanity. The former was the power, the latter the occasion, for that obedience. Now, however, He makes available to us this power to be obedient and overcome temptation (see 2:17-18; 4:14-16).

Psalm 40:6-8 helped the preacher to understand the relationship between animal sacrifices and obedience. He finds these verses appropriate as the declaration of the Son of God at the time He became a human being: **when Christ came into the world** (Heb. 10:5) could be translated "as Christ was coming into the world." Within this context, the words **I have come** (from Psalm 40:7, quoted in Hebrews 10:7) have become a reference to the Incarnation. The preacher quotes Psalm 40:6-8 in Hebrews 10:5-7 as a declaration of Christ's obedience. In Hebrews 10:8-9a, he indicates the parts of the quotation he feels most important. In 10:9b, he interprets the quotation, and in 10:10 applies its significance to his hearers.

We turn our attention first to the quotation of Psalm 40:6-8 in Hebrews 10:5-7. **Therefore** (10:5) links this quotation to 10:4. Because the blood of animal sacrifices was ineffective, Christ declared (in the words of Psalm 40:6-8) that God wanted and Christ himself provided obedience instead of those sacrifices.

The way in which the preacher has quoted the words of Psalm 40:6-8 differs in several ways from that passage in our English Old Testaments. Some of these differences occur because he used a Greek translation of the Old Testament instead of the Hebrew text from which our Old Testaments are translated. Some differences may come from the preacher's quoting the psalm from memory and paraphrasing its words. None of the differences alter the basic meaning and impact of the psalm, though some of them do facilitate the preacher's use of it in this context.

The most obvious difference appears in the second line of the quotation (see Hebrews 10:5): **but a body you prepared for me.** A comparison of the New International Version and New King James Version translations of the Hebrew original behind Psalm 40:6 shows that scholars disagree even about that original: "But my ears you have pierced" (NIV); "My ears you have opened" (NKJV). The marginal reading of the New Revised Standard Version gives us a literal rendering of the Hebrew text and helps us to understand this divergence in interpretation: "ears you have dug for me." Does "dug" signify the piercing of the lobe or the opening of the ear so that one can hear, and obey? Probably the latter. It is difficult to see what significance piercing the ear lobe would have. "My ears you have opened" makes much better sense. The New Revised Standard Version follows this same line of interpretation: "But you have given me an open ear." God gave the psalmist an "open ear" to understand God's will and to obey it. The psalmist understands that God wants obedience, not sacrifice, and so the psalmist "hears and obeys."

Those who translated this psalm into Greek also struggled with the meaning of "ears you have dug for me." They took "ears" as a figure of speech in which a part of something represents the whole. (We do the same thing in English when we say that we need new "wheels." We mean that we need a new car. The part of the car has been used for the whole.) Thus they translated this line, "but a body you prepared for me." If the words "My ears you have opened" signified the psalmist's ready obedience, the "body" God prepared for him probably signified the means of obedience, the means of doing the will of God. The writer of Hebrews could still have used this psalm if the Greek translation of the psalm had read "ears you have opened for me." Hebrews says much about hearing and obeying the word of God. Yet the use of the term **body** facilitates his application of the psalm. He quotes it to portray Christ's taking on a human **body** in which to live a life of obedience.

Hebrews 10:6 reads, **with . . . you were not pleased,** while Psalm 40:6 says, "you did not require." To say that God was not **pleased** with the sacrifices is a stronger statement than saying He did not "require" them. In one sense God did require them, for in the law of Moses He commanded that they be offered (see 10:8).

Finally, in the last line of 10:7, **I have come** is joined closely with **to do your will, O God.** Psalm 40:7-8 reads, "I have come . . . I desire to do your will, O my God," thus separating "I have come" from direct connection with "to do your will, O my God." The preacher himself probably made this paraphrase. He brought **I have come** and **to do your will** together by ending the quotation before the Greek word for "I desire," which comes last in the Greek sentence. This paraphrase does not change the meaning but makes clearer the connection between the **I have come** of Christ's becoming a human being and the purpose of that coming: **to do** God's **will.**

Let us take one more look at the last line of this quotation. The NIV of Psalm 40:8 reads, "I desire to do your will, O my God"; Hebrews 10:7 reads, **I have come to do your will, O God.** The preacher has omitted the word "my" before **God,** but this omission is not our main concern.[6] He has rearranged the words of 10:7 in a way not shown by the NIV. A literal translation of the preacher's arrangement of this verse in Greek would be, "I have come to do, O God, your will." The preacher emphasizes the **will** of God by putting it at the end of the sentence. This is His main point. Christ came to do God's **will.** The preacher's interpretation of Psalm 40:6-8 in Hebrews 10:8-10 makes this main point clear.

In 10:8-9a, the preacher highlights portions of the quotation with which he wants to work. He first gathers together the four expressions used in the first and third lines of the quotation to describe the sacrifices: **Sacrifices and offerings, burnt offerings and sin offerings.** By bringing these terms together, he makes one powerful and comprehensive description of the Old Testament sacrifices. Then he brings together from the same lines the terms used to show God's rejection of these sacrifices: **you did not desire, nor were you pleased with them.** Through this psalm, Christ completely rejects the Old Testament sacrifices as the means of pleasing God or gaining access to His presence.

The preacher is still careful to state that **the law required** these sacrifices **to be made** (10:8). He says this because it is true, but it also has theological significance. He has explained God's purpose for these sacrifices. They did not "please" Him because they did not cleanse from sin and bring people into God's presence. Nevertheless, they gave a picture of the sacrifice of God's Son which would "please" God by effectively accomplishing these purposes. As we have seen, their very inadequacy pointed forward to His sacrifice (see commentary on 10:4 above).

The preacher next cites, in 10:9, the elements from Psalm 40:7-8 by which Christ affirms His obedience: the words **Here I am** (see Psalm 40:7, cited above in Hebrews 10:7) and a shortened form of the quotation's final words: **I have come to do your will** (see Psalm 40:8, cited above in Hebrews 10:7). The omission of **O [my] God** from the quotation's final words puts an even stronger emphasis on **your will.** Christ's fulfilling of God's **will** is the reason His sacrifice does what the animal sacrifices of the old covenant could not.

The preacher introduces the quotation in 10:9 with a verb in the Greek perfect tense, translated **he said.** The perfect tense of the verb emphasizes the fact that what Christ has said here possesses continuing validity. Christ our High Priest continues to be the One who can help us be victorious because He has done the **will** of God.

The preacher has shown the direction of his thought by the way in which he has selected and arranged materials from Psalm 40:6-8. Only one interpretive comment is necessary: **He sets aside the first to establish the second** (Heb. 10:9b). The words **sets aside** denote the removal of **the first. The first** refers to the animals sacrificed and to everything associated with them—the Tabernacle in which they were sacrificed, the priesthood that sacrificed them, and the first covenant under which they were offered. In 10:8b, the preacher stated that these sacrifices were **required** by the Mosaic **law,** the ineffective old covenant. If they were set aside, then the whole system that pertained to them was also removed (see 7:11-14).

The first system, however, was removed only so that **the second** could be established. **The second** refers, first of all, to the **will** of God fulfilled by Christ. Christ established the **will** of God by doing it and thus by enabling others to do it. His doing the **will** of God served as the effective sacrifice which atoned for sin. Through His obedience, he established the new covenant characterized by forgiveness of and cleansing from sin. He put into effect God's will that His people be cleansed from sin, be empowered to obey, and have access into His presence. His obedience establishes a covenant that enables God's people to obey.

Hebrews 10:10 makes this truth clear by applying what has been said to the readers and to all of us who are Christians. By Christ's doing **that will** of God, **we** Christians **have been made holy,** forgiven, cleansed, and be empowered to obey. It is only those who have thus **been made holy** who can come into the presence of and have intimate fellowship with the living God. The preacher clarifies the **will** of God which Christ has done in the last clause of 10:10: **through the sacrifice of the body of Jesus Christ once for all.** Here it is Christ's **body** rather than His blood that is mentioned. This is the **body** He assumed when He became human ("a body you prepared for me" [10:5]). It was in this **body** that He lived as a human being on earth. The preacher further emphasizes Christ's earthly life by using the name **Jesus,** a name the preacher employs when he wants to refer to the concrete human existence of the Son of God on earth (see commentary on 4:14). It was in this **body** that He practiced complete and perfect obedience to the **will** of God. Thus His sacrifice consists in His entire human life of obedience climaxing in His obedient death. It was this obedience that effected a sacrifice that was **once for all.**

According to 9:25 through 10:3, the once-for-all character of Christ's sacrifice demonstrated its effectiveness. In 10:5-10, however, the preacher does more than give evidence that Christ's sacrifice is effective. He gives the reason for its effectiveness. Christ's sacrifice was of a different quality: It was not the blood of dumb animals but the perfectly obedient human life of the Son of God climaxing in His obedient death. His life of obedience is the sacrifice that enables us to live obediently. How wonderfully appropriate!

Thus we can see how Christ's sacrifice consecrated Him to His heavenly High Priesthood. His perfect obedience has made Him the heavenly High Priest who is able truly to meet our need.

4. "HE SAT DOWN AT THE RIGHT HAND OF GOD" 10:11-14

In Hebrews 10:11-13, the preacher gives further evidence that proves the effectiveness of Christ's sacrifice: Christ "sat down" at God's right hand. This evidence comes directly from Psalm 110:1, quoted in Hebrews 1:13.

Use of Psalm 110:1 takes us back to the beginning of Hebrews in 1:3 and to the beginning of this great section on Christ's sacrifice in 8:1. As we have seen, the preacher bases his understanding of Christ's High Priesthood on Psalm 10:1-4 (see commentary on 5:5-6; 6:20; 7:1-10; and 8:1). This High Priest can meet our needs because He has "sat down" at God's right hand (4:14-16; 7:26-28). He has "sat down" there because He is the Son of God who has offered the only sacrifice of obedience which does away with sin.

Remember, Hebrews 9:25 through 10:14 is a sandwich: 9:25 through 10:4 is the top piece of bread; 10:5-10, the meat; 10:11-14 the bottom piece of bread. The preacher's argument in this bottom piece of bread (10:11-14) takes the form of a contrast between Christ and the old priests just as it did in the top piece of bread (9:25–10:4). In the top piece of bread, the preacher first gave a positive assessment of Christ's once-for-all sacrifice (9:25-28), then a negative assessment of the old high priests' repetitive sacrifice (10:1-4). In this bottom piece of bread, the negative assessment of the old priests (10:11) precedes the positive assessment of

Christ (10:12-14). The first piece of bread contrasted Christ's once-for-all sacrifice with the repetitive old covenant sacrifices. This second piece contrasts Christ's sitting at God's right hand (after offering His sacrifice) with the old priests' standing. Both pieces of bread give evidence of the effectiveness of Christ's sacrifice.

At first, 10:11 looks merely like a review and intensification of what the preacher already said about the repetitive nature of the old sacrifices in 10:1-3. In those verses he considered the repeated annual sacrifice of the high priest on the Day of Atonement. In this verse he looks not only at the high priest but **every priest.** He pictures not just "every year" but **day after day** and **again and again.** Priests continually perform their **religious duties** (described in 9:6 as mere "ritual duties" [NRSV]), outward ceremonial rites. They continually repeat the **same** sacrifices to no effect. These sacrifices, no matter how many times they are offered, cannot definitively deal with **sins.**

Hebrews 10:11, however, introduces a new element in this comparison: every day the Aaronic priest **stands** while he performs his duties. To stand in the presence of a king, and especially of God, was an honor. The Levites had been chosen to "stand" before God (see Deuteronomy 10:8; 18:5). But remember what the preacher has said about Christ, quoting Psalm 110:1. In comparison to Christ, the fact that the priests continue to stand demonstrates the ineffectiveness of their priesthood. For when this new **priest,** Christ, **had offered for all time** the **one sacrifice for sins** (10:12) described above, **he sat down. For all time** is the same phrase that is translated "forever" at the end of 7:3. The New King James Version here translates that phrase by the word "forever." Christ's sacrifice is valid for all time and eternity.

His sitting down demonstrated the once-for-all character of His sacrifice because He does not have to get up to offer it again. But it has even greater significance when we observe where **he sat down—at the right hand of God.** In 1:3 and 8:1, the preacher has substituted "the Majesty in heaven" or "the throne of the Majesty in heaven" for the word "God" in order to emphasize God's greatness and thus the greatness of Christ's position at God's right hand. Here he focuses on clarity: Christ is **at the right hand of God** and of no other. His sacrifice is complete because He has **sat down** in the greatest place of authority in the universe, and beyond! Remember, Christ by no means usurped this position. Psalm 110:1 proves that God the Father invited Christ to receive this honor.

Hebrews 10:13 alludes to the rest of Psalm 110:1—"until I make your enemies a footstool for your feet"—and develops the significance of those words. The preacher quoted Psalm 110:1 in Hebrews 1:13. His exposition of Psalm 8:4-6 in Hebrews 2:5-9 has shown that Christ's **enemies** will become a **footstool** for His feet at the Second Coming. At that time, His "enemies," those who have rejected Him, will be judged. The preacher here repeats this truth to complete the thought of 10:12 and also to emphasize that Christ is not presently engaged in sacrificial ministry. His "sitting" at the Father's right hand continues until that time when **his enemies** have become **his footstool.** He presently **waits** for that time, just as His faithful followers eagerly await His return to bring them into the full blessings of "salvation" (9:28).

Hebrews 4:14-16 describes Christ's activity during this period of waiting. He is interceding for us. He is giving us help in our time of trial or temptation. The fact that He sits at God's right hand reminds believers that His present intercessory ministry does not involve getting down on His knees to beg. The Father and the Son are together in ministering grace to God's faithful people.

Hebrews 10:14 brings this section on the effectiveness of Christ's sacrifice to a grand climax by showing how it applies to us, God's faithful people. He is no longer engaged in sacrificial ministry **because by one sacrifice he has made perfect forever those who are** continually **being made holy.** Christ has become "perfect" as our Savior by offering His sacrifice (see commentary on 2:9-10; 5:9; 7:28). Thus by that same sacrifice He has **made** us **perfect forever.**[8] He has provided for us to be cleansed from sin, live in obedience, and have access to God's presence. He has done this finally and definitively. **Forever** denotes the eternal quality of this provision. But only **those who are** continually **being made holy** experience this provision.[9] God's people whom Christ has cleansed from sin and given the power to obey are already holy. Yet there is a sense in which they are still **being made holy.** They must continually and regularly appropriate the grace of God available in Christ to live in holiness. "Holiness" is not something I possess, it is something I live by the grace of God. The preacher offers his final affirmation of the work of Christ (see 10:11-14) as a great incentive to continue in God's grace.

5. A COVENANT THAT DELIVERS FROM SIN 10:15-18

In Hebrews 8:7-13, the preacher quoted the new covenant prophecy found in Jeremiah 31:31-34 to show that the very prophecy of another covenant, especially a "new" covenant, meant the old covenant was obsolete. In Hebrews 10:15-18, he quotes selected verses from that same prophecy to show the quality of the new covenant. The quality of this covenant shows that no further sacrifice is necessary. Under this covenant, sin has been definitively dealt with. Obviously, then, no further sacrifice for sin is either appropriate or necessary.

Hebrews 10:15 introduces a biblical quotation as a word from God relevant for today. The **Holy Spirit** who inspired Jeremiah **testifies** to us today through the word He inspired Jeremiah to write. The Spirit **testifies** to the finality of Christ's sacrifice because it effectively deals with sin (10:14).

The preacher cites two selections from Jeremiah 31:31-34. In Hebrews 10:16, he introduces a citation from Jeremiah 31:33 (already quoted in Hebrews 8:10) with the words, **First he says.** Then in Hebrews 10:17, the preacher cites the last part of Jeremiah 31:34 (quoted in Hebrews 8:12) with the phrase, **Then he adds.** The preacher relates these quotations to Christ's sacrifice in Hebrews 10:18.

The quotation from Jeremiah 31:33 in Hebrews 10:16 emphasizes the change that God's grace makes in the human heart. When the preacher first cited this verse in 8:10, he followed the Old Testament wording: "This is the covenant I will make with the house of Israel." Now he paraphrases, **This is the covenant I will make with** *them* (my emphasis). The preacher believes there is *one* people of God made up of those who were faithful to God's promises, whether they lived before or after Christ. This paraphrase is the preacher's way of emphasizing that the new covenant promise is for all the people who live by faith in God and His promise, rather than for those who are merely physical descendants of Abraham. Indeed, outside of biblical quotation, he does not use words like "Israel" or "Judah" to describe God's people before Christ came.

So, the first two lines quoted in 10:16 show that the new covenant promise is for God's people of faith today. The next two lines begin to describe the quality of the new covenant: **I will put my laws in their hearts, and I will write them on their minds.**[10] Here is a description of the way God deals with sin in the human heart. These two statements reinforce and supplement one another. The terms **heart** and **mind** reinforce each other and show that the entire inner being of the human person is conformed to the will of God. God transforms the thoughts, emotions, and actions of the will. He enables people to know, desire, and do His law. Thus He has overcome the problem with the old covenant. Hebrews 3:7-19 made clear that the problem under that covenant was the problem of a rebellious heart. "The law written on the heart is . . . the 'law' of willing obedience that Christ embodied and that serves as a model for Christians."[11]

The further quotation from Jeremiah 31:34 in Hebrews 10:17 shows how God views our sins now that we live under the new covenant: **Their sins and lawless acts I** [God] **will remember no more.** The preacher has again done a bit of paraphrasing by adding the words **lawless acts** to this quotation. Here he focuses on sin that is intentional, indeed rebellious, that goes against God's "law." The preacher could have used the other word for "sin" that occurred in Jeremiah: "wickedness" (NIV) or "iniquity" (NKJV), the word he used in Hebrews 8:12. However, **lawless acts** fits well with what has been said in 10:16. God will put His **laws** in their hearts and minds. He will no longer remember the **lawless acts** that they used to practice before they had His laws in their hearts.

I will remember no more is a very strong statement (10:17). If God himself will never remember them, never take them into consideration, they have no more validity. In the sacrifice of Christ God himself has taken the punishment for the breaches of covenant made by His people. No one should separate this provision from the words of 10:16. God forgets the sins of those whose hearts are being conformed to His will and who therefore practice faithful obedience. This is why the preacher often exhorts his hearers to remain faithful.

Hebrews 10:18 relates the quality of the new covenant to the effectiveness of Christ's sacrifice as described above. **And where these have been forgiven.** Every word is important. **Where** refers to the new covenant based on the sacrifice of Christ; and **these,** to the "sins and lawless acts" of 10:17.

"Where forgiveness of these is" would more literally translate the preacher's original words. That phrasing shows that the preacher has emphasized the Greek word translated "forgiveness."

Although this Greek word is often translated "forgiveness," it probably has a broader meaning in this context. The New King James Version translates it by "remission." Although this "forgiveness," "remission," or "release" is primarily related to God's no longer remembering sin (as described in 10:17), it also includes His bringing the human heart into conformity to His will (as described in 10:16). Since under the new covenant Christ has dealt with sin decisively and definitively, **there is no longer any sacrifice for sin** that is being offered or needs to be offered. Christ's sacrifice, which the preacher has been discussing since 8:1, is completely sufficient and final.

ENDNOTES

[1]Hebrews 9:26

[2]In the book of Sirach (a book in the Apocrypha [the fourteen or fifteen books (or parts of books) that were considered by some to have been written during the time between the Old and New Testaments] written by Ben Sirach; also called Ecclesiasticus, or the Wisdom of Jesus the Son of Sirach) we find a description of the return of high priest Simon the Just from offering the sacrifice on the Day of Atonement: "How glorious he was, surrounded by the people, as he came out of the house of the curtain" (NRSV). Sirach was written in the second century B.C. It is somewhat similar to the Old Testament book of Proverbs.

[3]The New International Version translators have added the words **did he enter heaven** at the beginning of 9:25 to clarify the meaning of the passage. There is no equivalent in the Greek text. This addition, however, is confusing because it implies that entrance came before offering. The New Revised Standard Version is clearer: "Nor was it to offer himself again and again."

[4]See commentary on 2:9-10; 5:8-9; 7:28; 10:14.

[5]Hebrews 10:9a

[6]Both the Hebrew original and the Greek translation of Psalm 40:8 read, "O my God." "My" is the last word of the sentence in Greek. The preacher omitted it by ending his quotation before the Greek word for "my."

[7]Hebrews 10:12b

[8]For Hebrews' special use of the word "perfect," see commentary on 10:1.

[9]"The writer locates the decisive purging of believers in the past with respect to its accomplishment and in the present with respect to its enjoyment" (William L. Lane, *Hebrews 9–13,* vol. 47b, Word Biblical Commentary, New Testament ed. Ralph P. Martin, gen. eds. David A. Hubbard and Glenn W. Barker [Dallas: Word Books, 1991], p. 267).

[10]The Old Testament order is reflected in Hebrews 8:10: "I will put my laws in their minds and write them on their hearts." The reversal of the words "minds" and "hearts" in 10:16 does not appear to have any interpretive significance.

[11]Harold W. Attridge, *The Epistle to the Hebrews,* Hermeneia—A Critical and Historical Commentary on the Bible, ed. Helmut Koester (Philadelphia: Fortress Press, 1989), p. 281.

15

LIVE IN THE POWER OF THE HEAVENLY HIGH PRIEST

Hebrews 10:19-31

The preacher introduced his exposition of Christ's High Priesthood by exhorting his hearers to live in its benefits (see Hebrews 4:14-16). In 5:1-10, he gave a preview of his argument. In 5:11 through 6:20, he urged his hearers to greater spiritual depth so that they could receive and benefit from his deeper exposition of the truth of Christ's High Priesthood. In 7:1 through 10:18, the preacher explained the significance of Christ's being our High Priest. He explained Christ's call to High Priesthood (see 7:1-28), and He discussed the sanctuary in which this High Priest ministers, the covenant which He mediates, and especially the effective sacrifice for sin which He has offered (8:1–10:18).

Now, in 10:19-31, he applies what he has said about Christ's High Priesthood (see 4:14–10:18) to Christian living. In 10:19-25, he urges his hearers to make use of the benefits provided by the Christian's High Priest. In 10:26-31, he warns against the consequences of rejecting those benefits. Finally, in 10:32-39 he encourages his hearers by affirming their faithfulness and prepares them for further exhortations to faith and endurance (see 11:1–12:29).

There are certain parallels between 10:19-39 and 5:11 through 6:12. In 5:11 through 6:12, the preacher encouraged his hearers to receive the deeper knowledge of Christ's High Priesthood. In 10:19-39, he urges them to act on the basis of that deeper knowledge which he has now explained to them. Hebrews 5:11-14 parallels 10:19-25; 6:1-8 parallels

10:26-31; and 6:9-12 parallels 10:32-39. In 5:11-14, he urged them to be spiritually alert and to receive this teaching; in 6:1-8, he warned them of the consequences if they did not; and in 6:9-12, he affirmed his confidence in them that they would. In 10:19-25, he urges his hearers to enter into the benefits of Christ's High Priesthood now described; in 10:26-31, he warns them of the grave danger if they reject these benefits which he has now explained; and in 10:32-39, he again expresses confidence that they will respond in faith and obedience.

In 10:19-39, the preacher speaks more intensely (as compared to 5:11–6:12) because he has now explained the great privileges Christ's High Priesthood offers. The preacher follows up both passages (5:11–6:12 and 10:19-39) with examples of faithfulness. Hebrews 6:13-20 describes the faithfulness of Abraham and climaxes in 6:19-20 with Christ's entering behind the veil. Hebrews 11:1-40 gives many examples of faith which lead up to Christ's entrance into heaven in 12:1-3. Hebrews 10:32-39 introduces these examples of faith in 11:1-40 and therefore will be considered in the next chapter of this commentary.

1. LIVE IN THE PRIVILEGES OUR HIGH PRIEST HAS PROVIDED 10:19-25

Hebrews 10:19-25 reminds us of the way the preacher introduced the section on Christ's High Priesthood in 4:14-16. Both passages begin by describing the privileges that **we have** (10:19) and then explain what we should do to take advantage of those privileges.[1] From beginning to end the preacher expresses his urgent concern that his hearers enter into the grace their High Priest makes available. He wants them to live lives that demonstrate an appropriate response to that grace.

Hebrews 10:19-21 summarizes the privileges that **we** as Christians **have** through Christ's High Priesthood (as it is described in 4:14–10:18). Hebrews 10:22-25 explains what we should do with these privileges. The phrase **we have** (10:19) is in the present tense. Christ makes these privileges continually available in the present. He makes them available to those who are **brothers** and sisters (3:1, 12) because they are His brothers and sisters (2:11-12) and children of God (2:10), part of His household (3:1-6), and beloved (6:9: "dear friends"). Hebrews 10:19-20 describes the first privilege, **confidence to enter the Most Holy Place;** and 10:21 describes the second, having **a great priest.**

The fact that Christ has cleansed us from sin gives us **confidence to enter the** heavenly and true **Most Holy Place** (10:19). This is the language of worship. We can come into the very presence of the living God! The word translated **confidence** refers to more than a feeling. We might translate it "the right" or, better yet, "authorization" to enter God's presence. Of those two, "authorization" speaks most clearly. We usually think of "rights" as something we have in ourselves, but we receive "authorization" from someone else.

What makes us "authorized personnel," authorized to enter into God's presence? **The blood of Jesus.** The preacher has explained (10:5-10) that the phrase **the blood of Jesus** is a symbolic way of describing Christ's completely obedient human life, culminating in His obedient death as a sacrifice for us. We must not, however, miss the power of this descriptive term. Christ's obedience took Him all the way to the shedding of His blood. His sacrifice has taken care of sin and authorized our entrance into God's presence. The translation of the New International Version, **by a new and living way opened for us** (10:20), is misleading. Note the New Revised Standard Version: "by the new and living way that he opened for us." He has **opened a new and living way** for us to enter. This way is **new** or fresh—that is, new in quality—and it is **living.** The word **living** reminds us of a number of passages in Hebrews which refer to the Son's eternity (see 7:8, 16, 25; 9:14). God (10:31) and God's word (4:12) are also "living." Here the word **living** means that the power of the eternally living God has opened this **way.** Thus, this way works; it actually brings people to God.

Christ opened this way for us **through the curtain.** Hebrews 9:3 reminded us that a curtain separated the Holy Place of the Tabernacle from the Most Holy Place where God, in some sense, dwelled. That curtain served as a barrier to keep people from the presence of God. By analogy, 6:19-20 described Christ as passing behind the "curtain" into the "inner sanctuary," the heaven where God dwells. Thus, when the preacher says in 10:20 that Christ "opened [the new and living way] for us through the curtain" (NRSV) it appears to mean that He has broken through the barrier and opened the door for us. The way is truly open.

However, the rest of the verse seems to identify **his body** with **the curtain.** Commentators have found it very difficult to make sense out of this identification. Christ's **body** was certainly not the barrier between us and God. Some have suggested that instead of understanding **the curtain** as a barrier, we should understand it as the point of entrance. Christ's **body** was the point of entrance into heaven. It is possible, however, to translate the NIV phrase **that is, his body** in another way: "that is, *by* *means of* His body." By this alternate translation, Christ's **body** is seen as the means of His breaking through the barrier into God's presence. The phrase **his body** would then be parallel to the earlier phrase **the blood of Jesus** (10:19). Both would refer to His sacrifice.[2] The word the New International Version translates **body** is usually translated "flesh" (see NASB; NKJV; NRSV). No word better describes the frailty of the humanity which the Son of God assumed than "flesh" (see commentary on 2:14; see also 5:7). By means of offering His true humanity in obedience to God, He has breached the barrier and enabled our entrance into the presence of God.

Hebrews 10:21 describes the second benefit that is ours. **We have a great priest** who is now in heaven ministering grace to us every day (see 4:14-16). **Great priest** is a literal translation of the Hebrew words that we usually translate as "high priest."[3] The preacher uses the word **great** to emphasize the greatness of the High Priest he has just described in 7:1 through 10:18. This High Priest is greater than any priest ever has been or will be. This High Priest is **over the house** or household **of God.** (And we are that house [see 3:6].) We Christians are His people whom He represents, His family. The blessings He provides are for us.

Christ's sacrifice was the key that established both these blessings. Because His sacrifice truly cleanses from sin, we are authorized to enter God's presence (see 10:19-20). Because His sacrifice was a sacrifice of complete obedience, He has become our **great priest** who ministers daily grace to us from the Father's right hand. He has opened the way to God, and He is in God's presence to enable us to enter by that way. Since we are His household, the exhortations that follow apply to us!

Because of these great benefits, there are three things that we should do: the preacher describes the first and most fundamental in 10:22; the second, in 10:23; and the third in 10:24. Verse 25 expands the instructions given in verse 24. The first of these exhortations encourages us, among other things, to faith; the second, to hope; and the third, to love. The preacher subsequently expounds these themes: faith in 11:1-40; and endurance because of hope in 12:1-29. Chapter 13 has much to say about love.

Once we receive authorization to come into God's presence, what is our most obvious foundational response? Hebrews 10:22 answers that question: **Let us draw near to God.** This phrase is a picture of worship. The writer of Hebrews describes the Christian life as the true worship of God. Everything else that God's faithful people do is based on their drawing near to Him. By drawing near to Him they leave all that is sinful and unholy. Their thanksgiving, praise, and acts of love are the "sacrifices" that they bring when they draw near (see commentary on 13:1-17). The most important thing the faithful do is to enter God's presence!

The two great images the preacher uses to explain what Christ has done for us describe access to God's presence: entrance into the promised land (heavenly "city," "rest"; 4:1-11; 11:8-10, 13-16; 12:22-24) and entrance into the most holy place (4:14–10:18). Both the promised land and the most holy place represent life in the presence of the living God. The preacher's emphasis on Christ's High Priesthood makes "entrance into the most holy place" the dominant image of the two, thus reinforcing the imagery of worship. Underlying everything else we do, we as Christians approach God through Christ in prayer and worship.

The rest of 10:22 describes how we carry out this worship. We come **with a sincere** or "true" (NKJV) **heart.** This is the kind of heart God produces through the new covenant (see Jeremiah 31:31-34, quoted in Hebrews 8:8-12). The **sincere heart** is tuned to God; it is "true" to Him, ready to obey Him. This heart is the exact opposite of the hardened and rebellious hearts evidenced by the Old Testament wilderness generation (see Hebrews 3:7-19). The phrase **in full assurance of faith** describes an attitude of complete trust in the reality of God and the provision that He has made in Christ. We trust neither in ourselves nor in any sacrifice other than Christ's.

The next two phrases in 10:22 describe the inward and outward holiness that enable this approach to God. **Having our hearts sprinkled to cleanse us from a guilty conscience** means that we have allowed Christ to cleanse our inner beings of sin. We enter God's presence in that cleansed state. Literally translated, the phrase **guilty conscience** is "evil conscience" (NASB). Christ cleanses our inner selves from the guilt and power of sin. He gives us an inclination to obey God. The phrase **having our bodies washed with pure water** may refer to baptism, but it also indicates that we have allowed Christ to clean up the outside of our lives, the actions that flow from our hearts. Thus it is clear that we approach God only through the atoning sacrifice of Jesus. Just as the Aaronic high priest had to be ritually clean in order to enter the earthly Most Holy Place, so Christians must be truly holy through Christ in order to live this life of worship toward God.

The second exhortation follows from the first. We must persevere in that true worship based on trust in God and empowered by Christ's sacrifice: **Let us hold unswervingly to the hope we profess** (10:23; see 4:14). We receive the power to follow this exhortation by obeying the previous exhortation to draw near to God.

Consider the New American Standard Bible translation of this statement: "Let us hold fast the confession of our hope." What is "our **hope**"? The ultimate salvation God has for us, that final entrance into His presence. We have made a "confession" that this ultimate salvation is what we are seeking. We must "hold" that confession, or that profession of faith in God's final reward **unswervingly,** "without wavering" (NASB). "Keep your eye on the prize, hold on!"

We can be sure that the salvation for which we hope will become a reality because *God* guarantees it. He has **promised** it and He is absolutely **faithful.** We can depend on Him without question. Nothing less than the faithfulness of God guarantees that those who endure to the end will receive the "hope" God has prepared for them.

The first two exhortations (**Draw near! Hold unswervingly!**) have related to God and His promises. The third relates to our brothers and sisters in Christ. As we have seen, the first two deal with faith and hope. The third, and longest, deals with love. Throughout this sermon, the preacher does not deal with love for others as much as he does with our approaching God in faith and keeping on until we receive the hope God has promised us. Nevertheless, this love is very important. In Hebrews 13, the preacher describes love as the sacrifice proper to Christian worship (13:16). Faith and hope are barren without the sacrifice of love.

Let us consider how we may spur one another on toward love and good deeds (10:24). **Let us consider** means that we are to give attention to this matter. We are to seek to understand others and the best ways to encourage them to such **love and good deeds.** The New King James Version reads "stir up" rather than **spur . . . on.** The Greek term behind **spur . . . on** has the same connotation as the English phrase "stir up." Ancient writers usually used it for stirring up people in the wrong way, for irritating or angering. Some people are good at just "stirring others up." Christians should practice the same zeal in stirring up people to **love!** This **love** expresses itself in **good** or appropriate **deeds.** These **deeds** meet the needs of and bless those who receive them.

Hebrews 10:25 offers specific examples of how Christians should love each other. First of all, their love keeps them from giving **up meeting together** for worship, encouragement, and Christian fellowship. Some of the preacher's first hearers appear to have developed a **habit** of not participating in the church gatherings. Such a habit is a breach of love. Meeting times provide a context for the most important kind of mutual care: **let us encourage one another.**

The New King James Version uses the word "exhorting" rather than **let us encourage.** The Greek word in question has a wide range of meaning which includes encouragement, instruction, exhortation, and even warning. The preacher is speaking of encouragement in the Christian life: encouragement to draw near to God and to hold on to our hope, encouragement to love one another. Encouragement for those who are falling away or growing lax takes the form of exhortation or warning! By means of this very sermon-letter, the preacher is seeking to encourage his friends. In fact, he calls his letter a "word of exhortation" or a "word of encouragement" (13:22).

The urgency of this mutual concern and encouragement is intensified by the fact that **the Day** of judgment, of Christ's return, is **approaching.** The preacher has already spoken of the judgment and of Christ's return in 9:27-28. He shows the importance of this to them by concluding the main body of his sermon with a warning about the final judgment (12:25-29). Our hope of salvation is real. So is the judgment for those who disobey (see 2:1-4).

This final note of coming judgment makes a smooth transition to the next section of exhortation which warns us of the possibility of ultimate loss.

2. WE ARE ALL THE MORE ACCOUNTABLE BECAUSE WE HAVE RECEIVED THESE PRIVILEGES 10:26-31

In Hebrews 10:19-25, the preacher urged his hearers to put into practice the privileges they have received through Christ's High Priesthood and sacrifice. In 10:26-31, he warns against rejecting those privileges by persisting in deliberate sin. The "if" statement in 10:26a affirms the possibility of such sin. Verses 26b through 27 describe its consequences, first in terms of blessing lost (10:26b), then in terms of punishment gained (10:27). Verses 28 and 29 intensify the severity of this punishment by comparing it with the punishment for violators of the old covenant. If their punishment was severe, how much more serious will be the punishment of those who violate the new? Verse 30 adds support to the paragraph by citing Scripture. Verse 31 concludes this section with a solemn warning.

In 10:26a, the preacher uses two short words to describe the sin of apostasy as a possibility for his Christian hearers: **If we.** If apostasy were impossible for the believer, the preacher would have no reason to discuss it at all.

Apostasy is the total and complete rejection of God. The preacher gives three characteristics of this sin. First, this sin occurs **after we have received**

the knowledge of the truth. This knowledge includes factual knowledge about Christ grasped by the intellect. The preacher, however, is talking about a knowledge that goes beyond the merely intellectual. He describes a knowing that involves experiencing the **truth** about Jesus Christ.

Those who first received the book of Hebrews had certainly experienced this **truth** at their conversion (2:1-4). However, the preacher has now exposed them to an even deeper understanding of **the knowledge of the truth** by instructing them in the significance of Christ's High Priesthood. Thus the warnings they receive here are more intense than the warnings of 6:1-8. In 6:1-8, the preacher was warning them against refusing to receive a deeper **knowledge of the truth.** Here he warns them lest they reject the truth they have received. Apostasy is the rejection of experienced truth.

Secondly, the preacher is not talking about an unintentional failure to keep some regulation. The first word of this verse in Greek is the word translated **deliberately.** He is addressing the deliberate rejection of the clearly known will of God. The refusal of the wilderness generation to enter the Promised Land offers a prime example of this kind of deliberate action (see 3:7-19).

Finally, this apostasy is the result of persistent sin: **keep on sinning.** The wilderness generation's refusal to enter the Promised Land was the climax of a series of disobedient acts. Deliberate, enlightened persistence in sin leads to apostasy, to being cut off from Christ and the salvation He provides.

The preacher describes the consequences of this sin by the awesome phrase: **no sacrifice for sins is left** (10:26). The implications of this statement are momentous in the light of all he has said about Christ's High Priesthood and sacrifice. The old sacrifices did not cleanse from sin. It is no use to turn back to them now. They merely reminded us of sin. They all served to point toward Christ's effective **sacrifice.** Only His sacrifice brings true cleansing and access to God. Those who practice conscious, deliberate, persistent sin will be cut off from the only **sacrifice** that can bring them into God's presence!

Hebrews 10:27 describes what *is* **left** for those who have rejected Christ's sacrifice. Instead of access to God and joy in His presence (see 12:22-24) they have **a fearful expectation of judgment.** Indeed, the first word in the Greek text of this verse is the word translated **fearful.** Without the sacrifice of Christ the future offers no "hope" (10:23), only dread! Their **judgment** involves condemnation, the punishment they will receive from God. The preacher paints a terrifying picture of this judgment: **raging fire that will consume the enemies of God.** We are reminded of the judgment on Korah and his followers in Numbers 16:35 and 26:10. Note also such Scriptures as Isaiah 26:11 and Zephaniah 1:18. Those who apostatize from Christ have put themselves in the category of **the enemies of God.** They will receive the awful consequences due the opponents of God.

In Hebrews 7:1 through 10:18, the preacher has shown how much greater the new covenant is than the old. It only stands to reason, then, that the punishment for violating the new would be greater. In 10:28, he describes the punishment of those who **rejected** the old covenant; in 10:29, the correspondingly much more severe punishment of those who turn away from Christ.

The preacher calls the old covenant **the law of Moses.** He is thinking especially of the **law** which prescribed death for the one who **rejected** God's covenant (see Deuteronomy 17:2-6). The word translated **rejected** means "to set aside, annul." It is often used to describe those who rejected God or His law (see Mark 7:9; Luke 10:16; John 12:48; 1 Thessalonians 4:8; compare Ezekiel 22:26). The preacher is not referring to people who experienced failures or mistakes, but to those who definitively set aside or rejected the law as a whole. The primary sin in the Old Testament which put one outside the bounds of the covenant was idolatry. Deuteronomy 13:6-10 and 17:2-7 show clearly that people who thus rejected God by practicing idolatry were to die **without mercy.** There was no reprieve. The law offered only one restriction: the certainty of the offense had to be substantiated **on the testimony of two or three witnesses.**

The Mosaic law was only a shadow and copy. Yet those who set it aside deserved death. **How much more severely do you think a man deserves to be punished** who has violated that shadow's reality—the new covenant? With the words **do you think** the writer appeals to his hearers to form their own conclusion. It is as if he said, "I've shown you how much greater the new covenant is than the old. In light of that superiority, how much worse could you imagine the punishment would be for rejecting that new covenant?"

The New King James Version translation of this statement helps us understand the preacher's emphasis: "Of how much worse punishment, do you suppose, will he be thought worthy?" This "punishment" will be "worse" not in degree but in kind. Under the Mosaic law people suffered physical death. Those who reject Christ's sacrifice will suffer eternal separation from God (see Hebrews 10:27). They "will be thought worthy" of this punishment by none other than God himself! There will be no judge to whom they can appeal; no two or three witnesses will be necessary.

The last part of 10:29 describes the person who has turned away from Christ and persisted in deliberate sin in the face of the truth. This verse offers a threefold picture of those who reject Christ. They have **trampled the Son of God under foot; treated as an unholy thing the blood of the covenant that sanctified** them; and **insulted the Spirit of grace.** By persisting in deliberate sin and rejection of Christ, despite a real experienced knowledge of the truth, a person does all three of these things. Thus this description shows the tragedy and horror of such rejection.

The first two of these statements relate directly to this sermon's two main themes. The first statement is built on the preacher's teaching about the **Son of God,** the second on His teaching about Christ as our High Priest.

In the first part of Hebrews, especially 1:1 through 4:13, the preacher has shown that the **Son of God** is God's final and complete revelation of himself (see especially 1:1-3). Those who have **trampled the Son of God under foot** have intentionally and persistently rejected this final revelation of God. The expression **trampled . . . under foot** strongly expresses rejection and disdain, both in Greek and English. It implies a repeated trampling, a complete and definitive rejection. Those who have rejected this revelation have no other source from which they can hear the word of God!

In the great central section of Hebrews, 4:14 through 10:18, the preacher has shown that the Son is our High Priest who has provided **the blood of the covenant** through which we are **sanctified.** He, and He alone, has made a way for us to be cleansed of sin and to come into God's presence. But, the one who perseveres in persistent rejection and disobedience has **treated** this precious **blood** of Christ which makes us holy as if it were **unholy,** profane, "a common thing" (NKJV). There is a sharp contrast between **sanctified** and **unholy.** To think of referring to **the blood . . . that sanctified** as **unholy** would have shocked the preacher's original hearers. There is no other way into God's presence but through this blood that he has rejected.

The preacher does not speak of the Holy Spirit as much as some other New Testament writers. Nevertheless, he shares the New Testament conviction that through the work of Christ the Holy Spirit indwells both individual Christians and the church. The Spirit purifies believers and empowers them for service. Through the work of Christ the Holy Spirit is

the Spirit of grace (10:29). He is the agent through whom God ministers His grace to our hearts and lives. Those who persist in deliberate disobedience in the face of the grace they have experienced through the Holy Spirit grossly **insult** Him. The climax of this description of apostasy is this picture of insulting the gracious Holy Spirit.

Persistent, willful, knowing disobedience does all of this! Apostates have deliberately chosen to (1) reject Christ, (2) abandon the people of God, and (3) return to the world from which the blood of Christ had separated them. "In their lives the sacred has been collapsed into the profane."[4]

Hebrews 10:30 introduces scriptural support for God's judgment on the apostate. God himself is the One **who said, "It is mine to avenge; I will repay," and again, "The Lord will judge his people."** The first of these quotations comes from Deuteronomy 32:35, the second from 32:36.

The point of these quotations is, first of all, simply that God does judge wickedness. He is the judge. Thus He certainly judges those who turn away from Him in deliberate, persistent disobedience, those who treat as nothing the great provision He has made for their salvation.

The preacher may also have been thinking of the significance of these quotations within their Old Testament context. The first quotation describes God's judging the nations because of their idolatry. This might imply that believers who turn away from Christ in apostasy become no more than idolatrous pagans. The preacher may have included the second quotation because it specifically mentions **his people.** God judges those who have been His and apostatized, but He vindicates His faithful people. These citations reinforce the awesomeness of God's judgment on those who deliberately and persistently reject the grace they have experienced.

Hebrews 10:31 concludes this section of warning on a most solemn note. The word translated **dreadful** is the same word translated "fearful" in 10:27. Just as in 10:27, it appears first in the Greek sentence. Verse 31 portrays an even greater sense of dread than verse 27, for the preacher has now described the enormity of apostasy (see 10:29) and the awesomeness of God as judge (10:30).

Under the old covenant (10:28) "two or three witnesses" were responsible to initiate the punishment of execution. Here (10:31) it is **the living God** himself who executes sentence. We have seen above that the quotations from Deuteronomy 32:35-36 came from a context describing God as judging the nations and His own people for idolatry. Within that context He refers to himself as the God who lives forever (see Deuteronomy 32:40). He is not like the idols. He lives. He is active in the affairs of human beings.

With the foreboding phrase, **To fall into the hands of,** the preacher indicates the complete helplessness of the apostate before God. The apostate is totally at the disposal of the one and only true and living God whom he has rejected! The preacher concludes this warning by impressing on his readers the holiness and awesome majesty of this One who is the living God!

The preacher did not give this warning to trouble the person with sensitive conscience. Those who are concerned about their spiritual state have not turned away in apostasy. As we have seen, this apostasy results from the deliberate, persistent, open, public practice of sin, despite a thorough knowledge of God's grace and in the teeth of the warnings of Scripture. The preacher gives this warning to goad us on to faithfulness, not to depress us. He does not want us to have a compulsive preoccupation with an analysis of our own feelings. He reminds us of the treasure we have by bidding us consider the magnitude of its loss.

The preacher has not implied that his readers have apostatized. If they had, there would have been no point in his warning. The "we" of 10:26 tactfully implies the possibility of their falling away. However, from verse 28 on he has been speaking impersonally of the person who apostatized under the law of Moses and the person who does the same under the new covenant.

In the concluding section of this exhortation, 10:32-39, the preacher reassures his hearers by referring to their previous faithful conduct and directs their attention to the examples of faithfulness and endurance coming in Hebrews 11. Thus 10:32-39 forms a transition between the preacher's discussion of Christ's High Priesthood (and its consequences) and these wonderful examples of faith and endurance. The preacher, however, does not forget what he has said about Christ's High Priesthood. He makes statements which assume this knowledge at crucial points, such as 11:39-40; 12:1-3, 18-24; and 13:7-16. We consider 10:32-39 at the beginning of the next section.

ENDNOTES

[1] See also 6:19; 8:1; 13:10.

[2] William L. Lane, *Hebrews 9–13,* vol. 47b, Word Biblical Commentary, New Testament ed. Ralph P. Martin, gen. eds. David A. Hubbard and Glenn W. Barker (Dallas: Word Books, 1991), p. 275j.

[3] See the discussion at 4:14.

[4] Lane, p. 295.

Part Four

THE PILGRIMAGE PICTURE: HOLD FIRMLY TO YOUR FAITH UNTIL YOU ENTER THE HEAVENLY HOMELAND

Hebrews 10:32–12:13

We have seen that there is one people of God throughout history. God called that people into being by revealing himself and inviting them to be His own. God's people are those who by faith inherit the promise of Abraham (see Hebrews 6:13-20). God spoke on Sinai and formed them into a people (see commentary on 1:1–2:4). God's eternal rest has always been their appointed goal (4:1-11). It was to that people, "Abraham's descendants" (2:16), that the Son of God came with God's final revelation of himself. He is the High Priest of this "house" of God (3:1-6). Through His effective sacrifice, He cleanses God's people from sin, enabling them truly to enter the presence of God and thus achieve their God-designated goal (see 7:1–10:31).

In Hebrews 10:32 through 12:29, the preacher gives us a spiritual history of this people of God. In part 4 he uses the Pilgrimage Picture to paint their history from the past to the present (10:32–12:13). In part 5, he uses the Sinai Picture to carry us from the present to the future (12:14-29). The first half focuses on the need for faith and endurance in order to receive eternal reward. The second clarifies the wonderful privileges God's people now enjoy and looks ahead to future judgment.

The preacher does not write this history because he is interested in ancient times. He uses it to show us how to live as God's people today. Hebrews 10:32-39 is the introduction to this history. This introduction is an invitation for his original hearers, and for all who will obey God's voice, to take their place in the history of the glorious and faithful people of God!

16

TAKE YOUR PLACE AMONG THE PEOPLE OF GOD

Hebrews 10:32-39

The preacher's description of his readers' past faithfulness under suffering (see Hebrews 10:32-34) reminds them that they have been and are a part of God's faithful people. In 10:35, he urges them to continue in this way of life. In 10:36-39, he strengthens this exhortation by quoting Habakkuk 2:3-4. This key verse introduces the main themes of the history of the people of God: faith (Hebrews 10:38a, citing Habakkuk 2:4b), perseverance or endurance (Hebrews 10:38b, citing Habakkuk 2:4a), and final judgment (Hebrews 10:37, citing Habakkuk 2:3b). In Hebrews 11:1 through 12:29, the preacher spells out these themes in greater detail. Faith is the theme of 11:1-40, endurance of 12:1-24, and final judgment of 12:25-29.

We can divide this large historical block the following way. Hebrews 11:1-40 describes the people of God in the past. The people of God who have gone before show us what it means to live the life of faith. The coming of Christ in Hebrews 12:1-3 is the transition point from past to present. Christ has brought God's people the privileges of cleansing from sin and access to God. These privileges enable us to experience God's presence and to endure suffering. In Hebrews 12:4-13 the preacher urges his readers to endure their present sufferings. In 12:14-24, he reminds them of the wonderful privileges God's people now enjoy through Christ their High Priest. Finally, in Hebrews 12:25-29, the preacher turns to the future. The final judgment is coming. It will bring God's faithful people to their anticipated goal.

We now turn to a more detailed consideration of 10:32-39. The preacher has warned of the dire consequences of rejecting the great salvation Christ has brought (10:26-31). He does not, however, believe that his hearers have rejected this salvation. In 10:32-35, he encourages them by reminding them of their past faithfulness. He asks them to **remember** their **earlier days** (10:32), the days right after they had **received the light**—that is, after their conversion. At that time, when they were new Christians, they **stood their ground,** they "endured" (NASB) a **great contest.** The preacher pictures them persevering in a great athletic event. He is fond of using the race (12:1-3) or the boxing match (12:12-13) as an example of Christian endurance.

They endured despite the fact that they had to face **suffering.** He describes this suffering in the two statements of 10:33 and the first two of 10:34. The first and fourth statements describe the suffering they experienced personally; the second and third, their identification with others who suffered. Verse 33's New International Version translation **sometimes . . . at other times** is a bit weak. Those words seem to imply that the two types of suffering did not overlap. The "partly . . . and partly" of the New American Standard Bible and New King James Version are more accurate. At the same time they both suffered and identified with others who were suffering for their faith. They were publicly put to shame by both verbal **insult** and actual physical **persecution.** They also **stood side by side** others who were so treated. By associating with others receiving mistreatment for Christ, they only increased the chances that they too would be abused.

Hebrews 10:34 states specifically how these first recipients of Hebrews **stood** by (10:33) other suffering Christians and how they suffered persecution themselves. First, they **sympathized with those in prison** for their faith. The word **sympathized** implies much more than merely *feeling* compassion.[1] These Christians acted concretely to help those in prison. Government authorities did little to supply the necessities of prisoners in the first century. The Christians to whom Hebrews was addressed helped their imprisoned fellow believers by bringing them food and supplying their other needs, as well as by visiting and encouraging them.

These Christians also suffered themselves through the **confiscation** of their **property,** perhaps as part of their being banished from their homeland. As noted in this commentary's introduction, this confiscation and banishment might have occurred when the Roman emperor Claudius banished the Jews from Rome. Christian Jews may have been the prime target of this persecution. However, the preacher has mentioned confiscation of property for a special reason. They **joyfully accepted** this confiscation of their **property** because they **knew that** they had **better and lasting possessions** that could not be taken from them if they persevered in faith. The New International Version translation masks the fact that the word **property** is plural but the word for **possessions** is singular. They willingly gave up earthly "possessions," plural, because they anticipated a **better and lasting** "possession," singular. The New Revised Standard Version contrasts the earthly "possessions" that they lost with "something better and more lasting" that they possessed.

The words **better and lasting** are significant. As we have seen, "better" pertains to the things of the new covenant, sanctuary, and sacrifice (see 7:22; 8:6; 9:23). Their "better" possession includes cleansing from sin, present intimacy with God, and especially the assurance of future heavenly fellowship with Him in the "enduring city" (13:14) that God has prepared for His people.[2] These blessings are **lasting** and eternal in quality. The essence of faith is to live for this heavenly reality instead of for earthly possessions and pleasures. This is the kind of faith that Abraham and the others listed in Hebrews 11:1-40 enjoyed. This is the kind of faith that bears the fruit of obedience and endures until the end. In 10:32-34, the preacher goes beyond saying that his hearers did reasonably well after they were converted. They showed the very faith he is urging upon them! They themselves are the first example that he gives them to emulate. The preacher will spend the next two chapters urging his hearers to continue in this kind of faith.

He begins this exhortation in 10:35-36. He supports this exhortation by quoting Habakkuk's prophecy of judgment in Hebrews 10:37, and concludes this section with a word of encouragement in 10:38. His hearers must not **throw away** this **confidence** that they have. Their **confidence** was more than a feeling (see commentary on 10:19). They have "authorization." Through the sacrifice and High Priesthood of Christ they have been cleansed from sin and thus "authorized" to come into God's presence. The preacher says, "Do not throw away what Christ has done for you!" **It will be richly rewarded.** Note the New American Standard Bible, "which has a great reward." This "great reward" that God has prepared is the **better and lasting** possession to which reference has already been made. It refers especially to that eternal fellowship with God that is the climax of the journey of faith.

Verse 36 makes clear one thing that is necessary to maintain this "confidence" and receive this "great reward"—**You need to persevere.** Perseverance is the theme that will be developed in 12:1-13.

Perseverance means doing **the will of God** according to the example of and through the power made available by Jesus (12:1-3), who has accomplished our redemption by doing God's will (10:9-10). Only by "keeping on keeping on" can they receive the **better and lasting** possession that God has **promised.**

In 10:37, the preacher introduces Habakkuk 2:3-4 to warn his hearers of the consequences if they fail to persevere. The prophet knew that the time until God's judgment would be, from the eternal perspective, **just a very little while.**[3] **He who is coming will come and will not delay.** Habakkuk looked forward to God or His Messiah coming to deliver the righteous and judge the wicked. The preacher urges his readers to endure until Jesus' certain return. He **will not delay** beyond God's appointed time. The preacher will discuss this time of judgment in 12:25-29.

My righteous one (10:38) is the person who pleases God. This person endures, continuing to do the will of God until Christ returns. He is able to endure because he **will live by faith.** Habakkuk lived by faith. He kept trusting God, even though he faced persecution, because he believed in God's power and in His promise that He would vindicate His own. So the preacher wants his hearers to live by this kind of **faith.** It is this kind of faith that will enable them to "live," to have eternal life, to experience the ultimate "saving of the soul" (10:39 NKJV). He wants them to continue to depend on God's power for the help they need in the certainty that God will keep His promises of future reward.

That power has been made effective and those promises verified by the work of Christ. Nevertheless, this faith is the kind of faith that God's people have always had, as 11:1-40 will show. This faith will enable the preacher's hearers, who live after Christ's High Priestly work, to endure suffering (see 12:1-13). Those who do not endure **shrink back** (10:38). By this phrase the writer again refers to apostasy. The one who does not endure in faith and **shrinks back,** as Esau did (12:14-17), will have to endure God's displeasure at the judgment (discussed in 12:25-29). Indeed, that person will be **destroyed** (10:39).

The preacher portrays a clear contrast between faithfulness that leads to life and unfaithfulness that leads to destruction. He bases this contrast on his understanding of the continuity between the old covenant and the new covenant, of which Christ is the Mediator (see 8:6) and the Guarantor (7:22). Both covenants are based on God's absolute faithfulness. Both lay down clear options that lead to life or death. But under the new covenant the stakes are much higher, because the greater privileges available through Christ mean greater responsibility.

The author returns to the hearer's own situation in 10:39 by affirming that **we are not of those who shrink back** in apostasy and are thus eternally **destroyed** at God's judgment, **but of those who believe and are saved.** Thus he both affirms his reader's faith and introduces his models of faith (see 11:1-40) as a means of informing and strengthening that faith.

ENDNOTES

[1]See commentary on 4:15 where the same word is used of Jesus.

[2]The same Greek word is translated **lasting** in this verse and "enduring" in 13:14.

[3]The preacher has paraphrased the quotation from Habakkuk. In his most significant adaptation, he reverses the two sentences in Hebrews 10:38. Habakkuk has the clause "And if he shrinks back, I will not be pleased with him" before "but my righteous one will live by faith." The arrangement in Hebrews makes it clear that the one to whom "if he shrinks back" refers is the "righteous one" who will live by faith. In Habakkuk, the one who "shrinks back" could be understood as the one "who is coming" and "will not delay." Despite these sequence changes, the preacher uses the Habakkuk quotation in a way that is faithful to the prophet's original intention. Habakkuk does not understand why the wicked are prospering and oppressing the righteous. He is told to patiently wait, to endure, because God will surely come in judgment and set things right. In Hebrews, too, the preacher addresses the quotation to a situation in which the wicked are persecuting the righteous. The righteous are told to have endurance, not to give up, because they will receive an eternal reward at the judgment soon to come. While both writers deal with the situation of persecution which will be set right in coming judgment, Habakkuk's emphasizes theodicy, the justification of God's action. The preacher encourages his hearers to endure and not to turn away from faith to apostasy.

17

FOLLOW THE EXAMPLE OF THE FAITHFUL BEFORE YOU

Hebrews 11:1-40

Hebrews 11:1-40 describes the history of God's faithful people from creation up until the coming of Jesus. By means of this description the author demonstrates the nature of that faith by which, according to Habakkuk 2:4 quoted in Hebrews 10:38a, the just will obtain eternal life. The preacher knows his hearers share this faith (see Hebrews 10:39). He urgently wants them to persevere in it.

Hebrews 11 is usually divided into two major sections, verses 1 through 31 and verses 32 through 40. The first section's examples of faith all begin with **by faith.** These verses cover the history of God's faithful from the creation (11:3) and from Abel, the first example (11:4), to the conquest, the fall of Jericho, and the faith of Rahab (11:30-31).

Hebrews 11:1-31 falls into three subsections: verses 1 through 7, 8 through 22, and 23 through 31. Each of these subsections gives examples of faith from a different Old Testament era. Verses 1 through 7 give examples from the very beginning of the world (described in Genesis 1-11); verses 8 through 22, from the period of Abraham and the patriarchs (see Genesis 12–50); and verses 23 through 31, from the period of Moses up through the conquest (recorded in the books that run from Exodus through Joshua).

1. THE FOUNDATIONS OF FAITH 11:1-7

The first subsection (11:1-7) makes it clear that faith is living life in light of the reality of God and in the assurance that He fulfills His promises. This kind of faith is necessary to **please God** (11:6).

Just as the early chapters of Genesis lay down the basic pattern of relationships between God, humanity, and the world, so 11:1-7 describes the basic structure of faith. Verses 1 and 2 introduce the whole section by defining faith as it functions in the lives of the faithful (verse 1) and by tying this definition to the examples which follow (verse 2). Verses 3 and 6 give the object or content of faith and enclose faith's first two examples—Abel and Enoch (verses 4-5). These verses show us that the person who has God-pleasing faith believes both in God's existence and creatorship and in His character as a rewarder of those who seek Him. Abel (verse 4) and Enoch (verse 5) set the tone for this whole chapter by demonstrating that faith anticipates this reward beyond death. Noah, the concluding example in this subsection, introduces several themes that will be developed in the following verses: the obedience of faith, persecution by the unbelieving world, and the certainty of coming judgment.

As noted above, 11:1 describes faith as it functions in the lives of God's people. Most English translations make it sound like faith is a feeling of certainty: **Now faith is being sure of what we hope for and certain of what we do not see.** The faith under discussion involves more than merely **being sure** and **certain.** We will better understand this verse if we translate it "Now faith is the reality of what we hope for and the evidence of what we do not see."

Before we discuss how faith is "reality" and "evidence," it is important to define the phrases **what we hope for** and **what we do not see. We hope for** the reward that God has promised His people, that "rest" (4:1-11), that heavenly city and homeland (11:9-11, 13-16, 26, 39-40), that eternal fellowship with God which we have begun to experience in this life through Christ our High Priest. **We do not see** God (11:6, 27), His power, faithfulness, or providence.

So what is faith? First of all, **faith** is living life depending on the fact that those things which God has promised, and for which we hope, are real. The person without faith lives for rewards of this world that he can see. The person of faith lives for what God has promised because he knows it is the truly real and lasting reward. In the second place, **faith** is the means by which God's promised rewards become a "reality" in our lives. It is by trusting God that we begin to experience them now and will experience them ultimately at Christ's return. **Faith** is also the "evidence" of God's unseen being and power because when we trust Him, we experience His power in our lives.

Thus **faith** involves living life on the assumption that God's promised rewards are real and that His power is active in the present; He is "the living God." At the same time the life of **faith** offers proof of the reality of God's future promises and present power, for the person of faith begins to experience God's power in the present.

The explanation of faith we have given thus far assumes that **faith** means "my" or "our" faith. However, the preacher's main focus is on the faith of **the ancients** (11:2), which he will describe in the following verses. *Their* **faith** demonstrates to us the "reality" of God's promises and gives "evidence" of God's power in the present. They are accredited witnesses of faith because they **were commended for** their lives of faith by none other than God himself. Their lives of faith document that God's promises do come true and that He does demonstrate His power in the lives of His people.

The writer begins his historical survey of the people of faith where the Bible begins, at creation. And yet his first example of faith is surprising. He does not begin with one of "the ancients," but with us: **By faith we** (11:3). The preacher is addressing people of faith in order to strengthen their faith (as 10:39 above has made clear). He invites his hearers to join him in the perspective of faith at a most basic level: fundamental to all else that he says is the conviction that God is the Creator. The entire visible **universe was formed at God's command. Formed** means more than merely brought into being. God shaped, arranged, and put together this universe, making it a wonderful functioning whole.

The forming of the world was accomplished merely **at God's command.** A more literal translation would be, "by the word of God" (NKJV; NASB; NRSV). This same word of God addressed Abraham with God's promise (6:13-20) and revealed God's law to His people at Sinai (see commentary on 2:2). This word brought God's final revelation of the way of salvation through the Son (1:1-3). God's word through the exalted Son continues to address us from heaven (12:22-24). It is this word to which we must give account (4:12-13) because it will speak the final word of judgment at the dissolving of the universe (12:25-29). God does all by His word.

Why is belief in God as Creator so fundamental to faith? Because by affirming creation believers assert that **what is seen,** the entire visible universe, **was not made out of what was visible** (11:3). This universe was not created out of some preexistent matter. God did not create it out of part of himself. He created solely by His word! Thus God is the ultimate reality. Faith is living on the basis that this ultimate reality is the ultimate reality! God is real, thus we can depend on His promise for the future and His power for today. Everything we see is derived in its totality from His word alone. Faith is living our lives for God and not for the universe He has made.

Throughout this paragraph the preacher is assuming what he will state in 11:6: faith is necessary to please God. Verse 6 is a crucial statement that clarifies the description of faith in verse 1. Thus it will be helpful to look at this verse before considering the examples of Abel and Enoch in verses 4 and 5.

And without faith it is impossible to please God (11:6). The preacher often uses a double negative to make a forceful positive statement. If one would please God, it is absolutely necessary to have faith! He considers this fact almost self-evident, but he proceeds to clarify and defend it.

Anyone who comes to him is the language of worship. Note the New Revised Standard Version's translation, "whoever would approach him." The preacher understands the Christian life as approach to God in worship. He knows we can do this only through the promise of God fulfilled in the High Priesthood of Christ. Thus faith is absolutely necessary for any worshiper. Who would consider approaching God without believing that God **exists** and **that he rewards those who seek him?**

God's faithful people believe that He **exists.** This reminds us of the earlier phrase, "things not seen" (11:1 KJV). The people of faith do not see God with their eyes, but they know that He "is." They experience the power of this "living God" in the present. The phrase **that he rewards those who earnestly seek him** reminds us of the earlier words "things hoped for" (11:1 KJV). God will fulfill His promises of eternal blessing. The more literal New King James Version translation is helpful: "that He is a rewarder of those who diligently seek Him." It is not just that God **rewards;** "He is a rewarder." This speaks of His character. He is the kind of person who can be depended on to reward "those who diligently seek Him." The preacher here describes worshipers as those who "diligently" seek God. He wants his hearers to be such diligent seekers.

Thus faith is living life on the assumption that the living God of the Bible, who can be depended on to keep His word, is the basic reality of existence. This faith has both a present and a future aspect. The person of faith depends on God's power for the present and trusts in God's promises for the future.

We turn now to the first two examples of faith, given in 11:4-5. The Old Testament does not say in so many words that either Abel or Enoch had faith. The preacher knows that they had faith because the Scripture does bear witness that they pleased God. As we have seen, the person who pleases God must have faith (11:6). We note also how both these men ended their earthly lives. The preacher uses these two first examples to demonstrate that the kind of faith he is discussing transcends death. Throughout the rest of this chapter he makes it clear that he wants his hearers to have resurrection faith (see 11:11-12, 17-19, 28, 35).

The account of Cain and Abel is in Genesis 4:1-16. These two brothers, the sons of Adam and Eve, each offered sacrifice. God accepted Abel's but rejected Cain's. Cain then killed his brother Abel. Abel became the prototype of the righteous person, and Cain of the wicked. In New Testament times, people often called Abel "righteous Abel" (see Matthew 23:35, 1 John 3:12), although the author of Genesis did not use the word "righteous" to describe him. Contemporary people often ask the question, "Why did God accept Abel's sacrifice but reject Cain's?" The preacher has the answer. Abel offered his sacrifice **by faith** (Heb. 11:4). He becomes the premiere example of the "righteous one" who "will live by faith" as described in Habakkuk 2:4, quoted in Hebrews 10:38. Through the **faith** expressed in that act of sacrifice **he was commended by God as a righteous man.** How do we know that God **commended** him? **God spoke well of his offerings,** thus showing that it was offered by faith. No other offering would please God.

By this act of **faith he still** continues to speak. He still offers a God-approved testimony to faith's validity. Why does the preacher state this point so clearly? After all, all of the people in this chapter "still speak" to us: Through Scripture, their examples of faith still witness to the faithfulness of God and the validity of the life of faith. And why does the preacher add the statement, **even though he is dead?** Obviously, all the people in this chapter are dead. Perhaps he makes these statements because Able is the first example the preacher gives, the example that sets a pattern for the rest. There is, however, a deeper reason for these statements. Abel's faith continues to bear witness to God's faithfulness, even though he died a martyr's death! His was a faith that affirms the faithfulness of God beyond death. It is possible to translate this verse, "By faith he still speaks because he died." His very death testifies to us that we can trust God to take care of us beyond the grave! Thus Abel becomes the prototype for all of those who suffer opposition for their faith (11:23-25; 35b-38), and especially for those who accept death in order to obtain God's eternal resurrection (11:35b)!

In order to understand what the preacher says about Enoch (11:5), it is helpful to consider the record of his life found in Genesis 5:21-24. Nothing more is said about Enoch than we find in this short passage:

> (21) When Enoch had lived 65 years, he became the father of Methuselah. (22) And after he became the father of Methuselah, *Enoch walked with God* 300 years and had other sons and daughters. (23) Altogether, Enoch lived 365 years. (24) *Enoch walked with God;* then he was no more, because God took him away [my emphasis].

Our English translations of Genesis follow the original Hebrew text. The writer of Hebrews, however, as we have seen elsewhere, used a Greek translation of the Old Testament. Note the clauses italicized in verses 22 and 24 above, "Enoch walked with God." Instead of this clause, the Greek Old Testament, which the writer of Hebrews used, read as follows: "Enoch pleased God." The people who translated the Old Testament into Greek thought they could best express the meaning of the phrase "walked with God" by the phrase "pleased God." And indeed, if "Enoch walked with God," then he did please Him. The writer of Hebrews knows that Enoch was a person of faith because he **pleased God.**

The Scripture bears witness that **Enoch was taken from this life** without dying because it says **he could not be found, because God had taken him away** (see Genesis 5:24). However, Genesis 5:22 says that before Enoch was thus taken by God he spent many years in which he "pleased God." That means, he lived many years by faith. It appears that God took him because of this life of faith. And this is exactly what the writer of Hebrews says, **By faith Enoch was taken from this life.**

The fact that Enoch **did not experience death** is very important. He, along with Abel, is a witness to faith in a God whose promises go beyond death. Each of them bear witness to this truth in a different way. Abel is a prototype of the faithful who suffer opposition for their faith without temporal deliverance in order to receive the reward of eternal life in the next world. Enoch is a prototype of the faithful whom God delivers from suffering and martyrdom in this life. At the conclusion of this chapter the preacher gives a catalog of each kind. He lists in 11:32-35a those faithful who had an "Enoch" experience of God's power in this life; he portrays those who had an "Abel" experience in 11:35b-38. Both types live by the same kind of faith. For them God's promise of deliverance is sure, whether experienced in this life or the next. The preacher encourages his hearers to have the kind of faith that will sustain them in the face of death by martyrdom!

We have seen that to have faith is to live life according to the unseen reality of God rather than according to the visible things of this world. We cannot see Him with our physical eyes, but His power is real in the present and His promise of eternal blessedness is certain for the future. Thus we can trust Him to take care of us even beyond death.

The examples that follow show how this faith works out in the lives of God's people. The example of Noah in verse 7 introduces a number of themes that the preacher develops in subsequent examples. Noah illustrates the clear connection between faith and obedience; the expected opposition of the unbelieving world against the people of faith; and the certainty of both future judgment and reward.

First, the example of **Noah** reveals the essential link between faith and obedience: **By faith Noah . . . in holy fear built an ark.** In doing so, he obeyed the warning God had given him. The New King James Version translation "moved with Godly fear" clarifies the meaning of the New International Version's **in holy fear.**[1] Noah was motivated to obey by his **holy** or godly **fear.** To have a proper godly fear is to be fully convinced of the reality of God, of God's power, of God's grace, of the faithfulness of God's promises and the seriousness of His judgment. Godly fear is almost another way of describing faith. Noah realized that God's warnings of judgment were just as sure as His promises of reward. The preacher would encourage us to live lives of obedience motivated by such wholesome godly fear.[2]

Noah demonstrates the future direction of faith. He was **warned about things not yet seen.** We have already seen that the phrase "things hoped for" (11:1 KJV) refers to the final fulfillment of God's promises, to our eternal reward. God rewards the faithful (see 11:6). In this case, however, the words **things not yet seen** refer to future judgment, the judgment coming in the flood. That historical judgment, however, is a type or picture of the final judgment, which the preacher will describe in 12:25-29 at the end of his spiritual history of God's people.[3] The emphasis throughout Hebrews 11 is on God's promised eternal blessings. Nevertheless, this chapter begins with a reminder of His final judgment. The two are opposite sides of the same coin: the final salvation of the faithful will be, at the same time, the final condemnation of the disobedient. However, it is faith that leads to obedience and not the toss of a coin that will decide the destiny of the preacher's hearers.

When Noah acted in faithful obedience to God's warning about the upcoming flood by building the **ark,** his actions necessarily **condemned the world.** By his obedience, he showed that the unbelieving world was wrong and was under God's condemnation. Yet today, those who follow the way of faith implicitly condemn the world because they live by a set of values at total variance with the world's values. Their lives are a warning to the people of the unbelieving world of God's condemnation at the final judgment (see 12:25-29). Thus, as we will see, the people of faith experience alienation (11:8-9) and persecution (11:24-26, 35b-38) because the world rejects them. This theme of rejection by the world grows in importance throughout this chapter, climaxing in a description of martyrdom and total exclusion from society (11:35b-38).

The example of **Noah** helps us to see that this type of faith is a condition for receiving God's approval and therefore his promised blessings, but it in no way merits them or earns His favor. We learn this from the words **heir** and **righteousness** in the statement: **Noah . . . became heir of the righteousness that comes by faith.** The New King James Version and New American Standard Bible translate "heir of the righteousness that *is according to* faith" (my emphasis). **Righteousness** here denotes right relationship with God and is virtually equivalent to the divine approval which God bestowed on Abel and Enoch. Noah did not earn this approval; he received it as an **heir.** God freely gave it to him. Faith, according to the preacher, is living in total dependence on God, His present power and His future promises. If the believer begins to think that he has merited God's favor he denies his faith, because he would then be depending on himself and not totally on God. Thus the faith of Hebrews 11 is the exact opposite of depending on one's own merit. At the same time, it is the God-ordained condition for His favor, because by living in true faith believers treat God as God. The phrase **the righteousness that comes by faith** concludes this first section of the preacher's examples of faith. It reminds us of the quotation from Habakkuk 2:4 with which the preacher introduced this catalog of the faithful in Hebrews 10:38. The preacher wants his hearers to continue to exercise this kind of faith so that they will be the righteous whom God approves.

Noah, then, inherited divine approval by living a life of faith. He also received the salvation of **his family** from destruction in the flood. Undoubtedly, he also became an **heir** of God's eternal blessings, of the

236

heavenly homeland. The preacher, however, has not yet developed this theme because its presentation in the Old Testament is based on God's promise to Abraham. Nevertheless, the last word in the Greek text of 11:7 is the word **heir.** The preacher thereby prepares his hearers for the story of Abraham and God's offer to His people of an eternal inheritance.

2. THE PILGRIMAGE OF FAITH: ABRAHAM & GOD'S PROMISE 11:8-22

The next two subsections focus on Abraham (11:8-22) and Moses (11:23-31), this chapter's two greatest exemplars of faith. By their lives they clarify faith's essential characteristics. The choice of these two, the emphasis put upon them, and the way in which they are interrelated, are firmly based on the role that they play in the Old Testament and on Hebrew's understanding of the continuing relevance of the Old Testament for Christians.

Within the Old Testament Abraham represents God's promise and Moses the fulfillment of that promise. However, the preacher has shown over and over again the Old Testament's own witness that God's promises did not reach their final fulfillment in Moses. God's revelation in Moses of the priestly-sacrificial system was a type or picture that pointed to Christ's fulfillment (see commentary on 3:5). In this chapter we see another important aspect of God's work in Moses. Although God did not bring the final fulfillment of His promises through Moses, He did demonstrate His power to deliver His people and to enable them to become victorious. Thus Moses and those associated with him become witnesses that God's power is a reality for the people of faith in their present need as they press courageously on to the promise of future eternal reward.

Note several parallels between the Abraham (11:8-22) and Moses (11:23-31) subsections. In each there are seven examples of faith. Each of these examples is introduced by the phrase **by faith.** The first four "by faiths" of each section relate to the main character of the section (Abraham in 11:8-9, 11, 17; Moses in 11:23-24, 27-28); the next three, to persons who were related to or came soon after the main character (Isaac, 11:20; Jacob, 11:21; Joseph, 11:22, associated with Abraham; the Israelites, 11:29-30; and Rahab, 11:31, associated with Moses). In both sections, the last example of the main character's faith involves sacrifice and deliverance from death (Abraham's sacrificing of Isaac, 11:17-19; Moses' keeping of the Passover, 11:28).[4]

In 11:8-22, and indeed throughout this entire chapter, the preacher describes two parts of the promise God made to Abraham: the promise of land and the promise of descendants. The former promise of land may overshadow the latter promise, but both are important. Note how the author alternates between the promises of land and descendants: Verses 8 through 10 introduce Abraham's obedient response to God's promise of the land; verses 11 and 12 his response to the promise of descendants; verses 13 through 16 explain the significance of the promise of the land; verses 17 through 19 bring out the implications of the promise of the descendants. Verses 20 through 22 describe how Isaac, Jacob, and Joseph, who are promised descendants, anticipated the promise of the land. So the author has structured his discussion in terms of land (11:8-10), descendants (11:11-12), land (11:13-16), descendants (11:17-19), land (11:20-22). The promise of the land occupies the initial, central, and final positions. Thus the importance of 11:13-16 is highlighted by its central position and by the fact that it has no parallel in the Moses section. These verses explain how God's promise is to be understood throughout the rest of the chapter by providing a commentary on the faith of Abraham, Isaac, and Jacob.

In order to understand the preacher's perspective on this promise, we must first understand the perspective of Genesis 12 through 50. According to Genesis, Abraham and the patriarchs received God's promise that they would become a great nation, inherit the land of Canaan, and be a blessing to the world. By responding to God's promise they lived as **aliens** (11:13) in the Promised Land, all the while anticipating the promise's future fulfillment. Genesis ends on a note of anticipation with Joseph referring to the coming exodus and giving instructions about his burial (see Genesis 50:25).

The preacher affirms the Genesis perspective. In both Genesis and Hebrews, Abraham is the example of one who lives in faithful obedience. He trusts God and believes that God will fulfill His promise of blessing even though he cannot see that fulfillment. In both books, he is referred to as an **alien** (Heb. 11:13) or stranger in this present world. Joseph's affirmation of God's future fulfillment (11:22) concludes Hebrews' discussion of the patriarchs just as it concludes the Genesis account.

Yet in 11:13-16, the importance of which we have demonstrated, the preacher brings out the deeper significance of the promise of the land. The promise of land was really a promise of a heavenly homeland. It was for this homeland that Abraham stepped out in obedient faith (see 11:8-10). It was this homeland that the patriarchs descended from him anticipated by faith although they could not see it (11:20-22). And it is in order to reach this yet invisible homeland that the author wants his hearers to live lives of faithful obedience like the patriarchs lived.

The promise of descendants, discussed in the second (see 11:11-12) and fourth (11:17-19) positions, reminds the readers that God will fulfill His promise to His people. Just as God provided Abraham a descendant through the birth of Isaac (11:11-12), and preserved him through the sacrifice of Isaac (11:17-19), so He will sustain His faithful people who are Abraham's descendants (2:16) and heirs of the promise. He will sustain them even beyond the grave. He will bring them to the promised heavenly homeland. His present power accomplishes His purpose.

Abraham, then, is the example of faith par excellence. The incidents given from his life make it clear that faith implies the obedience and perseverance of aliens living in an unbelieving world. The preacher calls us to live as Abraham lived in order to receive God's promised blessing, which is eternal, not temporal.

As we have seen above, Abraham's first two acts of faith, described in 11:8-10, are closely related to each other, and both pertain to the promise of land. They describe how the life of faith begins and how one continues in it.

The life of faith begins with ready obedience. **Abraham, when called . . . obeyed and went** (11:8) could be translated, "As Abraham was called . . . he obeyed and went." To understand the nature of his obedience we must understand the divine call. God called him **to go to a place he would later receive as his inheritance.** The New King James Version more accurately translates the verb **to go** as "to go out." Abraham was called "to go out" from the country where he lived to an indefinite **place** which only **later** he would **receive as his inheritance.** He was to leave the security of home for "someplace" which he would inherit "sometime." Despite all of this insecurity, from the unbelieving world's point of view, he **obeyed and went** out, **even though he did not know where he was going.** The preacher probably used the word **place** instead of "country" or "land" because the **place** he has in mind is more than an earthly country.

Abraham was called to make a definitive break with the unbelieving world and its whole set of values. He was called to live for the heavenly reward that he could not see any more than we can. Yet he **obeyed.** The preacher urgently calls his hearers to make such a definitive break with the world. They are not to depend on the world for their security or to seek in it their ultimate happiness. They are to depend on God to take care of them and to satisfy them with His promise of eternal blessing.

Abraham not only obeyed immediately, he obeyed continuously. His obedience led him to live in a manner that separated him from the unbelieving world. Verse 9 makes it clear that, when he got to the Promised Land, he lived there as a stranger: he **made his home . . . like a stranger,** "stayed for a time" (NRSV), "lived as an alien" (NASB). He was continually on the move and never at rest. (See Genesis 23:4, where Abraham says, "I am an alien and a stranger among you.") He resided in a foreign country without rights. The phrases **promised land** and **a foreign country** form a sharp contrast. The earthly **promised land** was not the final fulfillment of the promise, as we will see. Furthermore, it is a matter of record that he lived there **in tents,** the mark of a nomad or alien. He did not settle down and become part of an unbelieving society that disregarded God.

God still calls people of faith to live as aliens in this sinful world even though they have been given the promise of an inheritance. People of faith do not depend on this world for their security, seek in it their happiness, or live by its sinful values. **Isaac and Jacob** followed Abraham's lifestyle (11:9). Here the preacher calls them **heirs with him of the same promise.** He will tell us more about their faith in 11:20-21. Abraham's life of faith led him to a lifestyle that was not uniquely his, for it belongs to all people of faith.

But what is this **promise?** Verse 8 indicates that it was "a place he [Abraham] would later receive as his inheritance." Verse 9 has referred to "the promised land," but indicated that Abraham was living in it as a stranger and alien. So the promise must refer to more than the real estate of Canaan. Verse 10 gives the content of the promise and explains why Abraham was willing to live in Canaan as a stranger. He **was looking forward to** the eternal city. Abraham was not merely searching for that city; he was anticipating it with confidence. He **was looking forward.** Such confident anticipation was the continuous habit of his life. The phrase **the city with foundations** offers a direct contrast to the description of Abraham as dwelling in tents (11:9). This phrase portrays permanence. Compare the Revised English Bible's translation, "with firm foundations." The preacher bases this description on the "biblical representation of Zion as the city firmly established by God."[5]

This is an eternal city because its **architect and builder is God** himself. The words **architect** and **builder** indicate one who planned and then carried out the plan. Using both words, the preacher emphasizes that the establishment of this city was God's work from beginning to end. Therefore He can offer this city as the permanent, eternal inheritance for

His faithful people. Abraham did not look for one of the fortified cities built by the Canaanites of his day. Abraham, and all the faithful people of God, anticipate the revealing and the attainment of the heavenly city. Any home that we have in this world is only temporary.

To summarize, Abraham separated himself from the unbelieving world, its security, its source of happiness, and its values, in order to receive God's promised inheritance. He continued to live separate from the world as he faithfully anticipated the final fulfillment of God's promise. How could he be sure that God would fulfill His promise?

Hebrews 11:11-12 addresses this question by turning to the other part of the promise, the promise of descendants. The important point is that Abraham began to experience the fulfillment of God's promise, even within his lifetime, through the miraculous birth of Isaac. Thus Abraham experienced God's faithfulness. This faithfulness was evidence that God would remain faithful in the future. We today can see even more evidence, for we can look back and see even more ways that God has fulfilled His promises.

God's promise of descendants also opens the way for others to be included in the promise to Abraham. God promised an inheritance to Abraham and his descendants. The examples of faith that follow in this chapter are the spiritual, if not the physical, children of Abraham. The people to whom Hebrews was addressed are his spiritual "descendants" (2:16). If we answer God's call in faith and obedience, we become part of Abraham's descendants and heirs of the eternal blessing God promised to him.

Abraham[6] experienced God's faithfulness when he trusted God to give him a son. Two great impediments stood in the way of Abraham's fathering the promised son: Abraham himself **was past** the **age** when he could be expected to have children.[7] Even more serious, **Sarah herself was barren** and had been throughout all her childbearing years. But Abraham **considered** that God was **faithful**[8] to keep His **promise** of a son. The word **considered** describes the entire course of Abraham's life, from the time he received the promise until the birth of Isaac and beyond. He lived his life from this faith perspective. Therefore, he received God's promised son.

Hebrews 11:12 gives the long-term results of Abraham's faith. Note the huge contrast between **one man,** referring to Abraham, and the number of his descendants, as innumerable as the stars and grains of sand. And the one (Abraham) was not a young man; he was **as good as dead** as far as his ability to reproduce a son with Sarah was concerned.[9] The preacher is already implying that Abraham's faith went beyond death. God could bring life from death. We have seen how foundational this concept is to faith in the examples of Abel and Enoch. The preacher develops this idea more thoroughly in 11:17-19, 23, 28, and especially 11:35-38. He urgently desires that his readers have this kind of faith.

God kept His promise! The last part of 11:12 paraphrases God's words to Abraham (see Genesis 22:17) promising Abraham a multitude of descendants. The preacher and his readers can see how God has fulfilled this promise in the many faithful spiritual descendants of Abraham. These words, spoken by God after Isaac was offered as a sacrifice, look forward to the next example of Abraham's faith (see Hebrews 11:17-19).

We next turn to 11:13-16. We have shown above that the preacher has emphasized these verses by putting them in the center of his discussion of the faith of Abraham and those associated with him (see 11:8-22). He uses these verses to show the proper perspective from which this whole section is to be viewed. Before going any further, he must make clear the true identity of the promised homeland. He must make this clarification while discussing Abraham, because it was to him, as well as to Isaac and Jacob, his son and grandson, that this promise was given. Clarification of this promise clarifies all of the examples to be given in this chapter. All of these people of faith were the descendants of Abraham pursuing the promise of a homeland that had been given to him.

Verse 13 vividly describes the relationship of **all these people** (Abraham, Sarah, Isaac, Jacob and Joseph, and others) to the fulfillment of God's promise when they died. None of them lived to see it. They were **still living by faith** at the time of their death. The words translated **by faith,** "in faith" (NKJV; NASB; NRSV), "according to faith," appear first in the preacher's original sentence for emphasis. When these people died they were living **by faith,** not by sight. They had still **not** received **the things promised.** They **saw** them only by the eyes of faith. They **welcomed** or "greeted" (NRSV) them **from a distance** as people greet their hometown when they see it from far away. By these actions they **admitted that they were aliens and strangers on earth** (see commentary on 11:9; compare Genesis 23:4). **Admitted** is a weak translation of the original. They "confessed" (NASB; NKJV; NRSV) their alienation on earth. They were by no means ashamed of it. They ended their lives still looking for the fulfillment of the promise. They still saw themselves as aliens in an unbelieving world. We are reminded that death itself did not destroy their faith.

The phrase **people who say such things** (11:14) may refer first of all to Abraham, Sarah, Isaac, Jacob, and Joseph, but also includes all people of faith. The kinds of things that they affirmed and "confessed" (11:13 NRSV) **show that they are looking for a country of their own. A country of their own** is better translated "a homeland" (NKJV; NRSV). They are not looking for a country that they can make their own. They are looking for the country that already is their native land. The translation **looking for** is also weak. "Seeking" (NASB; NRSV; compare NKJV) is much better. They were not trying to find it here on this earth. They were anticipating it. They were preparing for it by living lives of faith.

From what has already been said, it is obvious that the "homeland" sought by Abraham, Isaac, and Jacob was not the land of Canaan. They were already in that land. But some of the preacher's hearers might object—especially when he used the word "homeland"—that these patriarchs had a homeland. They were natives of Mesopotamia. They could have gone back to this homeland from which God had called them and which they had **left behind.** The preacher answers this objection in 11:15. If that was what they had had in mind when they thought of a **homeland,** they would have had plenty of **opportunity to return.** It is obvious that they did not go back.

The "homeland" was not Canaan in which they lived. The "homeland" was not Mesopotamia from which they had come. What was it? Hebrews 11:16a has the answer: **Instead, they were longing for a better country—a heavenly one.**

This homeland was a **better** one. The preacher uses the word **better** throughout Hebrews (6:9; 7:19, 22; 8:6; 9:23; 10:34; 11:35, 40; 12:24) to describe the work of Christ, fully sufficient and effective in redeeming us from sin, and the eternal blessings that come from that work. **Better** does not contrast with what is "good," but with what is temporary, ineffective, weak, and useless. God has called His people to the **better** homeland of heaven (3:1), and has made a way for them to enter through the **better** or truly effective work of Christ (10:19-22).

The homeland the patriarchs sought was the eternal **heavenly** presence of God, a homeland appropriate for those made perfect through the fully sufficient work of Christ. It was this homeland for which the patriarchs **were longing** because it is the native place of those who live by this kind of faith in God and His promise.

Hebrews 11:6 made clear that this kind of faith brings God's approval. The last half of 11:16 affirms in the strongest way God's commendation of these people. Because of their faith, **God is not ashamed to be called their God.** They **admitted** (11:13) and boldly confessed that they were

God's, so God was not ashamed to call them His own (see Mark 8:38; Luke 9:26; Romans 1:16; 2 Timothy 1:8, 12, 16; Hebrews 2:11). Abraham and his faithful descendants confessed that they were waiting for the heavenly homeland, that they were trusting in God (see Hebrews 11:13-16a). He, then, is by no means **ashamed** to acknowledge that they are His people. In fact, He has already prepared for them the very thing they are longing for—an eternal **city.** By faith they have acted on the basis of what He has already done for them. They are His and He acts on their behalf. The image of the eternal **city** is another way of describing the promised rest that the disobedient wilderness generation lost (3:7–4:14), and is, of course, the equivalent of the **heavenly** homeland (11:16) and of the "city of the living God" (12:22). Each description emphasizes a different aspect of the reality: "rest" emphasizes the end of distress and the enjoyment of blessing; "homeland" the place of belonging; **city,** the idea of fellowship with others and especially with God. Underlying all these picture is the idea of eternity!

Now that the preacher has described the nature of true faith in God's promise, he turns to Abraham's greatest crisis of faith—the command to sacrifice Isaac (see 11:17-19). Verse 17a states the facts of the case: **By faith Abraham, when God tested him, offered Isaac as a sacrifice.** We find the original account of this event in Genesis 22:1-18. The Old Testament makes it clear that God was testing Abraham's faith by commanding him to sacrifice Isaac. This was more than any test a father who loved his son would face. This test was special because of who Abraham was and who Isaac was. The last half of Hebrews 11:17 makes this clear by identifying Abraham as **He who had received the promises** and Isaac as **his one and only son** of the promise.[10] Verse 18 makes clear the promise under consideration: **It is through Isaac that your offspring will be reckoned.**

So here's the test Abraham faced: How could God keep His promise to give Abraham many descendants if Abraham sacrificed the very person through whom God had promised to give those descendants? The preacher and his hearers know, of course, that God did not require Abraham to go through with the sacrifice. That is why he says that Abraham **was about to sacrifice his one and only son** or, better, "was ready to offer up" (NRSV) his only son. However, as far as Abraham's faith was concerned, the deed was as good as done.

There is only one explanation that explains how Abraham could go through with this sacrifice: **Abraham reasoned that God could raise the dead.** Note especially, the preacher does not say "raise Isaac." He says **raise the dead.** The Greek word behind **dead** is plural; the preacher spoke of "the **dead** ones." Both Abraham and the preacher believed that God had power over death for all His faithful people!

The preacher is establishing a pattern of faith that believes in God's power over death. Abel witnessed to this power by a faith that transcended martyrdom (see 11:4). Enoch witnessed to it by a faith that overcame death itself (11:5). Abraham has already witnessed to it by a faith that kept believing God although he was "as good as dead" (11:12). Now Abraham witnesses to God's power to raise the dead by sacrificing Isaac. Those who first received the book of Hebrews needed this kind of faith to face the future (see 11:35b-38). God always calls His people to this kind of faith.

The New American Standard Bible translation of the last part of verse 19 connects the deliverance of Isaac very closely with the coming resurrection: "from which he also received him back as a type." The New American Standard Bible's translation, "as a type," has replaced the New International Version's phrase, **figuratively speaking.**[11] This translation more clearly shows that Isaac is a "type" or picture of the general resurrection to which people of faith look forward.

Abraham passed the test of faith by trusting God to raise Isaac. Even if He had killed Isaac, God could still have fulfilled His promise. Isaac's symbolic "resurrection" is a type of what God will do for all the faithful. These verses emphasize the faithfulness of God to Abraham even more than Abraham's faith. We too can trust Him!

The author has described Abraham's faith at the birth (see 11:11-12) and offering of Isaac as a sacrifice (11:17-19). He has told us that Isaac and Jacob were "heirs with" Abraham of "the same promise" of a heavenly homeland (11:9). Thus he has prepared us for the examples of faith given to us by Isaac (11:20), Jacob (11:21) and Joseph (11:22). Obviously they possessed the faith the preacher described in 11:13-16. They believed that God would fulfill His promise of a heavenly homeland. Their faith in this promise transcended death.

Hebrews 11:20 refers to Isaac's blessing of Jacob and Esau (see Genesis 27:27-40, 28:1-5). The preacher, in his original Greek text, emphasizes the main point of this verse by placing it first: It was **in regard to their future** that Isaac blessed Jacob and Esau. The New American Standard Bible or New King James Version translations of this phrase clarify another point: "regarding things to come" or "concerning things to come." Isaac did not merely bless them for the future, but his blessing pertained to what God was going to do in the future. Genesis 28:4 records how Isaac gave Jacob "the blessing of Abraham." Thus Isaac looked forward to the same promised blessing that Abraham had anticipated. This blessing finds its fulfillment in Christ's High Priestly work which makes the heavenly homeland accessible. Isaac's faith is, indeed, a chip off the old block. "Things to come" fits very well with the preacher's other descriptions of the coming salvation (see Hebrews 2:5; 6:5; 9:11; 10:1; 13:14).

Verse 21 describes how Jacob then passes on the blessing to each of Joseph's sons (see Genesis 48:1-22). He also looks forward to what God is going to do. He gives this blessing **when he is dying** (Heb. 11:21). His faith in God's future salvation, in the city to come, went beyond his death. Within the Old Testament the period of Jacob's dying begins in Genesis 47:28 and runs through Genesis 49:33. It is significant that the preacher picked Jacob's blessing the sons of Joseph (see Genesis 48:1-22) as the example of Jacob's faith. He could have described Jacob's blessing his own twelve sons (see Genesis 49:1-28). The preacher probably chose the former incident because Jacob specifically blessed the sons of Joseph in the name of the God of Abraham. Jacob said that they would be called by his name and by the names of his fathers Abraham and Isaac. He also gave them the promise of numerous descendants, which God had given to Abraham and Isaac (see especially Genesis 48:15-16). This blessing associates them closely with the faith of Abraham and Isaac. Jacob's blessing of Joseph's sons prepares for the example of Joseph's own faith in Hebrews 11:22.

The statement **and worshiped as he leaned on the top of his staff** is a quotation from Genesis 47:31.[12] These words describe what Jacob did after he gave Joseph instructions concerning his burial, but before he blessed Joseph's children (see Genesis 48:1-21). A **staff** is a sign of a person on a journey. Perhaps the preacher wanted to portray Jacob at his death worshiping God on the way to the heavenly homeland.

The preacher concludes this series in 11:22 by noting the example of Joseph's faith. Joseph believed so strongly that God was going to deliver the children of Israel from Egypt and bring them into Canaan that he commanded them to take his **bones** with them and bury him there (see Genesis 50:24-26). This incident concludes the book of Genesis on a note of faith in God's future deliverance and prepares for the next book's description of that deliverance under Moses. Here in Hebrews it also prepares for the next group of faith-examples which center around Moses and the exodus from Egypt. By speaking in faith about the Exodus, Joseph affirmed his faith in God's future deliverance. This faith was strong enough that it led him to take action: he commanded his children to take his remains with them.

Like the faith of Abraham before them, the faith of Isaac, Jacob, and Joseph transcended death by looking forward to God's fulfillment of His promise.

3. THE PILGRIMAGE OF FAITH: MOSES & GOD'S POWER 11:23-31

It is not difficult to see why the preacher would associate Moses and Abraham as the two leading examples of faith. Within the Old Testament context both men looked to the Promised Land as their goal. God promised Abraham that He would give him numerous descendants and that they would inherit the Promised Land. Moses led those descendants out of Egypt toward that Promised Land. The alien existence of the patriarchs in Canaan foreshadowed the oppression of their descendants in Egypt. Moses identifies with their suffering and leads them out of Egypt. Under him they are welded into a people, the people of God, at Sinai. He leads them to the boundary of the Promised Land. His handpicked successor Joshua leads them into the Promised Land. Thus Joshua 21:45 says, "Not one of all the Lord's good promises to the house of Israel failed; every one was fulfilled." The last chapter of Joshua records the burial of Joseph's bones. This burial indicated that God had fulfilled the faith of Joseph who saw the future exodus and conquest (compare Genesis 50:24-26 with Joshua 24:32). Thus, within the Old Testament, Abraham and the patriarchs correspond to Moses and Joshua as promise corresponds to fulfillment.

Even a cursory reading of the Old Testament shows, however, that Abraham's descendants did not enjoy the ideal life in the earthly Promised Land, the life they may have envisioned. The writer of Hebrews agrees with the Old Testament prophets that the sin of God's people marred their enjoyment of God's blessing. We have seen his evaluation of their sinfulness in his discussion of the wilderness generation in Hebrews 3:7 through 4:11 and also in his use of the new covenant promise from Jeremiah 31:31-34 in Hebrews 8:1-13. However, he also agrees with the prophets that God has promised something better. In Psalm 110:1, 4, God promised a new High Priest who would minister in heaven (see Hebrews 7:1-28). This High Priest would mediate the new covenant promised in Jeremiah 31:31-34. Under this covenant God's people could be cleansed from sin and have access to himself (see Hebrews 8:1–10:18). They would be able to join Him in a heavenly homeland, of which the earthly Promised Land was but a picture.

The central unit of the Abraham subsection, 11:13-16, has shown clearly that God's promise of a land refers ultimately to the heavenly homeland. Thus Moses and Joshua cannot have brought the final fulfillment of God's promise to Abraham. What role does Moses play? Earlier chapters of Hebrews state that God's revelation through Moses was a picture, type, or prophecy of what was to come in His Son (see commentary on 3:5). The deeds of Moses, however, also demonstrate faith in the face of opposition. A look at the structure of the Moses subsection in comparison with the Abraham subsection will help us see the significance of Moses.

Note the similarities between the first three examples of Abraham's faith (11:8-12) and the first three examples of Moses' faith (11:23-27) when compared in reverse order. The chart below makes this clearer.

ABRAHAM AND MOSES
HEBREWS 11:8-31

THREE EXAMPLES OF ABRAHAM'S FAITH HEBREWS 11:8-12	THREE EXAMPLES OF MOSES'S FAITH HEBREWS 11:23-27
(A) By faith Abraham, when called to go to a place he would later receive as his inheritance, obeyed and went, even though he did not know where he was going (11:8).	**(C₁)** By faith Moses' parents hid him for three months after he was born, because they saw he was no ordinary child, and they were not afraid of the king's edict (11:23).
(B) By faith he made his home in the promised land like a stranger in a foreign country; he lived in tents, as did Isaac and Jacob, who were heirs with him of the same promise. For he was looking forward to the city with foundations, whose architect and builder is God (11:9-10).	**(B₁)** By faith Moses, when he had grown up, refused to be known as the son of Pharaoh's daughter. He chose to be mistreated along with the people of God rather than to enjoy the pleasures of sin for a short time. He regarded disgrace for the sake of Christ as of greater value than the treasures of Egypt, because he was looking ahead to his reward (11:24-26).
(C) By faith Abraham, even though he was past age—and Sarah herself was barren—was enabled to become a father because he considered him faithful who had	**(A₁)** By faith he left Egypt, not fearing the king's anger; he persevered because he saw him who is invisible (11:27).

made the promise. And so from this one man, and he as good as dead, came descendants as numerous as the stars in the sky and as countless as the sand on the seashore (11:11-12).

EXPLANATION—THE TRUE GOAL OF FAITH HEBREWS 11:13-16

ANOTHER EXAMPLE OF ABRAHAM'S FAITH HEBREWS 11:17-19

(D) By faith Abraham, when God tested him, offered Isaac as a sacrifice. He who had received the promises was about to sacrifice his one and only son, even though God had said to him, "It is through Isaac that your offspring will be reckoned." Abraham reasoned that God could raise the dead, and figuratively speaking, he did receive Isaac back from death.

ANOTHER EXAMPLE OF MOSES' FAITH HEBREWS 11:28

(D₁) By faith he kept the Passover and the sprinkling of blood, so that the destroyer of the firstborn would not touch the firstborn of Israel.

THREE EXAMPLES ASSOCIATED WITH ABRAHAM HEBREWS 11:20-22

(E) By faith Isaac blessed Jacob and Esau in regard to their future (11:20).

(F) By faith Jacob, when he was dying, blessed each of Joseph's sons, and worshiped as he leaned on the top of his staff (11:21).

(G) By faith Joseph, when his end was near, spoke about the exodus of the Israelites from Egypt and gave instructions about his bones (11:22).

THREE EXAMPLES ASSOCIATED WITH MOSES HEBREWS 11:29-31

(E₁) By faith the people passed through the Red Sea as on dry land; but when the Egyptians tried to do so, they were drowned (11:29).

(F₁) By faith the walls of Jericho fell, after the people had marched around them for seven days (11:30).

(G₁) By faith the prostitute Rahab, because she welcomed the spies, was not killed with those who were disobedient (11:31).

The first example of Abraham's faith (11:8) is lettered "A" and corresponds to the third example of Moses faith (11:27), lettered "A_1." In 11:8, Abraham leaves his homeland to receive an inheritance; in 11:27, Moses leaves Egypt. The second example of Abraham's faith (11:9-10), labeled "B" on the chart, corresponds to the second example of Moses' faith (11:24-26), labeled "B_1." In 11:9-10, Abraham lives as a stranger in Canaan because he is anticipating an eternal city; in 11:24-26, Moses experiences not only alienation but persecution in Egypt because he was anticipating an eternal reward. Finally, the third example of Abraham's faith (11:11-12), labeled "C" on the chart, corresponds with the first example of Moses' faith (11:23), labeled "C_1" on the chart. In 11:11-12, death is overcome by the birth of Isaac; in 11:23, death is overcome through the birth of Moses. The fourth examples of both Abraham and Moses recorded in 11:17-19 and 11:28 and labeled "D" and "D_1" both depict a faith that believes God can deliver from death. Three examples coming from people associated with Abraham appear in 11:20-22, labeled "E," "F," and "G"; three associated with Moses are recorded in 11:29-31, labeled "E_1," "F_1," and "G_1."

In each case, the second of the first three examples (11:9-10 and 11:24-26, labeled "B" and "B_1") is most important. The alienation experienced by Abraham in Canaan finds parallel in the persecution of and active opposition against Moses in Egypt. In this kind of situation, faith means the embracing of suffering, a theme which has roots in the example of Abel in 11:4 and prepares for the examples of suffering in 11:35b-38 at the conclusion of this chapter. This central example of Moses' faith emphasizes both the severity of the suffering God's people may face and the great value of the reward which they anticipate (see 11:26).

The first and third examples of each set—"A" and "C," "A_1" and "C_1"—show the different responses that faith makes under these varying circumstances. Abraham's example challenges the readers to keep on obeying God although they cannot yet see or understand how God will fulfill His promise. Moses challenges them to obey God in the face of strong and very visible social and physical opposition. Abraham's faith led to patient obedience in the face of alienation. Moses' faith led to courageous obedience in the face of suffering. Abraham modeled faith that patiently waits for God's answer. Moses modeled faith that courageously obeys despite danger. Both types of faith are based on a confidence in God's all-sufficient power and ever-faithful character. His power is real and His promises are true (see 11:1, 3, 6).

Compare also the fourth example on both sides of the chart: "D" and "D₁." Both of these examples are climactic. Both deal with God's deliverance from imminent death. Yet for Abraham (11:17-19) the crisis revolves around understanding. Moses experiences a crisis of God's power (11:28).

The three succeeding examples associated with Abraham ("E," "F," and "G"; see 11:20-22) emphasize again the need for patient obedience. We too must persevere because we have not yet entered into the final enjoyment of God's promised reward. However, the three examples associated with Moses ("E₁," "F₁," and "G₁"; see 11:29-31) encourage courageous obedience by showing God's power to deliver. They build on 11:28's climactic example of Moses' faith.

Moses does not bring the final fulfillment of God's promise, but his life demonstrates that God's people must face persecution and suffering with courage because the reward is inestimable and God's power to deliver is real. The first three examples of faith from Moses' life emphasize the need for courage. They come from the time before God had spoken to Moses at the burning bush. God had not yet revealed His power. It took courage to take a stand for Him. The fourth example from Moses' life, and the three following examples, are an encouragement to God's people because they demonstrate God's mighty power to deliver. The preacher is preparing his hearers for the persecution they may face. He wants them to practice the courageous obedience of Moses.

The first example of faith associated with Moses is found in 11:23. (see Exodus 2:1-10 for the original account). The New International Version makes it clear that this is the faith of **Moses' parents** at the occasion of his birth, **after he was born.** The God who enabled Abraham and Sarah to have Isaac, although they were old and Sarah had been barren (see Hebrews 11:11), preserved the life of Moses through the faith of his parents.

Like the examples of faith already given in this chapter, their faith involved acting in obedience to God's purposes that others could not see: **they saw he was no ordinary child.** This translation is more accurate than those given in other English versions, such as the New American Standard Bible, "they saw he was a beautiful child" (compare the NKJV; NRSV).¹³ Just as Isaac was Abraham's "one and only" son of God's promise (see 11:17), Moses also was **no ordinary child.** This phrase indicates much more than parents' natural affection for their son. They saw that God had a special purpose for him. Because they saw this with the eyes of faith, they acted in obedience to the perceived will of God and **hid him for three months.** The preacher does not need to tell the rest of the story of their faith since his hearers would have been familiar with it. Thus they acted contrary to the standards of this world, which took the form of an **edict** by the king of Egypt that all Hebrew male babies should be killed.

Their faith, however, required something the previous examples have not emphasized. The obedience that was an expression of their faith required courage. As already noted above, this theme characterizes the examples of faith in this Moses section. **They were not afraid of the king's edict.** They may have felt fear, but they did not give in to it. The Revised English Bible expresses the precise meaning of this statement: "They were not intimidated by the king's edict." Moses began life with the example of parents who demonstrated what it meant to have faith in the face of opposition and physical threat.

Hebrews 11:23 describes the faith of Moses' parents "after he was born." Verses 24 and 25 describe Moses' own faith **when he had grown up.** This phrase may refer to the phrase "after Moses had grown up" in Exodus 2:11. Exodus 2:11-12 relates the account of Moses' killing an Egyptian who was mistreating a Hebrew. The author of Hebrews probably thinks that by committing this deed Moses **refused to be known as the son of Pharaoh's daughter.** The word **refused** describes a definitive act on the part of Moses. He refused the status that would have been his as one of the sons **of Pharaoh's daughter.**[14]

Moses made this choice before he saw God at the burning bush and certainly before God manifested His power to deliver His people from Egypt. Thus he made this choice when it was costly to choose God's side. People often think Moses acted unwisely in slaying the Egyptian. They see this as an abortive attempt to deliver God's people in his own strength. The preacher says it was an act of faith, the time when Moses chose to be on God's side.

Hebrews 11:25 clarifies the consequences of Moses' choice by describing the options: **He chose to be mistreated along with the people of God rather than to enjoy the pleasures of sin for a short time.**[15]

First note what he chose: **to be mistreated along with the people of God.** The phrase **be mistreated along with** translates one Greek word. A similar word is used in the Greek translation of Exodus 1:11 to describe the suffering of God's people in Egypt. The preacher uses this word again in Hebrews 11:37 to describe the sufferings of God's faithful and in 13:3 to portray the situation of his own hearers. By identifying with the horrible suffering God's people experienced in Egypt, Moses identified with the suffering of God's people of all time, even the potentially imminent suffering of the preacher's hearers. He suffered mistreatment, but it was in good company, **along with the people of God,** the people who believe in the God who keeps His promises. Any mistreatment the preacher's hearers might suffer places them in that same honorable company. The preacher has said nothing yet about the possibility of God's delivering His people from suffering. Faith involves courageous obedience. Such obedience may require suffering!

Choosing one thing often means the rejection of something else. Moses' choice involved rejecting **the pleasures of sin** (11:25). The pleasures of Egypt were real pleasures. However, Moses could only have enjoyed them **for a short time,** the span of his life. He chose to look for something eternal. Furthermore, these pleasures are described as **of sin.** Even if some of Egypt's pleasures were not immoral in themselves, it would have been sinful for Moses to have chosen them. He would have been denying his faith in the living God and in God's promises of eternal reward. Even good things are wrong when they keep us from the will of God.

Verse 24 affirmed Moses' choice. Verse 25 made clear the two options between which Moses chose. Verse 26 describes Moses' thinking, his evaluation of these options, and thus explains why he chose as he did. The preacher hopes his hearers adopt as their own Moses' understanding of the situation. He puts the contrast sharply. The preacher does not say that Moses considered the "rewards" of Christ **of greater value than the treasures of Egypt** (11:26). He considered even **disgrace for the sake of Christ** as much more valuable that Egyptian **treasures.** The **treasures of Egypt** were legendary. Moses' world offered none greater. How could he prefer any kind of **disgrace** to those **treasures?** The last part of 11:26 explains why: **He was looking ahead to his reward.** The Greek text includes no word for "his." Obviously Moses expected to receive a share in this reward, but it is the reward anticipated by all of God's people. Can you picture how the preacher could have emphasized the value of the eternal reward any more than he has in this passage? Not only does that reward surpass the **treasures of Egypt,** most fabulous on earth. The very **disgrace of Christ** itself is inestimably greater than those earthly **treasures,** because that **disgrace** is the assurance that one will receive the eternal reward. The Christian may face persecution, *but it is worth it all! Hallelujah!*

Moses followed the pattern set by all God's people of faith: he saw what nonbelievers cannot see. Noah believed in "things not yet seen" (11:7);

Abraham and those with him "saw" and "welcomed" God's promised homeland from a distance (11:13); Moses' parents "saw he was no ordinary child" (11:23). By the eyes of faith, God's people can "see" His power for the present and His promises for the future, even when others cannot. Moses believed (in accordance with 11:6) that God rewards the faithful. The reproach of Christ guarantees the future eternal reward. May God give us the eyes to see what Moses saw! May we, along with Moses, be ready to embrace **disgrace for the sake of Christ** and consider it as nothing.

What does the preacher mean, **disgrace for the sake of Christ?** We have seen that the preacher believes God has had one people throughout history, the people of faith. There were people of faith even before Abraham, but since the time of Abraham God's people have looked forward to the fulfillment of the promise God gave to him. That promise reaches its fulfillment in Christ. God has one "house" or "household" in which Moses is a "steward," but over which Christ is the Son (3:1-6). If God has only one people, then Christ is the Mediator for those who lived before as well as those who lived after His coming. By trusting in God's promise, those who lived before Christ looked forward to Christ even if they did not fully realize this fact.[16] Thus by identifying with the disgrace of God's people, Moses was suffering **disgrace for the sake of Christ.**[17]

The description of Moses' sufferings here looks forward to the sufferings of Christ (described in 12:1-3) and serves to encourage Christians in their own sufferings for Christ. The Greek tense the preacher uses here indicates that Moses was continually and habitually **looking ahead to his reward** (11:26). Note the Revised English Bible's translation: "for his eyes were fixed on the coming reward." So we are to "fix our eyes on Jesus" (12:2) who has suffered much but is now at God's right hand. Entering into God's presence through Jesus is the **reward** (11:26) toward which Moses looked. It is the reward to which we look, although we already can enter it in a greater way than Moses could (see commentary on 11:39-40 below).

Moses endured suffering, but he was not any more intimidated than his parents had been (see 11:23). The next example of Moses' faith (11:27) makes this fact clear. **He left Egypt, not fearing the king's anger.** This is a bold statement. We might paraphrase, "He abandoned Egypt, not the least intimidated by the angry king." It is easy to see how this statement would encourage the recipients of Hebrews. They, like Abraham (see 11:8) and Moses, must abandon the value system of this world. They must be ready to face hardship and overcome fear, as both Moses' parents (11:23) and Moses himself did (11:27).

To what event, however, in the life of Moses does this verse refer? Does it refer to the time when he fled from Egypt after killing the Egyptian? Or, does it refer to his subsequently leading all God's people out of Egypt in the exodus? The author of Hebrews seems to be giving the events of Moses' life in chronological order. Exodus 2:1-10 describes the birth of Moses; 2:12-13 his killing of the Egyptian who was mistreating a Hebrew; and 2:13-15 his flight from Egypt after the king discovered what he had done. We have seen that Hebrews 11:23 refers to the birth of Moses. We have suggested that Moses' refusal to be considered part of Pharaoh's household in 11:24-26 is a reference to his killing the Egyptian. It is reasonable then to think that 11:27 refers to the next event in the book of Exodus, Moses' flight from Egypt after the king discovered his misdeed.

Furthermore, it is unlikely that the writer of Hebrews would refer to the exodus from Egypt at this point because he does not refer to the Passover until 11:28. The Passover preceded the exodus.

But there's a problem with this interpretation of 11:27: Exodus 2:14 says specifically that Moses was afraid after he had killed the Egyptian. The author of Hebrews is saying the same thing he said in regard to Moses' parents. Moses felt fear, but was not intimidated by it. He overcame his fear by faith in God. In spite of his fear, he left Egypt. This definitive break with Egypt and all for which it stood was the first step toward following God's plan, just as Abraham's leaving his home was the first step in his obedience (see 11:8).

The last part of 11:27 shows us how Moses could take this step: **He persevered because he saw him who is invisible.** Abraham's faith led him to patient perseverance as he separated himself from the unbelieving world until the time when he would receive the promise. The faith of Moses led to patient perseverance even in the face of suffering and persecution. Moses was able to persevere unintimidated because the continual habit of his life was to keep his eyes of faith on the God **who is invisible.** This seeing is a reference to the continual focus of his faith and not primarily to the appearances of God, such as at the burning bush (see Exodus 3:1–4:17). Moses kept the eyes of faith focused on God, His power, and His promises.[18] It is this kind of seeing that has been characteristic of other examples of faith in this chapter. It is only this kind of seeing that would encourage the preacher's first hearers. They did not have "burning bush" experiences of God, but they could "see" Him by faith. The phrase **he persevered** takes in the whole course of Moses' life. Because he kept his eyes on God, he endured to the end.

The central example of Moses' faith in 11:24-26 emphasized both the necessity for people of faith to endure opposition, persecution, and disgrace and the corresponding greatness of the reward to be gained. The preacher flanked this central example with two others (11:23, 27) which urged courage in the face of such suffering. The fourth and final example of Moses' faith (11:28) demonstrates God's power to deliver through faith.

By faith he [Moses] **kept** or established **the Passover.** God's instructions about the Passover are found in Exodus 12:1-20; the actual keeping of the first Passover, in Exodus 12:21-32. Moses' leading the people in keeping the first Passover was an expression of his faith. God had said that He was going to destroy the **firstborn** sons of Egyptian families, both human and animal. God would spare His people if they would properly kill and eat the Passover sacrifice and sprinkle its **blood** on the posts and lintels of the doors of their houses. By instructing the people to sprinkle this **blood** on their doors, Moses led them in affirming their faith that God would do what He said. Because Moses believed and obeyed God, both Moses and those who followed him were spared. The angel God sent as the **destroyer** did not even **touch,** much less slay, the Israelites' **firstborn** sons, although all the **firstborn** of those who did not sprinkle the **blood** died. The word **Israel** does not appear in the original Greek text but was supplied by the New International Version translators for clarity. This addition is unfortunate, for the contrast in this verse is not between Israelites and Egyptians per se, but between the people of faith and the people of unbelief; those who sprinkled the **blood** and those who did not.

The preacher does not relate the Passover to Christ's death. Yet the phrase **sprinkling of blood** must have reminded his readers of Christ's blood in 9:11-14. The deliverance experienced at Passover looks forward to those people of faith described in 11:32-35a who experienced God's deliverance even to the extent of being raised from the dead. The Passover also points forward to that final judgment, described in 12:25-29, when the faithful will receive God's eternal reward and the unbelieving His condemnation.

By faith Abraham experienced God's power to deliver from death when he offered Isaac as a sacrifice (see 11:17-19). By this action he affirmed his faith in God's faithfulness and in God's resurrection power. By faith Moses experienced God's power to deliver from death when he established the Passover with its sacrifice. Moses' faith led to a great demonstration of that power of God.

In rapid succession, the next three examples of faith (see 11:29-31) affirm God's power to deliver His people. The preacher is building an

256

image of the mighty power of God to deliver by quickly reinforcing the example of the Passover with these three concisely stated examples. The three examples that conclude the Abraham cycle emphasize the future aspect of faith, the need for faith to endure until the fulfillment of God's promises. These three examples emphasize the present power of God to deliver.

The first two examples (see 11:29-30) refer to the faith of God's people. The account of the Red Sea crossing is found in Exodus 14:15-31. God opened the sea so that deliverance was available to them, but they had to make that deliverance their own **by faith:** They had to obey God by walking through the sea trusting Him to keep the waters back.[19] Thus they demonstrated their faith when they **passed through the Red Sea.** The words **as on dry land** portray the magnitude of God's deliverance. They did not have to wade in the mud! Again, however, the preacher balances salvation for the faithful with judgment on those who did not believe: **But when the Egyptians tried to do so, they were** all **drowned.**

Between 11:29 and 11:30, the preacher skips from the crossing of the Red Sea under Moses to the conquest of Jericho in the time of Joshua (see Joshua 6:1-21). He has omitted the wilderness generation because they, as he has explained (see Hebrews 3:7–4:11), did not demonstrate faith!

Again, it was **by faith** that **the walls of Jericho fell, after the people had marched around them for seven days** (11:30). The preacher describes **the people,** not Joshua, as acting by faith. God told them to march around the city for seven days and He would give it to them. Rather than trying to conquer the city themselves, they trusted God's word and obeyed. After they had demonstrated their faith by walking **around** the walls **for seven days,** God demonstrated His power by causing the walls to fall. The **people** of this generation form a wholesome and encouraging contrast to the wilderness generation (3:7–4:11). People of faith are not always alone. They may be surrounded by a host of God's faithful followers.

The third and concluding example of faith in this series is closely tied to the previous example (see 11:31). One person in Jericho, along with her family, experienced God's power of deliverance. She was not the kind of person one might expect to have faith, for she was **the prostitute Rahab** (her story is found in Joshua 2:1-24; 6:22-25). **She welcomed the spies** that Joshua sent to spy out Jericho because she believed in the God who had brought His people out of Egypt and was giving them the Promised Land. She demonstrated her faith by choosing to go with God's people rather than remain allied with the people of her home city. Because of this she and her family were **not killed with** Jericho's people **who were disobedient.** The Greek word behind **disobedient** is the same word the preacher used in 3:18 to describe the unbelieving generation who died in the wilderness. He paints a subtle contrast between those people who had enjoyed so much of God's blessing, and yet disobeyed, and this **prostitute** who acted in obedient faith.

It will be helpful to summarize this Moses-section (see 11:23-31). The preacher used the first three examples of faith from the life of Moses (11:23-27) to show his hearers that God's faithful people must often suffer shame and persecution. Faith requires courage! He will continue this theme with the description of the intense suffering of the faithful in 11:35b-38. By the last example of Moses' faith in 11:28 and the three examples that follow in 11:29-31, the preacher has demonstrated God's power to deliver His faithful people in the here and now.[20] These examples lead directly into the intensified description of God's mighty power as a response to faith in 11:32-35a, and they assure us of God's final deliverance at the last judgment (12:25-29). The preacher urges his hearers to faithfully trust God in the face of persecution. God has the power to deliver them and will use it, perhaps in the here and now, and certainly at the final Judgment.

4. THE TRIUMPH OF FAITH: RESURRECTION 11:32-38

The preacher has given us a roll call of the great heroes of faith. The list is too long for him to describe all the examples he would like in detail. He begins this section by giving a few outstanding names to show that he is dealing with the history of God's people after the conquest. Then he groups the unnamed examples of faith together in great categories. This change of style was designed to impress the readers with the large number of faithful people and with the greatness of their triumphs and sufferings. Hebrews 11:32-35a continues the victories of faith described in 11:28-31. Verses 35b through 37, on the other hand, describe those who have suffered or been martyred for their faith. Thus they develop the theme of persecution begun with Abel (see 11:4) and continued in the description of Moses in Egypt (11:24-26).

The chart below demonstrates that the description of suffering faith in 11:35b-38 is the mirror image of the description of triumphant faith in 11:32-35a. First of all, the preacher balances political successes (the first three statements of 11:33) with disenfranchisement and alienation

(11:37b-38). Next he offers parallel pictures of three escapes from death (the last statement of 11:33 and the first two statements of 11:34) and three descriptions of death (11:37). Finally he portrays the military triumph of strength over weakness (the last three statements of 11:34) as parallel to the weakness of beatings and imprisonment (11:36). Verse 35 is the turning point of this passage; in it the preacher compares those who were raised from the dead to those who braved death by the power of their faith in the resurrection. This structure emphasizes the middle and concluding points: the comparison of the resurrections in verse 35 and the description of wandering in 11:37b-38.

Verse 35 is crucial. At this point two opposites meet: the triumphs achieved through faith and the suffering endured for and by faith. The greatest of those triumphs, resurrection from the dead (see 11:35a), pales before the **better resurrection** to eternal life which God offers to those who die for their faith.

The description of sufferings in 11:36-37 brings us back to the situation of the recipients of Hebrews (see 10:32-35; 12:3-4; 13:3). This description joins with the alienation of Abraham (11:9-10) and the suffering of Moses (11:24-26) to encourage those readers in their perseverance. Note that 11:38's description ends with those who are outcast wanderers. Abraham, too, was a wanderer and Moses was an outcast. It is likely that the recipients of Hebrews were themselves facing social ostracism with all its resulting emotional and economic consequences. These examples serve as the groundwork for the subsequent exhortations to endurance in 12:1-12.

A look at the crucial turning point of this section in 11:35, and the concluding description of total alienation in 11:38, reveals how the preacher's thought has gone beyond the thought of the Moses section. In the case of Moses and those who came after him, faithfulness which led to courage in the face of suffering brought God's deliverance in this life. And so it was with the victories described in 11:32-35a. But God does not always deliver His faithful in this life. Verse 35 says that some received a **better resurrection.** For some, God's deliverance comes only after death. Their final end in this world is alienation (11:38)! The preacher does not want to promise his hearers that they will be delivered in this life. When he described the suffering of Moses (11:24-26) he did not tell them to embrace suffering so that they would receive a temporal deliverance in the here and now. He told them to accept suffering because following God was worth it! The eternal reward is beyond calculation. And that is exactly what the faithful alienated and martyred received—a

better resurrection, the resurrection of those who live in the heavenly homeland! In 12:1-13, the preacher will challenge his hearers to take *their* place among God's suffering people!

VICTORY AND SUFFERING IN HEBREWS 11:32-38

> And what more shall I say? I do not have time to tell about Gideon, Barak, Samson, Jephthah, David, Samuel and the prophets (11:32).

Hebrews 11:33-35a Political Success (11:33a)	**Hebrews 11:35b-38** *Political Disenfranchisement* (11:37b-38)
Who through faith conquered kingdoms, administered justice, and gained what was promised.	They went about in sheepskins and goatskins, destitute, persecuted and mistreated—the world was not worthy of them. They wandered in deserts and mountains, and in caves and holes in the ground.

Escape From Death (11:33b-34a)	*Suffering of Death* (11:37a)
Who shut the mouths of lions, quenched the fury of the flames, and escaped the edge of the sword ...	They were stoned; they were sawed in two; they were put to death by the sword.

Military Victory (11:34b)	*Physical Punishment* (11:36)
... Whose weakness was turned to strength; and who became powerful in battle and routed foreign armies.	Some faced jeers and flogging, while still others were chained and put in prison.

RESURRECTION FAITH
(11:35)

Women received back their dead, raised to life again.	Others were tortured and refused to be released, so that they might gain a better resurrection.

The following discussion uses the chart on the previous page as its basis. The way in which 11:32 introduces the entire section indicates that the preacher is going to increase the intensity of his examples. The statement **And what more shall I say?** emphasizes the fact that he has made his point well. The next phrase **I do not have time to tell** indicates that he will abbreviate and move rapidly. Instead of naming particular people and their deeds of faith, he gives a suggestive series of names and then lists many broad categories of deeds of faith. This approach effectively communicates the impression that there are many, many more people of faith who have done many, many more deeds of faith than could ever be enumerated. Thus his hearers should be encouraged to join this great crowd. The names **Gideon, Barak, Samson, and Jephthah** summarize the period of the judges. **David, Samuel and the prophets** cover the period of the kings, prophets, and beyond.[21] This list of names suggests a multitude of people of faith extending indefinitely into the future. Some of the examples given reach into the time after the Old Testament was complete. The preacher introduces them with a brevity and rapidity that resembles machine gun fire.

The first three statements of 11:33 describe political victory and success through faith: **who through faith conquered kingdoms, administered justice, and gained what was promised.** It is easy to see how the list of names given in 11:32 suggested these victories. David **conquered kingdoms** and **administered justice.** Barak, Gideon, and David all **gained** victories that God had **promised** even though they did not receive God's ultimate promise of rest. The preacher's picture of just rulership, achieved through faith, stands in contrast to homeless wandering endured through faith (see 11:37b-38).

The next three statements, the last in 11:33 and the first two in 11:34, describe deliverance from certain death. The words **shut the mouths of lions** remind us immediately of Daniel (see Daniel 6:1-28), and **quenched the fury of the flames,** of his three friends (Dan. 3:1-30). These two events were associated in Jewish tradition as they are in the mind of every child who has regularly attended Sunday school. The third statement, **escaped the edge of the sword,** is a fairly general one and could apply to many people—such as David (1 Samuel 17:45-50), Elijah (1 Kings 19:1-3); Elisha (2 Kings 6:26-32), Jeremiah (Jeremiah 26:7-24), and perhaps many others. These three statements are set in bold relief by the first three statements of Hebrews 11:37 which describe those who died for their faith.

The next three statements in 11:34 focus on military conquest. Each one seems to prepare for the next so that the last is climactic. The first is the most general—**whose weakness was turned to strength.** Out of their previous weakness they were empowered by God. After their strengthening they **became powerful in battle** and this led to their routing **foreign armies.**[22] One can think of many biblical figures who fit the pattern these three statements lay out. Gideon would be one who was strengthened and ended up putting foreign armies to flight (Judges 6:1–8:35). These great triumphs must be understood in the light of Hebrews 11:36, which describes the faithful who were mocked, beaten, and imprisoned.

All these descriptions of triumph through faith (see 11:32-34) follow the pattern of this chapter's previous faith-empowered victories, such as the birth and restoration of Isaac to Abraham (11:11-12, 17-19) and the triumph of Moses and those who followed him by coming out of Egypt and entering Canaan (11:28-31). This pattern of victories reaches its climax in 11:35a: **Women received back their dead, raised to life again.** This phrase reminds us of the faith of Enoch who was delivered from death (see 11:5), and of Abraham's confidence that God could raise Isaac (11:17-19). The preacher is probably thinking of Elijah's restoration of the widow of Zarephath's son (1 Kings 17:17-24) and of Elisha's restoring the Shunammite's son (2 Kings 4:18-37). Their mothers were indeed people of faith who received a great blessing from God because of their faith.

Why has the preacher given this impressive list of the triumphs of faith? These exciting events brought victory in this world, which many people could see. These victories demonstrate that God's power is a reality! They encourage our faith! But the preacher has made it so clear that God's ultimate reward, His ultimate victory that "we hope for" (11:1), is beyond this physical world. Abraham anticipated the eternal city (11:13-16) and Moses an eternal "reward" far greater than the treasures of Egypt (11:26). Sometimes God does not deliver His people in this life in order to facilitate their entrance into that eternal reward.

Hebrews 11:35a gives the pinnacle of these earthly visible victories: **Women received back their dead, raised to life again.** Who could imagine anything greater than that? Yet, 11:35b offers something greater, infinitely greater: **Others were tortured and refused to be released, so that they might gain a better resurrection.** This is infinitely greater because it is a **better resurrection.** The women of verse 35a temporarily received their loved ones, but then of course they died again! Those who experience the **better resurrection** enter the full privileges of the heavenly homeland (11:13-16), of the city with foundations (11:9-10,

12:22-24), of God's eternal "rest" (4:1-11). They fully receive that for which Abraham longed, that reward for which Moses bore the "disgrace of Christ" (11:26). They could have been **released** if they had denied their faith, but they **refused** and were **tortured,** because that is what it took to keep their faith and **gain** this **better resurrection.** When God raises someone in the sense 11:35a describes, it merely shows that He can and will raise His faithful in the greater sense portrayed in 11:35b!

Thus all the suffering of 11:36-38 makes sense. The people these verses picture live for the eternal world. Their goal is heavenly, not earthly. They find their resources in God, not themselves or anything upon which others depend. Therefore they do not live in tune with this world. Their actions often convict the world, just as Noah's did (see 11:7), because they remind the world that it is neglecting God. Thus the unbelieving world may persecute people of faith. That very persecution is evidence that the faithful belong to God and that the **better resurrection** is theirs.

So, instead of the military victories described in the last three statements of 11:34, many of these faithful suffered the defeat of humiliating punishment, as described in the three statements of 11:36. They faced the shame of **jeers** while they endured the pain of public **flogging** (11:36). To be **chained** was a normal part of being put **in prison.** Some bore that painful restriction of liberty for Christ's sake. One may think, for example, of Jeremiah (Jeremiah 20:2, 7; 29:26; 37:15; compare 1 Kings 22:27). Even the first recipients of Hebrews may have experienced this type of suffering in the past (10:34; 13:3).

But this suffering went beyond imprisonment. The three statements of 11:37 stand in stark contrast to the last statement of 11:33 and the first two of 11:34. Verses 33 and 34 describe miraculous deliverance from death. Verse 37 describes the *death* of the martyrs, those who gave their lives to keep their faith and thus gain the ultimate reward. Zechariah, the son of Jehoiada, was **stoned** (2 Chronicles 24:21). Legend has it that Jeremiah was stoned in Egypt. Ancient legends state that Isaiah was **sawn in two.** Many, many were killed by the sword. The preacher may be thinking of the prophet Uriah (see Jeremiah 26:23), or even of John the Baptist (Mark 6:27).

Hebrews 11:33 showed that God sometimes demonstrates His power by giving His servants political success. The last part of 11:37-38 makes it clear that often His faithful people suffer complete political and social disenfranchisement. Although the New International Version starts a separate sentence in 11:38 for easier reading, 11:37-38 are all part of one sentence describing how these people **went about** or conducted their lives. Like Abraham, they were temporary residents in this world; like Moses, they suffered persecution. Their total exclusion by the world is indicated by the rough quality of their clothes, **sheepskins and goatskins.** These clothes remind us of John the Baptist and the prophets who lived separate from this world. They were **destitute** of daily needs, such as food, **persecuted** for their faith, and generally **mistreated** (11:37). Moses himself had suffered this mistreatment (see commentary on 11:25 above). The preacher's words reminded us of David who, pursued by Saul, **wandered in deserts and mountains, and in caves and holes in the ground** (see 1 Samuel 23:13-29). In summary, their total alienation and exclusion from the society of this world is marked by the following facts: Unbelieving society has allowed them only **sheepskins and goatskins** instead of proper clothes. It permits them only the **caves and holes in the ground** instead of proper housing. It has left them **destitute** of food and normal necessities.

But this very mistreatment by the unbelieving world means something wonderful—**the world was not worthy of them** (11:38). The unbelieving world thought that these faithful people were not worthy to associate with its society, but God knew that the unbelieving **world was not worthy of them.** That means that God was preparing something for them beyond this world—His eternal reward!

Countless Christians have received the persecution these verses portray. Modern times have seen an overwhelming abundance of martyrs and Christians who have suffered intensely for their faith. Perhaps the recipients of Hebrews were facing such situations. The preacher was preparing them for what he knew was coming. Indeed they were already experiencing the disdain of the world. Worse treatment was probably imminent.

But these verses describe the spiritual relationship of every Christian to the world. It is not our home. If we are true to our faith, people will not treat us like citizens. We focus on our eternal homeland. When the unbelieving world excludes us, it is treating us like it always treats God's people.

The world was not worthy of those people who suffered persecution before Christ came because they were faithful to God. God took care of them, but 11:39-40 makes it clear that they could not enter the fullness of God's promised blessing without the faithful who live after Christ's coming.

5. THE FULFILLMENT OF FAITH: "SOMETHING BETTER"[23] 11:39-40

Hebrews 11:39-40 concludes this last section and indeed the whole chapter by clarifying the relationship of these Old Testament believers to Christians. Those who lived before Christ were true examples of faith, but they did not yet enjoy the privileges of the new covenant which are ours in Christ. The preacher seems to imply that they have now entered into these privileges. His concern, however, is with his Christian hearers. Through Christ they have greater privileges than the Old Testament faithful had. Therefore they have a greater responsibility to live in faith and obedience.

All of these people were **commended** by God **for their faith.** They had the kind of faith that pleases God (see 11:6)! Many of them received various things that God had promised them, but none of them saw the fulfillment of *the* promise (11:39), access into the very presence of God. That **something better** that God **had planned** for us is the cleansing from sin and access into God's presence now available through the High Priesthood of Christ. The preacher uses the expression **made perfect** in a special way. Those who now receive this cleansing from sin that Christ has provided are said to be **made perfect.** The only way in which Christ makes us "perfect" in this life is by cleansing us from sin so we can come into God's presence. He gives us daily grace to live in victory over temptation.

Those people of faith experience this reality only **together with us,** we who live after Christ. We cannot be precise in determining the degree to which they by faith in God's promise participated in the benefits of Christ before He came. But now, they partake fully **together with us** of all those benefits. It is likely that they are included in the "spirits of righteous men made perfect" who, according to 12:23, dwell in the heavenly city. Of course they, like we, await that final judgment described in 12:25-29.

The preacher's point remains. They lived lives of faith before Christ came. In their day the benefits of Christ's High Priesthood were part of God's promise for the future. Today they are part of His power that is available for all God's people. If those before Christ lived lives of faith, we surely should be able, by the grace available to us, to do the same. As the opening verses of Hebrews 12 will show, the point is to keep focused on Jesus, the One who makes this difference!

ENDNOTES

[1]The "in reverence" of the New American Standard Bible is entirely too weak.

[2]The word which the New International Version translates "reverence" in 12:28 comes from the same root as the word translated **holy fear** in this verse. In 12:28 the preacher reminds us how we should worship God in light of the fact that He indeed is the judge.

[3]He also alludes to judgment in 11:28-29.

[4]And in each case, the ones delivered from death are associated with the main character. Isaac was the intended victim of Abraham's sacrifice. The people of Israel were involved with Moses in the Passover, and it was their firstborn who were saved. In each instance, the ones delivered become the next examples of faith—Isaac in verse 20; the Israelites, by implication, in verse 29.

[5]For example, Psalm 48:8; 87:1-3, 5; 122:3. See William L. Lane, *Hebrews 9–13*, vol. 47b, Word Biblical Commentary, New Testament ed. Ralph P. Martin, gen. eds. David A. Hubbard and Glenn W. Barker (Dallas: Word Books, 1991), p. 352.

[6]We follow the New International Version, which makes Abraham the subject of verses 11 and 12, rather than the interpretation represented by the New American Standard Bible and New King James Version, which makes Sarah the subject. The arguments concerning whether Abraham or Sarah should be the subject of this verse are rather technical. For arguments in support of the interpretation we have adopted, see Lane, pp. 344–45. For the opposite view, see *A Commentary on the Epistle to the Hebrews* by Philip Edgcumbe Hughes (Grand Rapids, Michigan: Wm. B. Eerdmans Publishing Co., 1977), p. 473.

[7]Abraham was one hundred when Isaac was born (see Genesis 21:5; Romans 4:19; Hebrews 11:12). Sarah was ninety. On her barrenness and age see Genesis 15:1-6; 17:15-22; 18:9-15.

[8]"would keep faith" (REB)

[9]It is true that Abraham had children by another wife after Sarah's death (see Genesis 25:1-6). But in his relationship with Sarah, considering his age, her stage in life and lifelong barrenness, he was **as good as dead.** See Hughes, p. 476.

[10]Abraham had fathered another son, Ishmael, by Hagar, Sarah's maid. Isaac, however, was the one and only son of Sarah, and the one and only son whom God had promised.

[11]For a defense of this interpretation, see Lane, pp. 362–63.

[12]This quotation is found in the Old Testament text of the New International Version. However, some English versions evidence a different understanding of this verse: "Then Israel bowed in worship at the head of *the bed*" (NASB, my emphasis). A slight difference in the pronunciation of one Hebrew word makes the difference between "staff" and "bed." The translators of the Greek Old Testament which the preacher used understood the word as referring to "staff." Many English translators have preferred "bed."

[13]The word translated **no ordinary** is the only word that Hebrews uses from the original account of Moses' birth in the Greek translation of Exodus 2:1-10. This word is also used to describe Moses in Acts 7:20, where it is qualified by

the phrase "to God" or "in the sight of God." Note the translation in the New International Version margin, "fair in the sight of God." In Acts, the NIV text translates the whole phrase, "fair in the sight of God," as "no ordinary." Here in Hebrews it is just the one word "fair" that is translated "no ordinary."

[14]The New Revised Standard Version translation "a son of Pharaoh's daughter" in place of **the son of Pharaoh's daughter** more clearly shows the preacher's emphasis on the status of sonship.

[15]The Revised English Bible uses the word "preferring" instead of "he chose": "preferring to share hardship with God's people. . . ." The Greek word in question can be translated in this way. "Preferring" makes the verse refer to the motivation for Moses' choice rather than the manner of the choice. In either case the meaning is very similar.

[16]The New Revised Standard Version translates the words behind the New International Version phrase **disgrace for the sake of Christ,** as "abuse suffered for the Christ." This translation seems to take Moses' point of view. He was suffering "abuse" for "the Christ" (the Messiah) who would come but whom he could not yet know as Jesus the Son of God. The preacher would probably have agreed that Moses did not understand the full significance of the "Christ" or the anointed one who would come. Both he and his hearers, however, knew that the Christ was Jesus, the Son of God, because God has now spoken in His Son (1:1-3). The **disgrace** Moses suffered was "the reproach of the coming Messiah with whom he was united by faith" (Hughes, p. 497). See John 5:46.

[17]The Revised English Bible translates **disgrace for the sake of Christ** as "the stigma that rests on God's anointed." The translators here have taken the word **Christ** to mean "God's anointed." Instead of seeing this word as a reference to Christ (Jesus), they see it as a title for Moses. Moses bears the disgrace that one who is "God's anointed" would bear. The problem with this interpretation is that nowhere in the Old Testament or in Jewish writings contemporary with Hebrews does anyone else call Moses "God's anointed." Neither is there anything in the context of Hebrews to suggest such an understanding. The preacher and his hearers would naturally associate the word **Christ** with the Son of God who came to earth and became Jesus.

[18]The New Revised Standard Version's translation, "as though he saw him who is invisible," is probably more accurate. This translation clearly implies that Moses saw with the eyes of faith. Compare the New King James Version, "as seeing Him who is invisible."

[19]Their fear of the sea (see Exodus 14:10-14) was overcome by their fear of God (Exodus 14:31).

[20]Just as in the example of Noah in verse 7, God's deliverance of the faithful entailed His judgment on the unfaithful.

[21]The preacher probably listed **Samuel** after **David,** though he preceded David, because Samuel was the first of the prophets.

[22]The preacher's growing intensity is shown by the fact that the verbs in these three examples move from passive to intransitive to active: **was turned . . . became . . . routed.**

[23]Hebrews 11:40

18

ENDURE SUFFERING AS CHRISTIANS

Hebrews 12:1-13

ebrews 12:1-13 brings the faith of the past to bear on the present suffering of Christian believers. The Revised English Bible editors placed a section heading before 11:1—"Faith in times past," and before 12:1, "Faith today." By their faithfulness Old Testament believers encourage Christians to faithfully endure suffering. The preacher has shown how true faith enabled past believers to endure great hardships, climaxing in his description of exclusion, abandonment, and martyrdom in 11:35b-38. He has reminded his hearers that they possess "something better" than those great people of faith ever knew. In this section he urges them to stand on the shoulders of those who have gone before (12:1). He reminds them of the "something better" that they have in Jesus (12:2-3). He urges them to endure the suffering appropriate for those with such privileges (12:4-13).

The preacher introduced this short history of God's people in 10:36-39. In that introduction he issued Habakkuk's clarion call for God's people to have a faith which produces endurance (see Habakkuk 2:4, see also Hebrews 10:37-38). In 12:1-13, he renews this call for endurance. He urgently wants his hearers to be "not of those who shrink back and are destroyed, but of those who believe and are saved" (10:39).

1. FOCUS ON THE PERFECTER OF FAITH 12:1-3

The preacher's main concern in this paragraph is expressed by the exhortation at the end of 12:1: **Let us run with perseverance the race marked out for us.** He has already expressed this concern for his hearers in 10:36. It is his reason for relating the great, crescendoing catalog of the faithful in 11:1-40.

The word **therefore** directs us back to his description of that **great cloud of witnesses** in chapter 11. The word **cloud** emphasizes the unity of this group. They were one in faith and purpose. The last verses of chapter 11 emphasized how **great** and impressive this body of faithful people is. They now are near us; they "surround" us. The preacher paints a picture of faithful champions in the stands cheering on Christians who are now running the race of faith. The preacher does not call them **witnesses** because they are "witnessing" what we are doing. The word **witnesses** does not mean "spectators." They may be watching us, but they are **witnesses** to us. They have completed the race of faith. They have stood on the victor's stand and received God's gold medal. God has accredited them as genuine examples of true faith. Their very lives say to us, "By God's grace, it can be done!"

In light of their testimony, run! But how? Hebrews 12:1's first two exhortations tell us something about how we should prepare for this race and the way we should run it. **Let us throw off everything that hinders.** The New King James Version translates the Greek behind the phrase **everything that hinders** as "every weight," the New American Standard Bible as "every encumbrance." The preacher's picture portrays a runner who removes all excess clothes, who trims off any excess body weight so that he has less to carry and less wind resistance. Even things that are good in themselves must be put aside if they hinder the Christian or distract from running the race. How many Christians are slowed or turned aside by concerns, interests, and entertainments that may be innocent in themselves. (Compare the thorny soil in Jesus' parable of the sower [Mark 4:3-20]).

If even good things must be set aside, how much more **the sin that so easily entangles.** Every sin **easily entangles.** All sin must be put aside. Picture a runner with his feet caught in vines or other plants or whose shorts have fallen around his feet. The runner trips and falls. That is what sin does to runners in the race of faith!

Then, when we have jettisoned any distraction and every sin, we are enabled to **run with perseverance the race marked out for us,** just as those watching (**witnesses**) have run their races!

Winners run the course **marked out** for the race. God has **marked out** our course. He has **marked** it **out** clearly **for us** through Jesus Christ. Christ has run this race and opened the finish line for us. He has opened the finish line by His High Priesthood and atoning self-sacrifice. That is why the preacher tells us to **fix our eyes on Jesus, the author and perfecter of our faith.** In 11:39-40, the preacher told his hearers that they had "something better" than all of those people of faith who lived before Christ. Here is the "something better." It is Jesus himself! It is all He has done to provide our salvation. Our resources for the race are much greater than theirs. The runner keeps his eye straight ahead on the finish line. The stands hold many witnesses to faith, but Jesus is on the other side of the finish line at God's right hand. To focus on the finish line is to focus on Him! Just as Abraham and Moses kept their eyes of faith focused on the eternal but invisible goal (see 11:10, 16, 26-27), so Christians must keep their eyes on Jesus!

The phrase **Jesus, the author and finisher of our faith** (12:2) is crucial. In the original Greek sentence, the preacher placed the words represented by **author and finisher** before the word **Jesus.** There is no Greek word for **our.** The word translated **author** is the same word that was used for Jesus in 2:10. In the commentary on that verse, we saw that the Revised Standard Version/New Revised Standard Version translation "Pioneer" was a more precise expression of its meaning. Thus, a more accurate translation of the Greek text might read, "the Pioneer and Perfecter of faith, Jesus."

Jesus is more than the "Pioneer and Perfecter" of "my" own personal faith. He is the Pioneer and Perfecter of the entire way of faith. He insures God's promise: Those who run the race of faith to the end will reach the eternal goal.

As our "Pioneer" He has run this race before us and opened the way to the finish line, the goal that was not yet attainable before His coming (see 11:39-40). He has been our true "Forerunner" (6:20). Thus He brings God's many children to "glory" across the finish line (2:10).

The "Pioneer" accomplishes this mission by becoming the "Perfecter of faith." It was sin that separated God's people from God and kept them from crossing the finish line. He is the "Perfecter" of faith in that He has decisively dealt with this sin. He himself was "perfected through suffering" (2:10). By His complete obedience and sacrifice of himself He became "perfect" as our Savior, "perfectly" able to save us (5:9-10). He exercises this ability to save by "perfecting" us—that is, by cleansing us from sin so that we can come into God's presence, across the finish line (see Hebrews 10:14; 11:40; 12:23; compare 7:11, 19; 9:9).

The preacher puts the phrase "Pioneer and Perfecter of faith" first because he wants his hearers to focus on the great salvation that Christ has provided. The name **Jesus,** however, reminds us that this Savior lived a real, daily human life in which He completely obeyed God despite the suffering He faced. He ran this race as a real human being.

The One who suffered is the One standing across the finish line at God's right hand.

The preacher now turns to this suffering, by which Jesus became the "Pioneer and Perfecter" of faith. **The joy** God **set before him** (12:2) was not so much the joy of returning to heaven, but the **joy** of bringing God's sons and daughters across the finish line into God's presence. For the sake of that **joy,** He **endured the cross.** The preacher has not previously mentioned the **cross,** but it symbolizes all he has said about Christ's sacrifice, with special emphasis on the great pain and shame that accompanied His death. Nowhere else does the New Testament says that Jesus **endured** the cross. The preacher has used this word here because he urgently desires his hearers to endure the pain ahead of them.

Jesus not only **endured** the great pain, but did so **scorning** the cross's **shame.** A modern person can hardly imagine the **shame** associated with crucifixion. The ancients could imagine nothing more shameful. The crucified person suffered painfully and publicly. His naked body was exposed to the whole world. He was ridiculed and ostracized from society. No doubt the preacher's hearers were suffering shame for their faith. Jesus "scorned" the great shame that was His. He considered it as nothing. He in no way let it determine his action or deter Him from faithful endurance. He faithfully moved toward the **joy set before him,** and that **joy** is our eternal blessing! Moses "regarded disgrace for Christ as of greater value than the treasures of Egypt, because he was looking ahead to his reward" (11:26). Jesus "scorned" His own great **shame** for the sake of the **joy** that is ours!

The hearers already know the conclusion of that suffering. The preacher mentioned it in his first allusion to Psalm 110:1 way back in Hebrews 1:3. Jesus' endurance resulted in victory—He **sat down at the right hand of the throne of God** on the other side of the finish line. He sat down there once-for-all. He continues to sit there in the seat of greatest power in all the universe and beyond. He lives in the presence of God with the power to bring us there! Through His work God's **throne** has become a "throne of grace" (4:16).

The preacher is concerned that his hearers **run with perseverance the race marked out** for them (12:1). Those Old Testament people of faith spur them on by watching them and, more importantly, by testifying to them that they can win the race by the grace of God! But the preacher calls them to keep their eyes fixed on Jesus because He is the One through whom that grace is available. He has endured. He makes possible the successful completion of their race of faith.

The preacher not only calls his readers to continually keep their eyes focused on Jesus across the finish line. In 12:3, he summons them to **consider him** in regard to His endurance. He calls them to calculate the greatness of the suffering He endured and to evaluate the significance it has for them. The **opposition** he endured climaxed in the cross with its unspeakable pain and unimaginable shame. He, like Moses (11:24-26), like the sufferers described in 11:35b-38, and like the readers of Hebrews (10:32-34), suffered this opposition **from sinful men.** But the preacher calls his hearers not just to consider Jesus as the greatest of all faith examples. He is that, but He is much more. Because He has overcome such suffering and shame, He can enable them to be victorious. If they look to Him for strength, He will supply it so that they need not **grow weary** of the race and thus **lose heart.** With His help, they can make the finish line.

2. EMBRACE THE DISCIPLINE OF LEGITIMATE CHILDREN 12:4-13

In Hebrews 12:4-11, the preacher quotes Proverbs 3:11-12 to encourage his hearers in their suffering. He quotes these verses in 12:5-6 and interprets them in 12:7-11. Verses 12 and 13 apply the interpretation to the situation of the hearers.

The preacher makes an easy transition from speaking of Jesus as the "Pioneer and Perfecter" of faith (12:1-3) to speaking of his Christian hearers as **sons** of God (12:4-11). He has already told his hearers (2:10-18) that Christ is the "Pioneer" of the "salvation" of God's "sons." Christ identifies with them as their "brother." By suffering as their High Priest, He enables them to enter the fullness of sonship and to reach their heavenly goal. Hebrews 3:1-6 describes Him as the faithful Son of God whose faithfulness they should emulate. Thus God's addressing His people as "sons," found in Proverbs 3:11-12 and quoted in Hebrews 12:5-6, is particularly appropriate for those the Son/Pioneer has enabled to become God's children.

In 12:4, the preacher describes the Christian life as a continual **struggle against sin.** He switches his metaphor from racing to boxing because the boxer is the one who faces hostile opposition. Verse 1's "sin that so easily entangles" referred to temptation and to sin in the human heart. The **sin** of verse 4, however, is more closely related to the opposition that Jesus suffered from "sinful men" (12:3). This **sin** is the wickedness in the world around us, the world's refusal to acknowledge God. Christians continually struggle against all that resists God. Thus, sinful people oppose them.

Those to whom the preacher wrote are engaged in this battle, but they have not yet had to resist **to the point of shedding** their **blood.** Jesus did! He endured the gruesome, painful, shameful cross (12:2). The readers of Hebrews may yet face a martyr's death. The preacher wants them to be prepared.

They, however, are in danger of discouragement. The tense and form of the Greek word translated **forgotten** (12:5) indicate that they have completely **forgotten** and not yet recalled the **word of encouragement** God gave them in Proverbs 3:11-12. Note that the preacher calls this whole sermon a "word of exhortation" (13:22). He and the writer of the proverbs he quotes share the same purpose: to exhort and encourage God's people to faithfulness despite difficulties.

The New American Standard Bible translates the words behind the phrase **that addresses you as sons** as passive, "is addressed to you as sons." The preacher may be implying that the words of Proverbs 3:11-12 are addressed to them by God. God is conversing with His children. The words address them in their capacity **as sons** of God. They have completely forgotten that the **sons** of God should expect hardship and persecution.

There is one significant variation in this citation of Proverbs 3:11-12 between the wording of the Greek version used by the preacher and the interpretation of the Hebrew original represented by our English Old Testaments. This variation occurs in the last line of the quotation: **He punishes everyone he accepts as a son.** The usual translation of the Hebrew text is represented by the New International Version of Proverbs 3:12: "as a father the son he delights in." This discrepancy arose because originally only the consonants of the words were used in writing the Hebrew Old Testament. Vowels were added when the text was pronounced. Two different ways of pronouncing this text led to the two different translations given above. The Greek translation of this last phrase of the quotation facilitates the preacher's purpose because it clearly affirms that God is the one who addresses the hearer as **My son** (verse 6, quoting Proverbs 3:11). The preacher includes this quotation to help God's children not **lose heart** at God's discipline, because that very discipline shows they are His true children.

The preacher interprets and applies this Proverbs quotation in Hebrews 12:7-11. His main point is encapsulated in the first statement: **Endure hardship as discipline** (12:7). The Greek word translated **discipline** is a bit broader than the English word. Ancient writers used it to describe the training of children. It includes both instruction and correction.

In 12:7-8, the preacher urges his hearers to endure the sufferings they face as formative discipline because of their status as **sons.** In 12:9-10 he strengthens his argument by showing them they should endure this hardship as discipline because of the Father whose children they are. Once the hearers see that the **hardship** they experience for Christ is God's **discipline,** God's training, then they can see that they should expect it as God's **sons.** Verse 8 makes the importance of this **discipline** clear: If they were not **disciplined** by God with the same discipline that all His children share, then they would be **illegitimate children** without the privileges of status, support, and inheritance that **true sons** have. They would lose the eternal reward that is the heritage of God's **true sons.**

Thus this hardship which is God's discipline marks us as His children and heirs. There is, however, more. We know how to respond to this discipline and understand the priceless benefits we receive from it only when we consider the Father who administers it. We see the quality of God as our Father by comparing Him with human fathers. The preacher makes this comparison twice, once in verse 9 and once in verse 10. He uses the first comparison to show us how we should respond to this Father's discipline. With the second he reinforces this proper response by showing the wonderful benefits of God's discipline.

Verse 9 compares the response appropriate for children to make to their **human fathers** with the proper response to **the Father of our spirits.** There is a strong contrast between **human fathers** and **the Father of our spirits.** A literal rendering of the Greek would read, "fathers of the flesh" and "the Father of spirits." "Flesh" describes humanity in all of its weakness and limitation (see commentary on 5:7 and 10:20). The "Father of spirits" emphasizes the transcendence of God. **Spirits** refers to human spirits. He is the ultimate source of our physical and spiritual life. He thus exists in a class totally above our "fathers of the flesh" through whose direct agency we received only physical life. If we **respected** our **human fathers** for the **discipline** with which they trained us, then we should completely **submit** ourselves to the infinitely greater **Father of . . . spirits.** The word behind **submit** is much stronger than the word the preacher used to describe respect for our human fathers. Our submission to the heavenly Father is to be complete.

This verse ends by stating the benefits we receive from this submission, a theme developed in the next verse. Those who submit themselves totally to the **Father of . . . spirits** will **live!** The Book of Proverbs says much about sons submitting to the instruction of their fathers. Such sons live a satisfying and wholesome earthly life. Much more is at stake here. God our Father is the **Father of . . . spirits.** The life that He gives is eternal! His discipline leads to the heavenly reward provided by the "living God" (3:12; 9:14; 10:31) through the eternal High Priest (7:25). This is the reward His people have always anticipated.

In 12:10 the preacher compares the discipline administered by our earthly fathers and Heavenly Father. He draws this comparison to show the great benefit that comes from the heavenly Father's discipline. Our earthly fathers' discipline was limited by time and judgment. They only disciplined us **for a little while,** the period of our childhood. They could only discipline us **as they thought best.** They may have used their best judgment, but they were human and so they may sometimes have failed despite good intentions. **God,** however, has infinite wisdom and disposal of all of our time. In His love He disciplines us inevitably for **our** very best **good.** This preacher defines this ultimate **good** as sharing **in his holiness.** Through Christ's sacrifice and High Priesthood we can already be cleansed from sin (9:11-14), have new-covenant hearts tuned to obey God (8:7-13; 10:15-18), access to His presence (10:19-25), and grace to overcome temptation (4:14-16). These Christ-provided benefits enable us to take advantage of the discipline of sonship. This discipline fosters continual growth in godly character and enables us to share more fully **in his holiness,** which is the very life of God himself. His children share in His life and reflect His character.

The preacher uses Proverbs 3:11-12 to show his hearers that they should not be discouraged by the suffering and persecution that they face for Christ. Rather, they should endure it as God's loving discipline and fully submit to Him. They should act in this way because this discipline marks them as the true children of God who are heirs of all God has promised and provided for them in Christ. Furthermore, their loving heavenly Father uses these sufferings as His means of discipline. He uses them inevitably for their best good, the best good imaginable, to enable them to share in His own nature and life. The preacher knows, however, that this discipline is still very painful. He concludes by addressing the pain (12:11).

The first half of 12:11 is a general statement; the second half pertains directly to God's loving **discipline. No discipline** of any kind **seems pleasant at the time** one experiences it, but **painful.** People undergo discipline only because it is worth the benefits to which it leads. God's discipline pays off big. **Later on . . . it produces** an abundant **harvest of righteousness and peace.** The phrase **righteousness and peace** describes a joyful wholeness of relationship with God and with God's family. We find this wholeness only in His presence. It is made possible only by His Own life dwelling within His purified people.

In one sense believers ultimately experience these blessings only at the **later on** of Christ's return. However, the results of all discipline are incremental. People of faith can experience these blessings in ever increasing degree if they submit to God's discipline. The important thing is to be among those **who have been trained** by this discipline. Those who have experienced God's discipline know its beneficial effects in their lives.

Verses 12 and 13 conclude this part of the author's exhortation to faith and endurance. **Therefore,** in light of the great cloud of witnesses to faith (11:1-40), in light of all that the "Pioneer and Perfecter of faith" has done for us (12:1-3), and in light of the true significance of the sufferings Christians presently endure (12:4-11), **strengthen your feeble arms and weak knees.** The preacher again assumes the role of sports announcer. The boxer is about ready to cave in. His arms are coming down. His legs are buckling. He needs to draw strength from the encouragement he has received.

The words **strengthen your feeble arms and weak knees** (12:12) appear to be a paraphrase of Isaiah 35:3. Isaiah addressed these words of encouragement to God's people in exile because God was going to bring them back home. The preacher addresses these words to his hearers because God is going to bring His people to their ultimate home.

He also urges them, **Make level paths for your feet** (12:12), a quotation from Proverbs 4:26. This exhortation fits well with the preacher's earlier description of the Christian life as a race. The preacher is instructing his hearers to run a straight path without turning aside. In the original Proverbs passage, a wise man is teaching his "son" to follow the straight path of obedience, not turning to wickedness on the right or on the left. Likewise, the preacher wants his hearers to pursue a straight path to the heavenly city. If they do, they will be an example to **the lame,** those who are becoming discouraged. **The lame** face the possibility of becoming **disabled** by giving in to their discouragement. Instead **the lame** can be **healed** by God's grace. The preacher's desire that his hearers show mutual concern for one another's spiritual welfare (4:1, 10:24-25) again finds expression in this concluding exhortation.

The preacher is about to introduce the example of Esau in 12:14-17 as a warning against turning from God's way. Then, in 12:18-24, he will balance his discussion of the "struggle" (12:4) that Christians face by describing the great privileges which are now available to people of faith.

Part Five

THE SINAI PICTURE: HEAR THE WORD SPOKEN FROM HEAVEN BY A HOLY GOD

Hebrews 12:14-29

The spiritual history of God's people begun in the fourth major section of Hebrews (10:32–12:13) finds its conclusion in the fifth (12:14-29). This history has portrayed a pilgrimage to the heavenly homeland. Hebrews 11:1-40 dealt with the past history of God's people from the creation to Christ. All of the faithful who lived before Christ anticipated that heavenly goal. Hebrews 12:1-3 focused on Christ. When He came, the past changed to the present. He completed the faith of those before Him and provided Christians with the means to reach the goal (12:1-3). Hebrews 12:4-13 addresses the present Christian experience. Throughout section four (see Hebrews 10:32–12:13) the preacher has urged his readers to have the kind of faith that perseveres in obedience despite persecution. For those who hang on, the reward will be great.

Hebrews 12:14-29 continues describing the present experience of Christians and moves on to the future and final judgment. While 12:1-13 focused on the opposition that Christians face and the reward to be gained; 12:14-25 considers the privileges now theirs through Christ and the consequently greater danger of judgment. The greatness of those privileges means the responsibility of Christians is great. The preacher introduces his description of the privileges (12:18-24) with a warning (12:14-17). The section ends in 12:25-29 with the final judgment.

In his introduction to this history of God's people, the preacher introduced the themes of salvation for the faithful and condemnation for the disobedient (see the quotation of Habakkuk 2:4 in Hebrews 10:38). These themes were prominent in the example of Noah's faith (11:7) near the beginning of this history. They reach their ultimate fulfillment in the description of the final judgment in 12:25-29.

This major section (12:14-29) turns from the Pilgrimage Picture to the Sinai Picture. It describes the privileges that Christians now have rather than the goal toward which they travel. "Sinai" is the mount of God's speaking, the place of revelation. God spoke in the past at Mount Sinai. God spoke in the past through the Son when He came to earth and accomplished our salvation as High Priest (see commentary on 2:1-4). But God now speaks from heaven through the exalted Son, our High Priest. We stand before this gracious mount of God's speaking in the present (12:22-24)! Through our Mediator we have direct access to the presence of God. There will be one more mount of God's speaking: God will speak again from heaven in the future at the judgment (12:25-29).

We turn, then, from the sufferings we Christian pilgrims face in this unbelieving world to the privileges that are ours in Christ as we stand before the heavenly mount. The preacher wants us to remember that these privileges entail responsibility, so he introduces this section with the warning example of Esau.

19

PURSUE THE HOLY LIFE

Hebrews 12:14-17

Before describing the great privileges Christ gives to faithful Christians, the writer of Hebrews offers a warning against squandered privilege. The preacher uses the example of **Esau** (Heb. 12:16) to speak urgent words of caution concerning his readers' present spiritual danger.

The rest of this passage is an explanation of the opening exhortation in 12:14: **Make every effort to live in peace with all men and to be holy; without holiness no one will see the Lord.** The translation of the New International Version is smooth but obscures some important aspects of the meaning of this verse, which are preserved by the New Revised Standard Version: "Pursue peace with everyone, and the holiness without which no one will see the Lord." The word "pursue" is much more graphic than the NIV phrase **Make every effort.** "Pursue" also reminds us of the race metaphor in 12:13. The Greek word translated "pursue" is plural. "Everyone" in the congregation is to "pursue" this peace together. In their mutual relationships, all Christians are to pursue wholeness and harmony with one another by drawing on the power that is theirs in Christ.

Christ also provides holiness, the basis of Christian peace, and the provision which enables us to **see the Lord** (12:14). The whole Bible emphasizes that human sinfulness separates people from the Holy God.[1] The Old Testament priestly ritual demonstrated this separation (see commentary on 10:1-4). Christ's sacrifice and High Priesthood have provided the means by which people's hearts can be cleansed of sin (see 9:14) and thus be enabled to have the holiness necessary to enter God's holy presence. The vision of God, described in 12:22-24, is now available to all of God's people. Christ has made available the holiness which God's people must "pursue."

The preacher urges his hearers to "pursue" peace and holiness. This does not mean that they presently lack those gifts and their benefits. They have already appropriated Christ's cleansing of their consciences from the guilt and power of sin (see 9:14). They have experienced the transformed heart available through the new covenant (see 10:15-18). Yet, by the daily practice of concrete obedience, they must intentionally make this holiness before God and the peace (wholeness) it brings with others a reality in their conduct. Participation in God's holiness must be lived out in daily life. We have seen that God's Fatherly discipline helps believers to grow in the practice of holiness (see 12:10) and thus to partake of His nature in a deeper way. Believers live in the holiness that Christ has provided, and yet they must also act. They must draw near to "the throne of grace" (4:16). They must persevere against difficulties each day to continue in holiness and enjoy its final consummation.

The three commands in 12:14-16 show how Christians carry out their common pursuit of peace and holiness. They strive *together,* seeking their own and each other's individual holiness, as well as the holiness and peace of the community. The preacher instructs all of his hearers to **see to it that no one misses,** "fall[s] short" (NKJV), or "fails to obtain" (NRSV) the **grace** of God available in Christ (12:15). Such failure to obtain God's **grace** can arise easily from slackness or negligence. Lagging in the Christian race or neglecting spiritual things may lead to a failure to obtain God's **grace** for daily living.

Failing to make use of God's **grace** leads to a **bitter root** growing up within the fellowship (12:15). The symbol of a **bitter root** represents a stubborn and self-seeking heart. How quickly such a **bitter root** will **cause trouble.** Pride and criticism soon surface. One selfish heart can mar the peace and wholeness of the entire body. If we do not arrest such bitterness, it will quickly **defile many.** Many will catch the same disease which fractures holiness toward God and harmony among His family. We must encourage, exhort, warn, instruct, and pray for one another to prevent such disaster.

We must guard against anyone's missing God's **grace** through neglect, and we must guard against the **bitter root** of rebellion and self-will. The first warning leads to the second. Failure to heed the second may result in people's becoming **godless like Esau** (12:16). We must by all means guard against such tragedy. The match of failing to appropriate God's **grace** leads to the bonfire of the **bitter root** of self-will, which leads to the forest fire of being **godless like Esau** (12:15-16). In this passage, to be **godless** is to reject holiness. Godlessness is total disregard for God and our responsibility to Him. As noted above, the faithful person trusts God's power for the present and believes that His promises for the future are sure. In contrast, the **godless** person lives totally for the things he or she can see and rejects the reality of God's invisible power and future promises.

Hebrews 12:16, in the original Greek, says that **Esau** was also **sexually immoral.** The Old Testament does not accuse Esau of sexual immorality, although Jewish tradition sometimes did so on the basis of his taking Hittite wives.[2] Old Testament writers did, however, often use adultery as a metaphor for idolatry. The two often went together: Those who rejected God and practiced idolatry often participated in sexual immorality. The person who rejects God and lives for the things of this world is often entrapped by lust, an enemy of God's holiness. "Licentiousness is the destroyer of holiness."[3] Perhaps the preacher mentioned this sin because some of his hearers were in danger of succumbing to it. He later warns them about such sin in 13:4. Avoiding this sin would help them to love each other appropriately and thus maintain peace and wholeness within the Christian family. The first readers certainly lived in a world where sexual temptation and sin were common. The preacher's warning is for first- and twenty-first-century hearers. Sexual immorality is a mark of the godless.

The preacher offers concrete evidence that **Esau** was **godless** (12:16). **Esau** lived for things he could see and rejected God's promises and power. He rejected God when he **sold his inheritance rights**—literally, his "rights as firstborn"—for a single meal (see Genesis 25:29-34). He turned away not only from material inheritance, but also from God's promise to his grandfather Abraham, the promise of a heavenly homeland (see Hebrews 11:9-10, 13-16). This was the promise pursued by Abraham, Isaac, Jacob, and all the faithful of Hebrews 11:1-40. Esau is their opposite, their foil. This is the promise that is fulfilled through Christ. Esau gave up his access to the promise of an invisible but eternal inheritance for the merest pittance of this world's goods—a single meal! God gives us the same opportunity that he gave Esau. All God's children are "firstborn." We all enjoy the blessings of that promise as we enter the very presence of God (see 12:22-24).

Esau would have received all the privileges of God's promise, but he squandered them for a mere bowl of soup. The preacher's hearers, then and now, have received the much greater privileges toward which that promise pointed. How tragic to trade those great blessings for earthly satisfactions. The key is to make use of God's grace so that no self-will or rebelliousness separates us from God and mars the harmony and wholeness of our fellowship (see 12:14-15).

Hebrews 12:17 explains the finality of Esau's situation by telling the rest of the story. The word **afterward** indicates the time after he had sold his right of the firstborn to the inheritance of God's promise. He then decided that **. . . he wanted to inherit this blessing . . .** (12:17a; see the whole story in Genesis 27:1-40). The material parts of the **blessing** attracted him (Heb. 12:17), for he possessed little interest in spiritual matters. **He was,** however, **rejected.** The preacher here describes more than Esau's being **rejected** by his father, Isaac. God himself rejected Esau. Esau is a prototype of apostasy. His totally **godless** attitude (12:16) cut him off from God.

The NIV's translation, **He could bring about no change of mind . . .** (12:17b), is a bit ambiguous. It might imply that Esau could not get his father, Isaac, to change his mind. Most versions translate **change of mind** as "repentance." Esau would not change his own **mind;** he would not repent of his godlessness. Note the NRSV: ". . . He found no chance to repent. . . ." **He sought** the physical benefits of **the blessing with tears,** but he was not willing to repent of his sin.

This desire for material blessing but refusal to repent shows how **godless** he was (12:16). He had no sorrow for anything that he had done wrong. He regretted only that he missed out on the material aspects of God's promise to Abraham. He wanted the part of **the blessing** that interested him (12:17).

Failure to appropriate God's grace may lead to a self-willed rebellious heart, which then leads to the kind of godless state we see in Esau. He lived totally for the things he could see and rejected God and His eternal reward. Even a negligent failure to appropriate grace may lead to apostasy. Let us pray for, warn, encourage, and support one another. Let us hold each other accountable. This mutual care and concern was an aspect of the "social holiness" for which the Methodists were once known!

The preacher has used this example of Esau to warn his hearers against the misuse of God-given privilege. They must not fail to appropriate the grace that God has made available. In the next section, 12:18-24, the preacher describes the privileges of grace that are theirs. He brings into focus all that he has said about the High Priestly work of Christ. He does this as he describes Christians in the presence of God at the heavenly Zion in 12:22-24. He puts this scene in perspective by comparing it with God's people before the visible mount where God established the old covenant (see 12:18-21).

ENDNOTES

[1]We think immediately of the sin of Adam and Eve, the murder of Cain, the sin of the world in Noah's day, the sin of Israel in the wilderness, the sin of the time of the judges, and finally the sin of Israel and Judah which sent them into exile (see, respectively, Genesis 3:1-24; 4:1-16; 6:5-6; Hebrews 3:1–4:13; Judges 2:1-23; 2 Kings 17:5-23). The whole sordid story is summed up by the prophets like Jeremiah who proclaim the sinfulness of the human heart (see Jeremiah 13:23).

[2]William L. Lane, *Hebrews 9–13,* vol. 47b, Word Biblical Commentary, New Testament ed. Ralph P. Martin, gen. eds. David A. Hubbard and Glenn W. Barker (Dallas: Word Books, 1991), pp. 454–55.

[3]Philip Edgcumbe Hughes, *A Commentary on the Epistle to the Hebrews* (Grand Rapids, Michigan: Wm. B. Eerdmans Publishing Co., 1977), p. 540.

20

ENJOY THE PRIVILEGES OF THE HOLY LIFE

Hebrews 12:18-24

n Hebrews 12:18-24, the Sinai imagery comes into full view. We are at the mount where God speaks to His people. The author of Hebrews, however, avoids using the name "Sinai," even though the description in 12:18-21 is clearly taken from the time when God's people stood before that mountain.

In 12:18-24, the preacher contrasts God's people before the mountain at which God established the Mosaic covenant (see 12:18-21), and before Mount Zion, the place of that covenant's ultimate fulfillment (see 12:22-24). In both situations, God is addressing His people. The sevenfold impersonal description of Sinai's terror (12:18-21) climaxes when Moses, the mediator of the old covenant, declares His fear because of the sin of the people. By contrast, the sevenfold description of the joyous fellowship of God's people at Mount Zion (12:22-24) climaxes in the proclamation of redemption through the blood of Jesus, the Mediator of the new covenant. This contrast emphasizes the great privileges God's people now enjoy through Jesus: cleansing from sin and access to His presence. Thus this section summarizes the main body of Hebrews which describes how these privileges have been made available through the High Priesthood of Christ.

The exhortations that build on the truth of this section form part of the next section (see 12:25-29), which describes the future of God's people: the final judgment. This close association between the present lives of God's people and the future judgment is no accident. What God's people do in the present, the way they appropriate the grace of God, profoundly affects their participation in God's final salvation at the judgment. Their use of present privilege determines their future destiny.

The phrases **You have not come . . .** (12:18) and **But you have come . . .** (12:22) describe approaching God in worship. The preacher again describes the Christian life as an approach to God in worship. It is not worship under the arrangements of approach depicted in 12:18-21, but rather under those gracious arrangements in 12:22-24.

The preacher offers a dreadful description modeled after God's revelation of himself at Sinai (see 12:18-21), but without using either the word "Sinai" or the word **mountain** (12:18). The New International Version has supplied the world **mountain** for clarity. However, the smoothness gained in translation mutes the awesome effect of the description. The preacher does not speak of **a *mountain* that can be touched and that is burning** (12:18, my emphasis). He speaks of *"something* that can be touched, a blazing fire, and darkness, and gloom, and a tempest, and the sound of a trumpet, and a voice . . ." (12:18-19 NRSV, my emphasis). He is not concerned with the place itself, but with the awesomeness of the presence of God.

The preacher draws the words of his description largely from the descriptions of Sinai in the Old Testament (see Exodus 19:15-21; 20:18-21; Deuteronomy 4:11-12; 5:22-27; 9:19). The presentation in Hebrews emphasizes Sinai's complete unapproachability. No person is mentioned to soften the description until the mention of Moses at the climax in 12:21. His admission of **fear** only intensifies the fearfulness of this scene.

Consider these seven features. The first descriptive feature, the phrase **can be touched** (12:18) indicates a visible, material mountain rather than an invisible and eternal one. **Fire . . . darkness, gloom and storm,** the next four aspects of this description (12:18), intensify the awesomeness of this foreboding picture. In fifth place comes the **trumpet blast** (12:19). It is a sound that announces an awesome presence, but has no content. The **voice speaking words,** the sixth descriptive element (12:19), is God's voice, but He himself is hidden. These **words** probably refer to the Ten Commandments. When the people heard this **voice** with God's **words,** they could absolutely take no more. They **begged that no further word be spoken to them** (12:19). **They could not bear** the least thing that **was commanded** them: **If even an animal touches the mountain, it must be stoned** (12:20). They **could not bear** to approach this unapproachable place.

Moses' words are the seventh and climactic element of this description. Moses was the mediator of the old covenant. In the Old

Testament, he approached God on Sinai. Moses went up the mountain and received the tablets on which the Ten Commandments were written. But here (Hebrews 12:21) the preacher says that the scene was so utterly **terrifying that Moses said, "I am trembling with fear."** It is important to note the occasion upon which Moses spoke these words. He did not speak them when he received the Ten Commandments. These words appear to represent what he said after the people had made the golden calf (see Deuteronomy 9:19). Moses' words, then, reveal the reason why the people could not approach God: their sin. The holiness of God and His people's rejection of Him bar their approach to Him.

The preacher's choice not to use the name "Sinai" has certainly enhanced the awesomeness of this picture. He may, however, have had an additional reason for its omission. The description is not of Sinai as it was. It is of Sinai as it would be for the recipients of Hebrews if they rejected Christ. This is a description of Sinai without the promise. The people of the Old Testament who stood before Sinai were the heirs of God's promise. Sinai exposed their sin, but gave no remedy for it. Sinai pointed forward to the fulfillment of God's promise that would adequately deal with sin. But Christ has come now and fulfilled the promise. To reject Him is to reject the promise toward which Sinai pointed and to be left with nothing but its condemnation! This description, then, sets the privileges described in Hebrews 12:22-24 in bold relief and warns the readers of the consequences they face if they refuse those privileges.

But the Christian recipients of Hebrews **have come** to a very different place (12:22; see 12:23-24). The preacher gave no name for the first mountain, but offers three for this one: **Mount Zion, . . . the heavenly Jerusalem, the city of the living God.**[1] The name **Mount Zion** establishes the parallel with the preceding description of (the unnamed) Mount Sinai. **Zion** and **city of . . . God** were terms that could be used to describe the earthly **Jerusalem** (12:22), especially in reference to its representation of God's presence among His people. The preacher has taken these terms to describe the **heavenly** eternal "place" where **the living God** dwells with His people. Here the preacher portrays "the city with foundations, whose architect and builder is God" toward which Abraham looked forward (11:10). This is the true "promised land" which the wilderness generation lost (see 3:7-19) and to which the faithful have always journeyed (see 11:13-16). This is heaven, the true "most holy place" into which Jesus has given His people access (see 9:24).

Within the Old Testament, the Promised Land was special because it was the place where God's people were to live in fellowship with Him. Jerusalem (also called Zion) with its Temple, became the focal point of that land and of God's presence among His people. The Most Holy Place of the Temple was the center of Jerusalem because it was the particular place where God promised to dwell among them. Thus, the Most Holy Place, Jerusalem/Zion, and the Promised Land were intimately linked within the Old Testament. All three came to symbolize God's dwelling with His people and their living in harmony and fellowship with Him. The preacher understood all three of these—the Most Holy Place, Jerusalem/Zion, and the Promised Land—as types or pictures representing the true heavenly presence of God into which His people enter through Christ their Pioneer and High Priest. All that has been said about Christ's cleansing people of sin and bringing them into the presence of God culminates in this passage. Here is a picture of God's people living in God's presence. This picture is both a present reality and a foretaste of what is to come.

And what a picture! The description of the first mountain, the mount of condemnation, offered nothing but impersonal, fearsome phenomena. This mountain offers a picture of joyful beings praising God! First we meet **thousands upon thousands of angels in joyful assembly** (12:22). Myriads of angels are present only where God is. This must be His dwelling place. They worship and honor Him in a great **assembly** of **joyful** worship.[2] God's people, living and dead, are here. They are **the church of the firstborn** (12:23). The word **firstborn** is plural, not singular. This is the church made up entirely of God's **firstborn** children. He has no other kind!

Firstborn children possessed inheritance rights. (Remember, Esau sold his right to the firstborn's inheritance [see 12:16-17]). All God's children are His heirs through Christ. All have a share in this wonderful heavenly city. Their **names are written in heaven.** Abraham and the other faithful were aliens on *earth* (see 11:13-16) because they were citizens of *heaven!* When we Christians do not feel at home in this sinful world, it's because this is not our home. But, through prayer, worship, and communion with God, we join the angels and all other believers, dead and living, in the presence of the living God.

The **church of the firstborn** (12:23) joins the great joyful company of angels in the worship of **God;** for, best of all, He is here on **Mount Zion** (12:22). It is His dwelling place. He is the center of worship and the cause of all the joy. Yet, in the middle of all this joyful fellowship,

God is still called **the judge of all men** (12:23). The original Greek text emphasizes the idea of **judge.** Literally translated, it reads, "to One who is Judge, the God of all." We would have expected God to be called **judge** in the previous description of the mount of condemnation (see 12:18-21), not here. There is no condemnation here, but there is judgment. God is still holy! No unholy thing enters here.

The preacher also emphasizes that no unholy thing enters God's presence by mentioning the next group of people: **the spirits of righteous men made perfect** (12:23). This description reminds us of the heroes of faith who lived before Christ (see 11:1-40). These heroes are **spirits** because they all have died. They were the **righteous** who lived by faith (compare 10:38). The preacher called the first of these examples, Abel, "righteous" (11:4). He implies that these righteous people have now been **made perfect** through Christ (12:23; see 11:39-40)—that is, they have been cleansed of sin so that they can come fully into the presence of God. Here they are! The preacher's description (**the spirits of righteous men made perfect** [12:23]) includes the Old Testament heroes of faith, but it also includes all God's people who have died. The fact that they have been **made perfect** or cleansed of sin corresponds to the fact that God is still **judge;** He is still as holy as He ever was.

Within the pictures of both mountains, God retains His holy character. But the second mountain (see 12:22-24) differs from the first (see 12:18-21) because of **Jesus the mediator of a new covenant** (12:24; see also 7:20-22; 9:15-21). The original Greek behind this phrase reads, "to the Mediator of a new covenant, Jesus." He has become the Mediator on the basis of all that He has done, as our sacrifice and High Priest, to cleanse us from sin and bring us to God.

You can see all that the preacher has said about these subjects concentrated in this word **mediator.** Even in heaven we are not allowed to forget that the One who is our **mediator** is none other than the One who came to earth as **Jesus** to suffer and die for us! All that Jesus has done has been done in association with the Father. We should not picture an angry God appeased by a loving Jesus. We have a loving God who has provided for our redemption through and along with His Son who became Jesus. Under and along with God, **Jesus** is the founder of this glorious heavenly party (see 12:22-24).

Jesus is the **mediator** here (12:24), not **Moses** (12:21). Moses could only tremble at the people's sin. Jesus' blood is **the sprinkled blood that speaks a better word than the blood of Abel** (12:24). **Jesus** brought cleansing from sin and established the new covenant with His **sprinkled**

blood (see commentary on 9:11-15, 18-21; 10:22). Cain spilt Abel's **blood** on the ground when he murdered him. The **blood of Abel** "cried out" to God as a witness to Cain's sin (Heb. 12:24; see Genesis 4:10). Abel's **blood** proclaimed the verdict, "guilty." Jesus' **blood, sprinkled** on our hearts, proclaims **a better word**—the verdict, "forgiven," "cleansed," "empowered for obedience." It is through this **blood** that we and all of God's people have access into the joyful presence of God on **Mount Zion** (12:22). If we reject this **blood** (12:24), we become subject to the awful separation from God and judgment depicted in 12:18-21.

God spoke on Sinai. God spoke in His Son on earth. He now addresses us from heaven with this gracious word (see 12:25) through the work of His Son, our great High Priest, Jesus. This is our "heavenly calling" (3:1), our invitation and authorization to come live in God's presence. However, the preacher has warned in 12:18-21 that there are dire consequences for rejecting this word. The blessings of acceptance and the consequences of rejection will both become a final reality at the Judgment, described in the next section (12:25-29). The preacher wants his hearers to be ready! What they do now will have momentous consequences then.

ENDNOTES

[1]The sevenfold nature of this description is as follows: (1) **Mount Zion, . . . the heavenly Jerusalem, the city of the living God** (12:22); (2) **thousands upon thousands of angels in joyful assembly** (12:22); (3) **the church of the firstborn, whose names are written in heaven** (12:23); (4) **God, the judge of all men** (12:23); (5) **the spirits of righteous men made perfect** (12:23); (6) **Jesus the mediator of a new covenant** (12:24); and (7) **the sprinkled blood that speaks a better word than the blood of Abel** (12:24).

[2]The New American Standard Bible reads "to myriads of angels, to the general assembly and church of the first-born" instead of **to thousands upon thousands of angels in joyful assembly, to the church of the firstborn** (12:22-23). The Greek word that the New International Version translates **joyful assembly,** the NASB translates "general assembly." The NASB associates this word with the "church"; the NIV with the **angels.** The New King James Version is in agreement with the New American Standard Bible; the New Revised Standard Version with the New International Version. Greek grammar allows either interpretation. In either case, the word denotes a joyful assembly of worship.

21

FEAR THE PERIL OF LOSING THE HOLY LIFE

Hebrews 12:25-29

ebrews 12:25-29 brings to a climax the spiritual history of God's people, which the author began in Hebrews 11:1. Here the preacher brings his hearers to the Judgment. He gives his most powerful appeal.

This section begins with an exhortation of warning (see 12:25) and ends with one of encouragement (see 12:28). The preacher supports the first warning by two contrasts: one in 12:25b, and one in 12:26-27. He bases his last warning on the second of these contrasts. Verse 29 ends this whole history of God's people with a reminder of the awesomeness of God.

Hear the preacher's warning: **See to it that you do not refuse him who speaks** (12:25a). The phrase **See to it** (see 3:12) expresses urgency. The word **refuse** describes a deliberate refusal to listen and obey. **Him who speaks** is a clear reference to the God in whose presence His people dwell, as described in 12:22-24. We are standing at Zion in God's presence. God himself is speaking!

The preacher began his sermon by telling us that the God who spoke in times past, especially on Mount Sinai, has now spoken definitively by sending His Son. This Son came as the historical Jesus to accomplish our salvation (see commentary on 1:1–2:4). The preacher now can say that the God who spoke on Mount Sinai speaks to us through His Son from heaven. We are not dependent merely on the past revelation when Jesus was on earth. God's present speaking from heaven is, however, based on

His previous historical revelation in Jesus of Nazareth, and would be impossible without it. God now addresses His gracious word of invitation to us through "the sprinkled blood" shed by Jesus when He was on earth (12:24). He now graciously speaks **from heaven** (12:25). God calls us **from heaven** and, through that "sprinkled blood," to **heaven** (see 3:1). The One who gave His obedient life and death as a sacrifice on earth is now, on the basis of that sacrifice, the High Priest at God's right hand. Through Him, God invites us into His presence.

The preacher here makes clear why it is so important to obey God's present invitation. When the preacher speaks of those who **refused him who warned them on earth** (12:25), he probably refers to the wilderness generation. They heard God speak on Sinai, but refused to trust Him to take them into Canaan. The preacher showed us clearly in 3:7-19 that they **did not escape** God's judgment (12:25). But now, as we have seen, God speaks from heaven through the blood of Christ, inviting us into His presence. This invitation is so much greater because it opens the way to heaven, not merely to an earthly Promised Land. God invites us to come in. It provides in reality that of which the speaking on Sinai was a mere shadow. What blessing is open to us! What tragedy if **we turn away from him** in apostasy (12:25). To whom or what would we turn? The preacher's next contrast (see 12:26-27) makes it absolutely clear that there is no one and nothing to whom we can turn if we turn away from God's heavenly call.

God spoke at Sinai and in His Son when He came as the historical Jesus (see 1:1–2:4). God spoke at Sinai and now addresses us from heaven through "the sprinkled blood," through the completed work of our heavenly High Priest. God spoke at Sinai, and He will speak one more time—at the Judgment. Hebrews 12:26-27 contrasts the "earth-shaking" quality of God's speaking at Sinai and "earth- and heaven-shaking" quality of His speaking at the final judgment. At Sinai, God's **voice shook the earth** (12:26). Hebrews 12:19 referred to the awesome voice speaking at the mount of condemnation. But God **has promised** through Haggai, **"Once more,** at the Judgment, **I will shake not only the earth but also the heavens"** (12:26).

The preacher has paraphrased this prophesy (see Haggai 2:6) in a way that deepens, but does not pervert, its meaning. Haggai's original words read, ". . . I will once more shake the heavens and the earth, the sea and the dry land." In Haggai's mind, "the heavens and the earth, the sea and the dry land" served as a description of the created order. The preacher has paraphrased this as **not only the earth but also the**

heavens (Heb. 12:26) in order to facilitate the comparison with Sinai when God shook only the earth. Haggai was prophesying to the exiles who had returned and rebuilt the Temple. They were tempted to be discouraged because the rebuilt Temple was so much less than the former Temple. Haggai prophesied that God was going to perform a great, final act of judgment and deliverance when He would overturn the present world order. The nations and kingdoms of the world would be overthrown, and Jerusalem would be glorified as never before.

Hebrews 12:27 shows the preacher's deeper understanding of this prophecy. He knew that by the words "once more" (Hag. 2:6; see Hebrews 12:26) God through Haggai referred to the final judgment. But the preacher knew that earthly Jerusalem is but a picture of the heavenly reality where God dwells. Thus, he understood this prophecy in a deeper way. This whole world we see will be overthrown so that the heavenly Jerusalem alone will remain stable. **The words "once more" indicate the removing of what can be shaken,** the visible heaven and earth— **that is, created things;** only the eternal realities, **what cannot be shaken,** will **remain** (Heb. 12:27).

The phrase **what cannot be shaken** (12:27) is to be identified with the **kingdom that cannot be shaken** (12:28). This unshakable **kingdom** is the reality already described as "Mount Zion, . . . the heavenly Jerusalem, the city of the living God" (12:22); "the city with foundations" (11:10); the "heavenly" "country" (11:14-16); and the "rest" that remains "for the people of God" (4:9). Here God's people dwell joyfully with Him in a state of blessedness as described in 12:22-24.

God "made" or created the heavens and the earth, this "universe," the worlds which we see (1:2). God also has established the eternal reality, an unshakable **kingdom** (12:28), but on a different level and in a different way. He is the "architect and builder" (11:10) of this eternal city which "he has prepared" for His Own (11:16). The discussion of "rest" in 4:4 helps us to understand the nature of this heavenly reality. We see in Genesis that God established that rest when, after the completion of creation, He himself "rested from all his work" (Gen. 2:2; compare Hebrews 4:4). This rest is His own rest beyond the creation. It is His own rest that He shares with us. This eternal order of rest is intimately related to God himself. When we enter it, we share His own life.

The opening exhortation (12:25) of this section (12:25-29) told us what to avoid. The concluding exhortation (12:28) tells us what to do. We have seen that the phrase **kingdom that cannot be shaken** (12:28) refers to this eternal reality that God has prepared for His own and that will remain untouched when the created world is removed at the Judgment. The preacher has used a number of different descriptions for this reality in order to help us understand it better. "Rest" (4:9) helped us to know that this reality brought ultimate wholeness. "Country" (11:14-16) or "homeland" reminded us that it is the place we belong and long for. "City" (12:22) assured us of its security and of the blessed communal aspect of this reality. At the heart of all of these terms has been fellowship with God. The preacher's last and final description is **kingdom** (12:28). This term emphasizes the central fact that God is at the center. He is the King. He has established this reality, and He sustains it. The subjects of the **kingdom** obey and have fellowship with Him. All the glorious blessings that the Bible associates with God's kingdom are fulfilled in this ultimate **kingdom.**

We who are faithful Christians, are in the process of **receiving** this **kingdom** (12:28). Verses 22 through 24 made it clear that we already participate in it. It is ours. We look forward to ultimate participation at the Judgment. How should people conduct themselves who are receiving such a treasure and who want to make sure that they enter into its ultimate enjoyment?

At first the preacher's answer is surprising, for he says only, **. . . let us be thankful . . .** (12:28). The first response of the faithful is deep, heartfelt, undying wonder and gratitude for what God has made available. By means of this thanksgiving, we **worship God acceptably** (12:28). The New Revised Standard Version's translation of this phrase is enlightening: "let us give thanks, by which we offer to God an acceptable worship." "Offer to God." All of life is worship of God. Christ has offered the only atoning sacrifice. Our thanksgiving for this sacrifice and all its benefits is our acceptable "offering." Worship through thanksgiving is accompanied by **reverence and awe** (12:28) because it truly acknowledges who God is and how we relate to Him. The Greek word translated **reverence** comes from the same family of words as the word translated "in holy fear," which the preacher used in 11:7 to describe Noah's obedience. Such offerings of thanksgiving imply the obedience of the worshiper.

The preacher envisions the Christian life as worship of God in the heavenly most holy place, made possible by the sacrifice and High Priesthood of Christ, and carried out by offerings of deep gratitude and thanksgiving accompanied by obedience. The ultimate blessing will be to experience this worship in its fullest when we have completely entered the eternal **kingdom** (12:28) we are now receiving. Hebrews 13:1-17 describes practical ways in which believers bring these offerings of thanksgiving and obedience within the Christian community. The kind of life that we live with God, as described in 12:22-24, will be reflected in the kind of life we live with one another in this world, as described in 13:1-17.

The preacher closes this section and the whole history of God's people with a quotation from Moses found in Deuteronomy 4:24: **our "God is a consuming fire"** (Heb. 12:29). Moses spoke these words to emphasize the gravity of breaking God's covenant. Over and over again the preacher has shown us how we share in privileges far greater than those who lived under the old covenant. He does not need to tell us that these words, as solemn as they were for Moses' hearers, have a far greater solemnity for people with our degree of privilege.

Part Six

FINAL APPLICATION AND FAREWELL

Hebrews 13:1-25

In this concluding section of Hebrews, the author addresses some practical questions about living the life of faith—questions faced by his hearers. However, he addresses these concerns on the basis of what He has said about the sacrifice and High Priesthood of Christ in 1:1–12:29. As those under the old covenant "drew near" to worship God with sacrifices at the Tabernacle, so we draw near and enter God's holy presence through the sacrifice of Christ our High Priest. The life of faith is a life of drawing near to God through Christ and offering the proper sacrifices—the sacrifices of praise and love. Thus the preacher fleshes out the life of faith by showing how we should separate from the world, draw near to God, praise Him, and practice love. The preacher shows his concern for his hearers by concluding this final chapter of Hebrews with news, greetings, and a prayer.

22

CHRISTIAN LIVING AS TRUE WORSHIP

Hebrews 13:1-17

In Hebrews 13:1-17, the preacher describes how to draw near through Christ and what sacrifices or offerings His people should bring. Virtually every aspect of the Christian life is involved in this drawing near and in these sacrifices. At the end of the last chapter, the preacher instructed us to bring the proper sacrifice (see Hebrews 12:28). In light of the wonderful privileges that are ours, we bring a sacrifice of thanksgiving offered with a true sense of the awesomeness of God. Hebrews 13:15-16 enlarges on this concept of our proper sacrifice. These verses tell us that alongside of and closely associated with thanksgiving, "praise" is a most appropriate sacrifice, and also doing "good" and sharing with others. Verses 1 through 6 give instructions concerning this sacrifice of doing "good" and sharing. The expressions of love shown to our brothers and sisters in Christ are pleasing sacrifices offered to God.

1. THE SACRIFICES THAT PLEASE GOD 13:1-6

This section consists of four pairs of exhortations: the first pair is in 13:1-2; the second in 13:3, the third in 13:4; and the fourth in 13:5-6. The first, third, and fourth pairs each have a supporting statement explaining why we should obey them.

The first pair of exhortations sets the tone for the whole: **Keep on loving each other as brothers. Do not forget to entertain strangers . . .** The New King James Version more literally translated the first of these, "Let brotherly love continue." *Philadelphia* is the Greek word that is translated "brotherly love," the same word behind the name for the Pennsylvania city of "brotherly love." "Phil" comes from the Greek word for "love," and "adelphia" from the Greek word for "brother." The word literally means "brother-love." The second exhortation is more literally, "hospitality do not forget." The Greek word used here for "hospitality" is similar to the word *philadelphia*. If we wrote it with English letters, it would be *philozenia*. It is easy to recognize the *phil* from the Greek word for love. *Zenia* is a Greek word meaning "hospitality." It's related to another word meaning "stranger," and thus we might translate this word "hospitality-love" or "stranger-love." The following literal translation reflects the terseness and power of these two exhortations in the original language: "brother-love, let it continue; stranger-love, do not forget." These two terms cover the broad spectrum of love.

The preacher has prepared his hearers for his encouragement to "philadelphia" or "brother-love." Previously he has shown them how Christians are God's children whom the Son of God calls His "brothers" (2:10-18). Christians are all God's "firstborn" who inherit His eternal blessings (12:22-24). The preacher has called his hearers "brothers" (3:1, 12; 10:19) and urged them to mutual concern for each other's welfare (10:25).[1] Outside of Christian literature, "philadelphia" or brother-love is used almost exclusively for the natural affection among actual blood brothers and sisters.[2] Thus this word would, for the first recipients of Hebrews, have spoken more powerfully of mutual care and concern within the Christian community than it might to us.[3] They have certainly been practicing this "brother-love," but the preacher urges them to continue. The second pair of exhortations in 13:2-3 give two specific ways in which this "brother-love" is to be carried out.

Philozenia, we have seen, is "hospitality-love" or "stranger-love." The preacher did not want his hearers to forget to express love outside their immediate circle. The first recipients of Hebrews probably lived in a situation where there was a great need to entertain traveling evangelists and other Christians. Most inns or hotels were centers of immorality. Non-Christians may have rejected their Christian relatives, thus not offering family hospitality. The Christian community could not neglect these traveling Christians any more than it could neglect to show hospitality to its own members. These traveling Christians were also "brothers." The preacher encourages them to practice this hospitality by reminding them that some people had **entertained angels without knowing it.** The hearers may have thought of Abraham and Sarah (Genesis 18:2-15). We never know what good may come from such hospitality.

The double exhortations in Hebrews 13:3 encourage the hearers to two specific ways of showing "brother-love." **Remember those in**

prison as if you were their fellow prisoners, and those who are mistreated as if you yourselves were suffering. The hearers had shown such love in the past (10:32-35), but it would be easy to forget these kinds of people. Those who associated with such sufferers might bring suffering on themselves. The word **remember** means to help them in concrete ways. Listen to a literal translation of the more forceful original Greek. We might translate the first, "Remember the prisoners as fellow-imprisoned," that is, feel their suffering and minister to their needs. Governments supplied few of the physical needs of prisoners in the first century. Their family or friends had to take care of them. Christians imprisoned for their faith may well have been abandoned by their non-Christian relatives.

Listen to the New American Standard Bible's more literal translation of the second exhortation: "Remember . . . those who are ill-treated, since you yourselves also are in the body." The preacher could not have stated this more strongly. Notice the double emphasis of the phrase **you yourselves.** The word here translated **mistreated** or "ill-treated" reminds us of the suffering of the heroes of faith (11:36-37) and Moses (11:25). The preacher probably thinks of those who are suffering *for their faith.* We should minister to the needs of those who suffer in this way because we, too, are "in the body," and therefore vulnerable to suffering and abuse. This way of speaking may have reminded the hearers that Christ took on a body and suffered in order to redeem them (2:14; 10:5-10). The preacher wants his hearers to show love in every practical form to those who need it, especially those who are suffering for their faith, even if by so doing they run the risk of bringing such suffering on themselves.

Hebrews 13:4 makes it clear that sexual impurity is not a private matter which affects no one else. Marriage is the bond of human society. Such sin has great consequences for the community. Sexual purity is a matter of Christian brotherly love. The second specific exhortation clarifies the meaning of the first broad one. **Marriage should be honored by all, and the marriage bed kept pure.** Those who honor marriage shun divorce. They keep the **marriage bed . . . pure** by refraining from fornication before and adultery after marriage. They abstain from all kinds of sexual perversion. We have already seen in the commentary on 12:14-17 that the "godless" person, one who has rejected God's covenant and God's eternal blessings, is often involved with sexual immorality.

In this series of instructions on brotherly love, only here does the preacher pronounce God's judgment on those who disobey: **For God**

will judge the adulterer and all the sexually immoral. The failure to practice hospitality or to minister to one in prison is a sin of omission and may easily arise from neglect. Sexual immorality is a sin of commission with the full assent of the will.

With his last pair of exhortations, found in verses 5 and 6, the preacher moves from sex to money. This pair of exhortations are opposite sides of the same coin: Unless you **keep your lives free from the love of money** you cannot be **content with what you have.** Greed and contentment are opposites. The first has no place in the Christian's life. The phrase **free from the love of money** actually translates one Greek word. Let's look at it closely so we can compare it with *philadelphia* and *philozenia* in 13:1. This word is *aphilarguros.* We can separate it into three parts: a-phil-arguros. You now recognize *phil,* the word for love used in *philadelphia* and *philozenia. Arguros* is the Greek word for "silver," used here more broadly to mean "money." The *a* gives *a-phil-arguros* a negative meaning, like the initial *a* in the English words *amoral* or *apolitical. Philarguros* would mean "money-loving." *Aphilarguros* means "not-money-loving."

The preacher began this chapter instructing his hearers to practice "brother-love" and "stranger-love." He concludes by telling them not to practice "money-love." The **love of money** destroys contentment. The **love of money** cancels out "brother-love" and "stranger-love" or "hospitality-love." The person who loves money keeps it greedily for himself and does not practice these other loves by doing good and sharing (see 13:16).

And really, the **love of money** is so needless. The God we serve has himself **said, "Never will I leave you; never will I forsake you"** (13:5). The New International Version accurately reflects the force of this statement. The original doubles, even triples, the negative for emphasis. Although the wording of this quotation is not exactly identical to any particular Old Testament statement, the preacher probably was paraphrasing God's words to Joshua (Josh. 1:5): "I will never leave you nor forsake you." Similar statements are made by Moses to Joshua in Deuteronomy 31:6, 8. The God who had shown His mighty power by delivering His people from Egypt did not abandon Joshua on the eve of his entrance into the Promised Land. This God who has redeemed us in Christ does not abandon us as we enter the true heavenly promised land of God's presence and eternal reward. Greed is not necessary, because God takes care of His Own. Greed is a denial of faith because the greedy person acts as if God would not take care of His Own.

The response of the Old Testament faithful (quoted in 13:6) should be our confident response: **The Lord is my helper; I will not be afraid. What can man do to me?** This is a Greek translation of Psalm 118:6. The preacher and his hearers know that in the psalms the word **Lord** refers to God, although it might have reminded them of the Lord Jesus who is the **helper** who gives "help" to the tempted (2:18; compare 4:16).

This affirmation of faith is a fitting conclusion for 13:1-6 which deals with the various aspects of love, of sharing and doing good (see 13:16). Trust in the living God frees us from self-centeredness, greed, and fear of unbelievers, all of which inhibit love. When we trust God to care for us, we can freely share and do good to others because we don't have to worry about ourselves. These loving actions toward others are loving sacrifices that Christians offer to God through Christ!

2. DRAW NEAR TO OFFER YOUR SACRIFICES 13:7-17

The preacher's hearers can properly offer these sacrifices when they follow Christ in separating from the sinful world and drawing near to God. This separation means breaking all ties with any kind of sub-Christian ritual worship with which they are still involved. Perhaps they were still tempted to participate in certain ritual meals that were celebrated throughout the Roman world but were associated with the sacrifices of the Temple (see 13:9-10). To continue in these practices would be a denial of Christ's sufficiency and a return from the reality of Christ to the emptiness of human ceremony. But they can continue in their break from old ways if they follow the example of and are obedient to their godly leaders (13:7-8, 17), hold on to true doctrine (13:9), and follow the example of Christ (13:12-13). In place of sub-Christian ritual worship they are to offer, through Christ, the sacrifices of praise and doing good (13:15-16).

The preacher has given his hearers many biblical examples. In 13:7 he begins his final appeal by asking them to **remember** their past **leaders** who faithfully **spoke the word of God** to them (see 2:3). He wants them to remember specifically and **consider** fully the **outcome of their** [the past leaders'] **way of life.** The hearers had seen the results of these people's lives. If they **imitate their** leaders' **faith, Jesus Christ** himself guarantees that they will have the same results. A literal translation of the Greek words behind 13:8 would read, "Jesus Christ yesterday and today the same, and forever." By placing the words **the same** in the very center of the sentence, the preacher emphasizes them. **Jesus Christ is the same** in the **today** of the hearers of Hebrews as He was in the **yesterday** of their former leaders. He was the exalted High Priest who had offered the effective sacrifice then. He is the same now. And He will be forever. He was able to cleanse and empower their former leaders and to bring them into God's presence. He can do the same for the readers of Hebrews in the present. He will be able to do the same forever. Guaranteed!

Thus, there is no reason for them to allow themselves **to be carried away** with **all kinds** of **teachings** which are **strange** to what they heard from their former leaders (note 2:3). These various inferior and **strange** teachings probably involved various **ceremonial foods** (13:9) that Jews throughout the Roman world ate in conjunction with certain rituals taking place in the Jerusalem Temple. By demonstrating the sufficiency of Christ's sacrifice, the preacher has shown clearly that ceremonies associated with any other sacrifice **are of no value to those who eat them.** The ceremonies of the old covenant dealt only with ritual cleansing (9:13; 10:4). The preacher has shown that through the new covenant **grace** is available to cleanse and transform **hearts** (9:14, 10:12-14). This grace can strengthen the hearts of Christians in God's way.

Instead of those **ceremonial foods, we** Christians **have an altar from which those who minister at the tabernacle have no right to eat** (13:10). Those who partake in ceremonies related to the old covenant have **no right** to partake of the blessings of Christ's sacrifice because they are seeking God somewhere else. When the preacher mentions the Christian **altar,** he does not refer to a new Christian ceremony which replaces the old covenant ways.[4] This **altar** represents the reality of participating in the heart-changing grace available through Christ.

Hebrews 13:11-13 shows why those still following the rituals of the old covenant have **no right to eat** at the Christian **altar.** Those sacrifices and Christ's sacrifice take place in mutually exclusive places, in two different spheres. The preacher here refers back to the Day of Atonement ritual (see Leviticus 16:27) which he discussed in Hebrews 9:1-14.

On that day the **high priest** carried **the blood of animals into the Most Holy Place as a sin offering, but the bodies** of those very same animals, were **burned outside the camp.** The place **outside the camp** was a ceremonially unclean place of exclusion from the society of God's people, a place as far removed as possible from the Most Holy Place where God dwelt. However, it is the very place where **Jesus also suffered. Outside the city gate** was the equivalent in Jesus' day of **outside the camp** in the Old Testament. And it is there that He offered His sacrifice **to make the people holy through his own blood.** The place that those who practiced the old sacrifices considered unclean was the very place where Christ's sacrifice, which makes His people holy, was offered. Those who participated in the old-covenant sacrifice would have nothing to do with people who were unclean outside the camp. How, then, can one participate in both the old-covenant rituals and in the benefits of Christ's sacrifice? The place that old-covenant people despise as unclean is the very place where new-covenant people are made holy and find God!

The preacher calls his readers, then, **to go to him** [Christ] **outside the camp.** When they follow this exhortation they will be excluded from the old sacrifices and from the approval of the unbelieving world, but they will be in the place of fellowship with Jesus. They would probably bear **disgrace** from both their Jewish and non-Jewish friends. Practice of the old-covenant rituals was legal in the Roman world and had a degree of social acceptance by non-Jews. Christian faith had no standing, But this **disgrace** is nothing other than **the disgrace he bore.** The **gate** they have left is not the gate of the **enduring city** that they **are looking for** and strongly anticipating (see 12:22-24). Only by separating from false teaching that requires participation in old-covenant ceremonial meals, only by bearing the shame of identification with Christ, could the hearers truly be made holy and attain that eternal **enduring city.**

The preacher has given his readers true teaching in place of the false teaching to which they were attracted. He has taught them about the fully sufficient sacrifice of Christ. It is time to show them the worship appropriate for those who believe that Christ's sacrifice truly cleanses from sin. How do those people worship who identify with Christ outside the city gate? Hebrews 13:15-16 answers this question. Verse 15's opening words **through Jesus** are important. Christians offer their sacrifices only **through Jesus.** He has offered the once-for-all sacrifice for sin. Thus He is now High Priest at the Father's right hand. He administers the new covenant through which we are cleansed. Our sacrifices do not atone for sin. God accepts our sacrifices because we have already been cleansed from sin through Jesus' sacrifice. Ours are acceptable through His and are a response to His. Thus our sacrifice is first of all **a sacrifice of praise** to God for all that He has done for us in providing this atonement (see 12:28). The Tabernacle had its daily sacrifices. Christians offer a continual sacrifice of **praise.** Make no mistake; believers offer no animal as their praise offering. They offer **praise** which is **the fruit of lips that confess his name** by declaring the greatness of what He has done!

Praise to God is our first sacrifice in response to Christ's sacrifice. But we must not neglect the second: **to do good and to share with others.** The phrase **to do good** translates a word that means to show kindness and compassion. **To share with others** also translates one Greek word which means to compassionately minister to the needs of others. The preacher here refers primarily to others' material needs, but would not want to exclude ministry to their spiritual needs. These words aptly summarize his description of the brotherly love, hospitality, and care for those in prison and suffering described in 13:1-3. They are the very opposite of the "money-love" forbidden in 13:5-6. Those who love money do not **share with others.**

Note that the preacher sees our care for others as part of our grateful sacrifice to God in response to His goodness toward us. The ultimate reason for offering these sacrifices is that **God is pleased** with them. They please the One whom it is our highest duty and ultimate joy to please. If He is pleased we need not be concerned about the "disgrace" we may endure from the unbelieving world.

The preacher began this section by urging his hearers to imitate their past leaders (see 13:7). He concludes it by urging them to obey their present godly leaders (13:17). This command might imply that some original hearers may have had a tendency to disobey. If those hearers were part of a house church in Rome, they may have fallen out with some leaders in the larger body of Christians. In any case, his encouragement to submit to godly leaders fittingly concludes what the preacher has been saying. If his hearers obey their faithful leaders, those leaders will affirm the true teaching about Christ's atoning work, about separating themselves from useless rituals, about bearing the reproach of Christ, and about offering sacrifices of praise and brotherly love.

The two Greek words behind the English words **obey** and **submit** are quite similar. They reinforce each other and strengthen the preacher's appeal.

The hearers should submit to these godly leaders because it is in their own best interest. These leaders are not building their own empires. They **keep watch over** the spiritual and eternal welfare of the hearers (13:17). They themselves **must give an account** (see 4:13) of their care to God.

If the hearers **obey** their leaders, their work **will be a joy** to them because they will see that those for whom they care are spiritually healthy. If the followers do not obey, the leaders' work will be **a burden.** The New American Standard Bible offers a more graphic translation, "with grief." The leaders would work with heaviness, "with sighing" (NRSV). Their hearts will groan with heaviness and grief because they care for those they lead.

The hearers' disobedience and the leader's corresponding grief will be absolutely **of no advantage to you,** the hearers. The commercial nuance of the word translated **no advantage** is caught by the New American Standard Bible and the New King James Version: "unprofitable." Your disobedience gives you the worst possible bottom line! Hebrews 13:17 also reminds Christian leaders of the way they should conduct their ministry and of the motivations that should drive them!

ENDNOTES

[1]"Christian brotherhood, therefore, is essentially *brotherhood in Christ;* for as he is the only Son (1:2, 5ff., etc.) . . . it is through union with him that we participate in the grace of sonship, and in him are accepted as the sons of God and, as sons, brothers and fellow heirs with him who is the heir of all things (1:2; Romans 8:14-17; Ephesians 1:5-7, 11-14; John 1:13)" (Philip Edgcumbe Hughes, *A Commentary on the Epistle to the Hebrews* [Grand Rapids, Michigan: Wm. B. Eerdmans Publishing Co., 1977], p. 562).

[2]4 Maccabees 13:23; 26:14 (a Jewish writing from the first century); Philo, *On the Embassy to Gaius,* p. 87 (Philo was a Jewish philosopher who lived until about the middle of the first century); Josephus, *The Jewish Antiquities* 4.5.4 (Josephus was a Jewish historian of the first century); see *The Epistle to the Hebrews* by Harold W. Attridge, Hermeneia—A Critical and Historical Commentary on the Bible, ed. Helmut Koester (Philadelphia: Fortress Press, 1989), p. 385, note 17

[3]Romans 12:10; 1 Thessalonians 4:9; 1 Peter 1:22; 2 Peter 1:7; 1 Clement 1:2 (a letter written from a pastor at Rome to the church of Corinth near the end of the first century); see Attridge, p. 385, note 18

[4]Neither does the preacher intend to forbid the use of ritual in Christian worship. He is concerned with rituals associated with the pre-Christ sacrifices of the Old Testament. If his hearers thought that participation in those rituals was necessary after the coming of Christ, then they were denying the adequacy of Christ's sacrifice.

PRAYER REQUESTS, BENEDICTION, NEWS & FAREWELL

Hebrews 13:18-25

The various issues the preacher addresses in Hebrews 13:18-25 are all natural for a letter's end. Although Hebrews has the form of a sermon, it concludes like a letter. The preacher has sent his sermon to his friends. A prayer request (13:18-19) is followed by a benediction (13:20-21), a final summarizing exhortation (13:22), some news (13:23), a final greeting (13:24), and a concluding blessing (13:25).

Pray for us. His prayer request (13:18-19) expresses the preacher's bond with his hearers and his sense of need for spiritual support. The word **us** may include other fellow workers, such as Timothy (mentioned in 13:23). The preacher clearly affirms the integrity of his motives. **We are sure that we have a clear conscience,** literally, "a good conscience" (NKJV; NASB). Not only has he been cleansed by Christ but he lives in integrity toward them. He demonstrates his character by diligently carrying out his **desire to live honorably in every way.** The last phrase could be translated "among all people." The preacher has the same kind of character and the same concerns as their local leaders whom he mentioned in 13:17.

The preacher is particularly urgent that his hearers pray for Him to **be restored to** them **soon.** We do not know the conditions or cause of his separation. This request, however, is in line with the urgency of the spiritual concern he has expressed throughout this sermon. His reasons for wanting to be **restored to** them are not just sentimental, though he no doubt loves them, but spiritual. If he is with them he can contribute to their spiritual well-being more directly, consistently, and thoroughly.

The great benediction in 13:20-21 is a fitting conclusion to this sermon. The preacher ends as a pray-er. He prays that God will truly effect what he has been urging in the lives of his hearers. The preacher has just requested prayer for himself, and now he gives this wish-prayer for them.

The God of peace is the God who through Christ's High Priesthood has brought peace between himself and His people. This peace between God and his people results in a restoration of wholeness within the Christian community (see 12:14). He achieved this peace **through the blood of the eternal covenant,** the means by which God **brought** Jesus **back from the dead** and equipped Him to be **that great Shepherd of the sheep.** The new covenant is **eternal** in duration and in quality. The eternal Son of God (see commentary on 7:16) established it by His perfect obedience (10:5-10).

The preacher uses the word **great** here to indicate Christ's peerless superiority as the **Shepherd of the sheep.** This title supplements and enriches the title of High Priest that the preacher has been using. It emphasizes Christ's constant, untiring, tender care for His Own. It reminds the hearers' leaders mentioned in 13:17 of their model and to whom they must given account. The caring Shepherd applies the blessings gained by the High Priest to His needy sheep. In Greek the words **Lord Jesus** come after the phrase **great Shepherd of the sheep.** The word **Shepherd** appears first for emphasis but the preacher is quick to identify the caring great Shepherd as the sovereign **Lord** of the sheep. This sovereign Lord is also the One who lived a human life as **Jesus.** The **Shepherd** image expresses the intensity of the care of the High Priest for His Own.

The benediction joins **God** and Christ inseparably together in this saving work. God himself effects salvation through the Son. In 13:21 the preacher prays that God will apply these benefits to his hearers. He wants God to **equip,** to completely furnish, his hearers with **everything good for doing his** [God's] **will.** The phrase **everything good** includes the full benefits of Christ's High Priesthood: cleansing from sin, joyful access to God and fellowship with God's people, grace to overcome temptation, and assurance of the heavenly city. Only possession of these gifts enables God's people to do his **will.** The preacher wants God to do in them **what is pleasing to him** [God] and nothing else. God himself is the true standard and Judge.

All that God does in and for us is accomplished **through Jesus Christ.** The magnificent greatness and glory of all the preacher has said requires a closing sacrifice of praise: **to whom be glory for ever and ever.**

It is interesting to note that the first half of this prayer, which focuses on the resurrection of Jesus, ends, in Greek, with a reference to **the Lord Jesus.** The title **Lord** emphasizes the sovereignty of the risen One. The last half of this prayer, which focuses on the application of His redeeming work in our lives, ends with a reversed title **Jesus Christ.** It is through the death of **Jesus** that we have been redeemed.

The concluding exhortation in 13:22 sums up the whole sermon: **I urge you to bear with my word of exhortation.** The word **urge** literally means "exhort." "I exhort you to bear with my word of exhortation." With the phrase **word of exhortation,** the preacher is describing his entire sermon (see Acts 13:15 NRSV). This phrase certainly describes the sermonic nature of Hebrews with its strong encouragement and sharp warning. This same phrase **word of exhortation** also describes the author's purpose. He wrote to exhort and encourage his readers to continue faithfully in their pilgrimage. He wants them to enter into the full privileges of cleansing and access to God that are theirs through Christ. He also has warned them of the consequences of turning away from Christ.

The phrase **bear with** is the preacher's polite way of appealing to his hearers to listen to and heed what he has said. His phrase **for I have written to you only a short letter** continues his polite appeal. He is politely saying that the letter is not too long for them to pay attention to it and profit from his instruction, exhortation, encouragement, and warning.

Hebrews 13:23 gives information about **Timothy,** no doubt the same one who is often seen as a companion of Paul. The New Testament offers no other information about **Timothy** being in prison. Timothy appears to be well known to both preacher and hearers, for he is called **our brother.** This verse indicates that Hebrews was probably written during the lifetime of people who knew Paul and had some association with him. The writer and Timothy appear to be close because the preacher hopes to **come with him to see** those who have received his sermon and thus fulfill his earlier prayer request (13:19).

In 13:24, the preacher appears to separate two groups: **your leaders** and **all God's people.** He also urges his readers to greet **all** members of both these groups. This may indicate that there was some friction between the recipients of Hebrews and other Christians or Christian leaders. This verse offers one reason why some feel that the preacher addressed this sermon to a house church that was part of the larger fellowship of Christians in the city. Perhaps the preacher's hearers were dissatisfied with some leaders in the larger church or with some factions within it.

The phrase **those from Italy** has two possible interpretations: It could refer to people then living in Italy. It could refer to people from Italy who were living outside their country near where the preacher was living. The latter interpretation is more likely. If the preacher were writing from Italy, he would probably have given the names of those who sent greetings instead of using a general term like **those from Italy.** Probably this phrase refers to Italians who lived away from home sending greetings back to Italy. In the introduction to this commentary we have suggested that this letter was written to a house church in Rome.

The farewell blessing (13:25), **Grace be with you all,** is brief and traditional, but full of meaning. This is the **grace of** God available in the new covenant for cleansing from sin through the High Priesthood and sacrifice of Christ (see 4:16; 12:15; 13:9). The preacher has been urging his hearers to receive this grace. Now he wishes it for them in the form of a blessing, a final prayer. May God grant that this prayer be answered in the life of everyone who listens to this "word of exhortation." Amen.

SELECT BIBLIOGRAPHY

This commentary has been written with the purpose of enabling the Christian in the pew to understand God's message in the book of Hebrews. Below is a list of resources that may help the reader who wishes to do further study. The first section consists of commentaries from the Wesleyan tradition that were previously mentioned in the preface. The second section consists of commentaries by evangelical scholars. It is not necessary to have a knowledge of New Testament Greek in order to use these commentaries with profit.

BOOKS IN THE WESLEYAN TRADITION

Carter, Charles W. "The Epistle to the Hebrews," *The Wesleyan Bible Commentary*. Ed. Charles W. Carter. Grand Rapids, Michigan: Wm. B. Eerdmans Publishing Co., 1966.

Cockerill, Gareth Lee. "The Epistle to the Hebrews," *The Wesley Bible: A Personal Study Bible for Holy Living*. Ed. Albert F. Harper, et al. Nashville: Thomas Nelson Publishers, 1990.

Murray, Andrew. *The Holiest of All*. New York: Fleming H. Revell, 1894. (Reprinted, Springdale, Pennsylvania: Whitaker House, 1996.)

Turner, George Allen. *The New and Living Way*. Minneapolis: Bethany Fellowship, 1975.

Walters, John. "Hebrews," *Asbury Bible Commentary*. Eds. Eugene E. Carpenter and Wayne McCown. Grand Rapids, Michigan: Zondervan Publishing House, 1992.

OTHER EVANGELICAL RESOURCES

Brown, Raymond. *The Message of Hebrews: Christ Above All,* The Bible Speaks Today. Ed. John R. W. Stott. Downers Grove, Illinois: InterVarsity Press, 1982.

Bruce, F. F. *The Epistle to the Hebrews,* The New International Commentary on the New Testament. Ed. F. F. Bruce. Grand Rapids, Michigan: Wm. B. Eerdmans Publishing Co., 1990.

Guthrie, Donald G. *The Letter to the Hebrews,* The Tyndale New Testament Commentaries. Ed. Leon Morris. Grand Rapids, Michigan: Wm. B. Eerdmans Publishing Co., 1989.

Hagner, Donald A. *Hebrews,* New International Biblical Commentary. Ed. W. Ward Gasque. Peabody, Massachusetts: Hendrickson Publishers, 1990.

Hughes, Philip Edgcumbe. *A Commentary on the Epistle to the Hebrews.* Grand Rapids, Michigan: Wm. B. Eerdmans Publishing Co., 1977.

Kistemaker, Simon J. *Exposition of the Epistle to the Hebrews.* Grand Rapids, Michigan: Baker Book House, 1984.

Lightfoot, Neil R. *Jesus Christ Today: A Commentary on the Book of Hebrews.* Grand Rapids, Michigan: Baker Book House, 1976.